M000215891

Talking to North Korea

'Based on dozens of visits to North Korea and dialogues with top party leaders, Glyn Ford offers an insightful and provocative analysis of the danger of North Korea's nuclear weapons as well as practical policy recommendations for the EU. Definitely worth reading!'
—William Ury, co-founder, Harvard Negotiation Project, co-author of *Getting to Yes: Negotiating an Agreement Without Giving In*

'A timely, perceptive, and penetrating analysis of North Korea. This is a must for those who are interested in contemporary North Korean affairs.'
—Chung-in Moon, Distinguished University Professor, Yonsei University

'With almost 50 visits to the DPRK, Glyn Ford is one of the top European experts on the Korean Peninsula. Readers, whatever their political views, will find much to stimulate their thinking regarding one of the most important political-security issues of our time.'
—Jeffrey D. Feltman, United Nations Under-Secretary-General for Political Affairs

'With direct access to North Korean government officials and a lifetime of observation and analysis of the country, Glyn Ford has an insight into the country like no other. A strongly recommended impartial read, revealing previous political tricks and failures of 73 years of miscommunication and stagnation . . . and a possible path out of this mess.'
—Nicholas Bonner, Founder of Koryo Tours

'Glyn Ford is a very rare case of a Westerner who has both political experience in the West and first-hand experience of dealing with North Korea. His book shows a possible way out of the continuous crisis through slow-motion change – the only way which might work.'
—Andrei Lankov, author of *The Real North Korea: Life and Politics in the Failed Stalinist Utopia*

Talking to North Korea
Ending the Nuclear Standoff

Glyn Ford

Parts of this work draw on *North Korea on the Brink: Struggle for Survival* by Glyn Ford with Soyoung Kwon, first published by Pluto Press 2008

First published 2018 by Pluto Press
345 Archway Road, London N6 5AA

www.plutobooks.com

British Library Cataloguing in Publication Data
A catalogue record for this book is available from the British Library

ISBN   978 0 7453 3786 9   Hardback
ISBN   978 0 7453 3785 2   Paperback
ISBN   978 1 7868 0303 0   PDF eBook
ISBN   978 1 7868 0305 4   Kindle eBook
ISBN   978 1 7868 0304 7   EPUB eBook

This book is printed on paper suitable for recycling and made from fully managed and sustained forest sources. Logging, pulping and manufacturing processes are expected to conform to the environmental standards of the country of origin.

Typeset by Stanford DTP Services, Northampton, England

Simultaneously printed in the United Kingdom and United States of America

'If at first you don't succeed, try diplomacy'

To Elise, Alessandro, and Ida

Contents

List of Figures and Tables

Figures

Tables

Map of North Korea

Country Leaders, 1990–2018

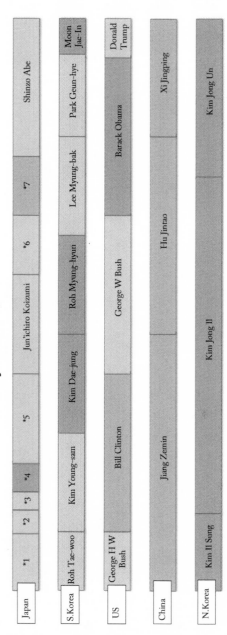

Legend: Left-wing, Centrist, Right-wing

Japan	*1, *2, *3, *4, *5, Jun'ichiro Koizumi, *6, *7, Shinzo Abe
S.Korea	Roh Tae-woo, Kim Young-sam, Kim Dae-jung, Roh Myung-hyun, Lee Myung-bak, Park Geun-hye, Moon Jae-In
US	George H W Bush, Bill Clinton, George W Bush, Barack Obama, Donald Trump
China	Jiang Zemin, Hu Jintao, Xi Jingping
N.Korea	Kim Il Sung, Kim Jong Il, Kim Jong Un

Timeline: 1990, 1995, 2000, 2005, 2010, 2015

*1 Liberal Democratic Party (LDP); Toshiki Kaifu (1989–91), Kiichi Miyazawa (1991–93); *2 Japan New Party: Morihiro Hosokawa (1993–94) *3 Japan Renewal Party: Tsutomu Hata (1994) *4 Social Democratic Party (SDP): Tomiichi Murayama (1994–96) *5 LDP: Ryutaro Hashimoto (1996–98), Keizo Obuci, (1998–2000), Yoshiro Mori (2000-2001) *6 LDP: Shinzo Abe (2006-07), Yasuo Fukuda (2007-08), Taro Aso (2008-09), *7 Democratic Party of Japan: Yukio Hatoyama (2009–10), Naoto Kan (2010-11), Yoshihiko Noda (2011-12)

Chronology since 1900

1904–05	Russo-Japanese war
1905	Japanese occupation begins
1910	Japanese annexation
1912	Birth of Kim Il Sung
1919	1 March movement in Seoul
1931	Japanese invasion of Manchuria/Kim Il Sung joins the Chinese Communist Party
1941	Birth of Kim Jong Il
1945	August – Japanese surrender and end of occupation
1946	8 February – Kim Il Sung becomes head of the Provisional People's Committee
1948	9 September – Birth of the DPRK
1950	25 June – Civil war starts
1953	27 July – Korean War Armistice
1956	Khrushchev denounced Stalin, putting Kim Il Sung at risk for the first time since the end of the war
1958	After an abortive coup, Kim Il Sung left in total command. The Kim personality cult ramps up
1961	July – Signature of Treaties of Friendship, Cooperation, and Mutual Assistance with the Soviet Union and China
1964	Tokyo normalises relations with South Korea
1966	North Korea in the football World Cup in England
1968	January – 'Peublo' captured off Wonsan. Blue House 'raid'
Late 1960s	North Korean economy starts to stutter. 'Second' Korean War
1970	Chinese Zhou Enlai visits Pyongyang. China-DPRK relations warm up
1972	New North Korean Constitution
1975	Kim joins the 'Non-Aligned Movement' and expands his diplomatic relations with Third World countries
1976	CIA-funded Cuban exile group blows up a plane killing five senior North Korean officials, amongst a total of 73 dead
1977–83	17 Japanese were abducted by North Korea, eight are still not fully accounted for

1978	September – Sino-Japanese Peace and Friendship Treaty
	December – China–US normalise relations
1983	October – Pyongyang assassination attempt against President Chun Doo-hwan in Rangoon, leaving 21 dead including five ROK Ministers
1984	Kim visit to Moscow and beginning of DPRK–USSR rapprochement
1986	The North Korean dual-use reactor goes critical
1987	Korean Air bombing, leaving 115 dead
1991	September – North and South Korea join the UN
	December – North and South Korea sign the Joint Declaration on the Denuclearisation of the Peninsula
1992	Rason Special Economic Zone created
	Signing of NPT and first IAEA Inspections
1993	IAEA demands that its inspectors be given access to key sites. North Korea threatens to quit the NPT
1994	June – Jimmy Carter visits Pyongyang
	July – Kim Il Sung dies
	October – US and North Korea sign the Agreed Framework
1995	March – the Korean Peninsula Energy Development (KEDO) Organisation is established
	Late 1990s – famine
1997	October – Kim Jong Il officially succeeds his father after thee-year 'period of mourning'
1998	February – Kim Dae-jung announces his 'Sunshine Policy'
	April – the US imposes sanctions on North Korea and Pakistan for exchanging missile technology
	August – Failed Kwangmyŏngsŏng satellite launch over Japan
1999	Missile talks with Clinton administration
2000	June – Kim Jong Il and Kim Dae-jung Summit
2001	July – UK Embassy opens in Pyongyang
2002	January – George W. Bush labels North Korea part of the 'Axis of Evil'
	July – North Korea carries out agricultural reforms
2003	January – North Korea finally withdraws from the NPT
	August – first round of Six Party Talks in Beijing
2004	December – the Kaesong Industrial Complex opens
2005	North Korea declares it has nuclear weapons
2006	July – North Korea tests a long-range missile

October – North Korea tests its first nuclear weapon

2007   February – North Korea agrees to close its Yonbyon nuclear reactor in exchange for $400 (€305) million of aid

May – a passenger train, carrying a North and South delegation, crosses the border for the first time since 1951

2008   June – North Korea destroys water-cooling tower at Yongbyon

October – the US removes North Korea from its list of 'state sponsors of terror'

December – Six Party Talks break down when North Korea refuses access to IAEA inspectors

2009   May – North Korea conducts its second nuclear test

December – North Korea conducts a currency revaluation

2010   The South Korean corvette *Cheonan* sunk

November – Shelling of Yeonpyeong Island

2011   December – Kim Jong Il dies and replaced by Kim Jong Un

2012   June – North Korea carries out further agricultural reforms, allowing family work teams

2013   *Byungjin* line adopted with simultaneous development of economy and a nuclear deterrent

February – North Korea conducts its third nuclear test

December – Jang Song Thaek executed

2014   February – The UN Commission of Inquiry reports on human rights abuses in North Korea

May – North Korea carries out industrial reforms, allowing managers to set wages

May – UNHRC publishes the Universal Periodic Review on North Korea

2015   August – North Korea claims to have miniaturised its nuclear weapons

December – North Korea carries out a ballistic missile test

December – US imposes further sanctions

2016   January – North Korea claims it has tested a hydrogen bomb (its fourth nuclear test)

February – Park Geun-hye unilaterally closes the Kaesong Industrial Complex

September – North Korea conducts its fifth nuclear test

November – UN tightens sanctions

December – Impeachment of Park Geun-hye

2017   February – Kim Jong Nam assassinated

May – Moon Jae-in wins special election
July – North Korea conducts an ICBM test
August – North Korea threats to strike Guam
August – UNSC imposes most stringent sanctions to date
September – North Korea conducts its sixth nuclear test
November – North Korea conducts an ICBM test
demonstrating the range to hit all of the mainland USA

2018   January – announces that it has completed its nuclear deterrent
and unilaterally halts both further nuclear and ICBM testing.
Agrees to send a team to the Winter Olympics
April – Kim Jong Un summit with Moon Jae-in in
Panmunjom border
May – Kim Jong Un summit with Xi Jinping in Beijing
June – Kim Jong Un summit with Donald Trump in Singapore

Acknowledgements

My first acknowledgement has to be to my staff, former and present, for their support. Soyoung Kwon continues to provide vital input from the point of view of someone who has studied the North, using material only available in Korean and with an academic knowledge only a native Korean speaker could possess. Kamila Kingstone helped draft the earlier chapters, later abetted on a voluntary basis by Alfy Birkett. Marialaura De Angelis, who was with me until earlier this year for close to a decade and travelled with me to the North on half a dozen occasions; Irina Kalashnikova, who came twice with her camera; and Cherry Burrow, who worked with me in the Forest of Dean. In Brussels, Chiara Zannini has taken over Marialaura's mantle, helped by Mathilde Séjourné there and John Price in Manchester. Special thanks are due to Kang Hye-yeon for translation from Seoul.

This book is informed by my dialogue with the vice-chairman of the International Department of the Party, led by Jonathan Powell, and his team at InterMediate, alongside my staff and me at Track2Asia. More recently we have been joined by Bill Ury and his impressive Korea Negotiation Initiative, part of the Harvard Negotiation Project, led by Liza Hester. It would have been impossible without them.

I also have to thank the East-West Center at the University of Hawaii for awarding me a POSCO fellowship in 2006 that gave me the breathing space needed to finish the penultimate draft of *North Korea on the Brink,* and in particular Dr Lee Jay Cho and all those associated with the Northeast Asia Economic Forum over the years, who have been and continue to be supportive and helpful in the extreme. The same is true of Rhee Tsang Chu and the staff of the Korean Global Foundation, with their annual World Korean Forum, and the staff and contributors to *NK News*. I also offer my thanks to both Dai Ichi Hoki (Tokyo) and Hans Media (Seoul) for translating and publishing *North Korea on the Brink* in Japanese and Korean, respectively.

It would be invidious to name those still serving their governments – in certain cases it might even detract from their career prospects – but I would like to thank those who provided help, assistance, and advice over the years – they know who they are – from the UK and Swedish embassies in Pyongyang; the EU embassies in Beijing, Seoul, Tokyo, and Washington; the Chinese Foreign Ministry and the International Department of the Chinese Communist Party; the Ministry of Foreign Affairs, Cabinet Office, Ministry for the Abductee Issue, and Diet in Tokyo. In Seoul, the Ministry of Foreign Affairs, Ministry of Unification, Blue House, and National Assembly; in Washington, the State Department, Pentagon, and White House; the Pacific Command in Honolulu; the UNC Command in Seoul; the United Nations in New York; the European External Action Service, European Commission, and European Parliament in Brussels; and the Foreign and Commonwealth Office in London.

Last but not least, I thank the staff and officials of the International Department of the Workers' Party of Korea, Ministry of Foreign Affairs, Ministry of External Economic Affairs, Korean Asia-Pacific Peace Committee, Koryo Hotel, and DPRK embassy to the United Kingdom. I would also like to thank the many individuals – and friends – who have talked to me and provided insights in a manner most commentators claim is impossible for North Koreans. I'm delighted to say it's just not true. The only two I'll name – the first because he is no longer directly involved in the process – is the man who was more responsible than anyone else in Pyongyang for getting me involved, Ri Ung Gil. The second is the one who carried it forward and who sadly passed away in May 2016, the late Kang Suk Ju.

Thanks also go to:

In Brussels: Laurens Brinkhorst, Nick Costello, Patrick Costello, Alexandre Dobolyi, Jas Gawronski, Coraline Goron, Thierry Jacob,

Mary Sun Kim, Marianne Mikko, Tereza Novotna, David O'Sullivan, the late Julian Priestley, Jacques Santer, Leo Tindemans, Kristian Vigenin, and Michael Wood.

Across Europe: Mike Cowin, Franz von Daeniken, Keir Dhillon, Stuart Emmerson, Joe Fisher, Kent Härstedt, Mary Hennock, Fariah Khan, Lorna McCaig, Wolfgang Nowak, Pär Nuder, Linda Price, Dessy Roussanova, Mark Seddon, David Slinn, Georgi Tolaraya, Morten Traavik, and David Yarrow.

In Beijing: Ginny Bai, Guo Wengui, Nick Bonner, Simon Cockerell, Zhang Lija, and Zhang Zhijun.

In Seoul: Hyung T. Hong, the late Kim Dae-jung, Moon Chung-in, Chad O'Carroll, James Pearson, and John Sagar.

In Tokyo: Paul Bacon, Yukihisa Fujita, the late Tsutomu Hata, Taro Nakayama, and Hajime Takahashi.

In New York: Sonja Bachmann, Jeff Feltman, Samuel Martell, and Stephen Noerper.

In Washington: Joe De Trani, Bob Carlin, Fred Krawchuk, Keith Luse, HR McMaster, Katherine Moon, Buzz and Alice Palmer, Rich Rubenstein, and Joe Yun.

Last, but by no means least, all at Pluto especially David Shulman, Chris Brown, Kieran O'Connor, Emily Orford, Neda Tehroni, and Robert Webb, plus my indefatigable editor Sarah Grey.

I apologise for anyone I've missed. That will be rectified in future editions.

I also must acknowledge my family. My son Alessandro, seeking somewhere interesting to spend his 'gap year' between school and university, became the first Western student at the Kim Il Sung University in 2014. His five months there provided insights no other source could match. He was grateful for a Pyongyang visit from sister Elise and mother Daniela, if only to provide fresh supplies of peanut butter. He brought back with him a taste for Taedonggang beer and soju. His taste might have been challenged by the new Rakwon.

Some of the thinking and ideas in this book appeared in articles published in a variety of newspaper and magazines, including *Global Asia, The Guardian, Il Manifesto, Japan Times, Korea Herald, Morning*

Star, New Statesman, Soundings, Tribune and China's Ministry of Foreign Affairs' *World Affairs*. They also found expression in conferences, workshops, and seminars organised in and by the Centre for Peace and Conflict Studies (Siem Reap), East-West Center (Honolulu), Friedrich Neumann Foundation (Pyongyang), Global Partnership for the Prevention of Armed Conflict (Den Hague), Jeju Peace Forum (Jeju), Keele World Affairs (Keele), Korea Society (New York), National Committee for North Korea (Washington, DC), National Human Rights Commission of Korea (Seoul), Nordic Institute of Asian Studies (Copenhagen), Peace Research Institute/Brookings Institution (Oslo), ROK-UN Conference on Disarmament and Non-Proliferation (Jeju), and US Institute of Peace (Washington, DC).

All the photographs are my copyright ©, unless otherwise indicated.

The opinions expressed in this book are entirely my own responsibility. All those acknowledged will disagree with some of what is written here; many will disagree with most. In particular, my North Korean interlocutors will be disappointed that I see the North through different eyes than their own. All I hope is that they recognise that I do this from the best of motives, in an attempt to present their country in a different light to the one in which it is normally seen in the West. We all, I believe, share a wish to find a settlement on the Peninsula that allows a progressive path to peace.

Note on Asian Names

With introduction of a spelling reform in South Korea in 2000, new forms for some very common words transformed Pyongyang into Pyeongyang, Kumgang to Geumgang, and Kaesong to Gaesong. Some have moved to the new system, but the North Korean press and the international media have generally stayed with the old spellings. This book uses the forms most familiar to the English-speaking reader, except in direct quotations, where the original is retained. Therefore, apart from this exception, the old versions of place names are used. Similarly, Korean terms follow the North Korean style: for instance, *juche* instead of *chu'che* and *rodong* instead of *nodong*.

For Korean names, I follow the DPRK style for North Koreans, with the family names followed by first names, capitalised and unhyphenated. Thus: Kim Il Sung, Kim Jong Il, and Kim Jong Un. For South Koreans, I follow their style, with a hyphen and a lowercased last particle. Thus: Kim Dae-jung, Moon Jae-in, and Park Geun-hye. This creates a problem for the period up to the end of the Korean War, but this has been resolved by selecting the style to reflect political identification.

Some names are given in a different form or order if they are already established in common usage, such as Syngman Rhee. For the Chinese names, the standardised pinyin transliteration is used: Mao Zedong rather than Mao Tse-tung, Beijing instead of Peking. Japanese names invert the name order (e.g., Junichiro Koizumi, Tomiichi Murayama, and Tsutomu Hata).

Preface

It was during the 1966 World Cup in England (North Korea 1 – Italy 0) that I first discovered the Democratic People's Republic of Korea (DPRK). It was longer before they found me. When I was elected to the European Parliament (EP) in 1984, one of my first interventions in committee was to propose that a report be prepared on EU–North Korea trade relations. In that report, the External Economic Relations (now International Trade) Committee concluded there were neither relations nor trade. The North was out of sight and out of mind. As with all EP reports, it concluded with a standard formula instructing that a copy of the report 'be sent to the Commission, Council, Member States and Government of the DPRK'. Two years later, when I finally visited the DPRK embassy to UNESCO in Paris for the first time, I asked them for their response to the EP Report. They replied that they'd never seen it. Back in Brussels, I asked the EP's administration what happened. The official response was, 'We didn't have an address'.

That was to change. By 2004 the EP had a standing delegation for the Korean peninsula. But it was not all for the better. Pyongyang has now spent a quarter of a century plastered across the world's front pages, as it apparently threatens the world with its nuclear weapons and missiles, if no longer with its ideology. I initially decided to write *North Korea on the Brink; Struggle for Survival* (Pluto, 2008) because the only books I found either – largely – painted it entirely black or – rarely – totally white; 'axis of evil' or socialist utopia. It's neither. The North is fifty shades of grey – some dark – rather than black or white, a product of its enemies as much as of its friends and itself. Ten years later, history has moved on. Everything has changed, and nothing. The last year has seen the Peninsula closer to war than peace. The book needed an update.

North Korea is a poor, beleaguered country run by an unpleasant regime that has served its people ill. However, the alternatives proffered by its enemies would only compound its pain. Do we really think that the changed regime in China – which has, since Deng Xiaoping, lifted more people out of poverty than live in the EU – is worse than the crony capitalism of the former Soviet Union, which has seen life expectancy fall by ten years and has driven thousands into poverty for each 'bandit billionaire'? Do we really think that the majority of ordinary people in Iraq, Libya, and Syria prefer the cruel, brutal chaos they now inhabit to the ordered authoritarianism that went before? Do ordinary Iraqis feel better placed now, in the midst of an almost decade long series of civil wars and insurrections, than they did under the brutal regime of Saddam Hussein? These questions are worth asking even if the answers aren't easy.

I wanted two things with the first book: first, to provide an appreciation and understanding of North Korea's history, politics, and economics, taking into account that the North went from feudalism to colony to Communism with no democratic detour or interregnum; second, to advocate the application of 'soft' rather than 'hard' power. I argued for 'critical engagement' – for 'changing the regime', not 'regime change' – to provide 'the greatest good for the greatest number'.

I still want to deliver on those two promises the second time around. But you can never step in the same river – or nuclear crisis – twice. Events and I have moved on apace. When I wrote *North Korea on the Brink* I had visited the country barely a dozen times; now I am approaching my fiftieth visit and for the last seven years have been involved in an extended political dialogue I established with the Vice-chairman of the International Department of the Party. In some facets I understand some things more and others less, but for both I have a more nuanced appreciation.

1
Introduction:
The Pyongyang Paradox

Pyongyang is trapped in a paradox. The very measures it has felt essential to ensure its long-term survival are precisely those that put it in short-term jeopardy. Kim Jong Un's *byungjin* line – which gave equal weight to building the nuclear deterrent and developing the economy – was designed to provide the security, time, and space to allow the economy to grow. The ultimate intention was to transform the country into an unattributed variant of Vietnam or China. Yet the nuclear strand of the policy threatens to precipitate a 'preventive' strike by Washington and its 'coalition of the willing', triggering a second Korean War – with devastating consequences.

Washington sees North Korea as an undeveloped Communist state in hock to Beijing, led by an irrational playboy with an odd haircut – and thus as a dangerous pariah that is unsusceptible to the normal political leverage of cause and effect. It would be more accurate, however, to see the Democratic People's Republic of Korea (DPRK) – as it prefers to be known – as constrained in a situation where its choices are narrow. With a failed industrial economy rather than an emerging one, its ruling regime has legitimate reasons to distrust the outside world and is desperate to ensure its survival in the face of clear existential threats. From Pyongyang's perspective, its actions are the inevitable corollary of this struggle for survival. Here the political stratigraphy of North Korea is revealing: the base feudal layer overlaid by the deep lessons of brutal Japanese colonialism (Japan occupied Korea from 1910 to 1945), then the careless division imposed by the United States in the aftermath of World War II. All followed by initial victory in a civil war, converted into a surrogate clash of civilisations that ended in a half-century stalemate, before it was in danger of being buried under the rubble of a collapsing Soviet empire. North Korea's recent behaviour is less a war cry than a cry for help.

There have been numerous attempts to explain North Korea, some less successful than others. Among the most risible is John Sweeney's *North Korea Undercover*, which parleyed a standard week's holiday into a heroic feat of daring and deserves marks for chutzpah, if nothing else. Victor Cha knows his stuff, without question; nevertheless, his *The Impossible State* reveals much about America's outdated misperceptions of the North. Yet Pyongyang hardly welcomes contemporary cutting-edge analysis. James Pearson and Daniel Tudor's *North Korea Confidential*, which illuminates the further shores of Pyongyang's market reforms, sufficiently irritated the North that Seoul felt it necessary to place the authors under round-the-clock protection.

For sheer encyclopaedic knowledge of the road to war, Bruce Cumings's two-volume *The Origins of the Korean War* is unsurpassed, but is matched page for page by Robert Scalapino and Lee Chongsik's *Communism in Korea*, charting the regime's first decade. For something to challenge the West's more recent received wisdom, Andrei Lankov's collection of books does exactly that. For those who like to cut fact with fiction, the pseudonymous James Church's early 'Inspector O' stories serve.

I first visited North Korea in 1997, during its darkest days since the war, at the height of the famine. I have been back almost fifty times since then, under a variety of guises. I served on a series of ad hoc delegations dispatched by the European Parliament consequent upon my visit in 1997 and in 2004 I successfully proposed the establishment of a standing delegation with the Korean Peninsula that still exists. Early on in my peregrinations it became clear where power lay in Pyongyang. Like in China, it was the Party, not the Ministries, that makes its mark.

Thus the majority of my visits have been under the auspices of the Workers' Party of Korea's (WPK) International Department.

In 2012 I was asked if I could set up a dialogue with politicians from the European Union. This I did, with Jonathan Powell, Tony Blair's former chief of staff and founder of the mediation charity Inter Mediate. Since then we've had an ongoing series of track 1.5 meetings; our current host is a member of the Politburo's Executive. In parallel, Pyongyang's perspective on the South is delivered by the Korea Asia-Pacific Peace Committee (United Front Department). In the twelve months leading up to this book's publication, I have been back to Pyongyang five times. This unique access has opened doors, from the White House to the Blue House, the Japanese cabinet office to the Chinese foreign ministry, the United Nations to the US Pacific Command, the EU's External Action Service to the National Security Councils.

One thing I have learnt is that the North is steeped in history and precedent. For them, history matters. They imbibe from birth a national narrative that shapes their comprehension of the world and their adversaries. Unlike in the West, where 'vision' means thinking beyond the next electoral cycle, North Koreans think long-term. The past is the key to the present. Thus any attempt to understand the DPRK and its people needs the vision to at least glimpse reality through their eyes. I hope this book will help you do that.

First, let us begin by dispelling the fabulous. The five biggest myths about the DPRK are that:

(1) **It's a Stalinist state run on the basis of Marxism-Leninism.** No, it's a theocracy with communist characteristics whose catechism is Kimilsungism-Kimjongilism.

(2) **Beijing and Pyongyang are like 'lips and teeth'.** No, the regime deeply distrusts and resents China. For the last decade they have barely been on speaking terms; Pyongyang is prepared to fight if necessary.

(3) **Pyongyang wants early unification.** No, the North's leadership is all too well aware that with its GDP at barely more than 2 per cent of the South's, early unification would only be assimilation by another name.

(4) **It's a command economy.** No, since the famine in the late 1990s it has increasingly become a malformed market economy. The future of the Peninsula is 'Two Countries, One System' until Pyongyang's 'tiger economy' and wealth of mineral resources allow it to catch up to Seoul.

(5) **Lifting American sanctions is the key.** No, the North has never exported or imported goods from the US. What they want from Washington is sufficiently robust security guarantees that liberate them to take the road to denuclearisation and allow China and South Korea to lift their sanctions.

North Korea's twentieth century was a turbulent one, as Chapter 2 explains in detail. Occupied by the Japanese from 1910 to 1945, the Korean Peninsula was divided after World War II by an arbitrary line of convenience drawn on a map to realise the promised Soviet and American zones. Neither North nor South was content with half; both wanted the whole. Seoul sought national unification and Pyongyang national liberation. The outcome was civil war (1950–53) that turned into a surrogate conflict between the world's two super-powers and a crusade against Communism by a US in the embrace of McCarthyism. After the end of the Korean War, North and South Korea continued to send informers, spies, and terrorists across the demilitarised zone (DMZ) to infiltrate and undermine their alter egos, but in the absence of their Cold War partners they were largely a threat only to each other.

North Korea had no history of democracy to fall back on, and its political architecture was constructed according to the 'people's democracy' paradigm used across the Soviet empire. After Soviet premier Nikita Khrushchev denounced Stalin and Stalinism in 1956, Kim Il Sung was under threat for the first time since the end of the war. He got his retaliation in first, purging the Party of those menacing him, leaving him and his fellow partisan generals to shift the country's focus from Stalinism to autarkic nationalism with the wand of Juche (self-reliance) ideology. Crucially, as Charles Armstrong points out in *The North Korean Revolution 1945–50* (2003), Kim fused Soviet socialism with indigenous Korean traditions and culture to create a state ideology that has outlived all the West's predictions.

Moscow and Beijing wooed Pyongyang simultaneously and the post-war economy, with its foundation of heavy industry, boomed. The North was global Communism's poster boy. By the late 1960s, however, the economic motor was beginning to stutter as the promised transition from heavy to light industry and increased delivery of consumer goods failed to materialise. Kim borrowed billions from the West in the early 1970s, but the turnkey projects he bought failed as the 1973 oil crisis spun the global economy into recession. Throughout the 1980s, from its acme as the world's 34th-largest economy, it slid. With the collapse of the Soviet Union it went from bad to worse. Aid from Moscow stopped and aid from Beijing braked.

Abandoned, the North looked to develop its own nuclear deterrent, but the economy went into a tailspin and the population went hungry. Millions died. So did Kim. For Kim it was biology, but the rest were the victims of failed policies and natural disasters. They became nameless victims of the worst humanitarian tragedy in the last quarter of the twentieth century. Washington knew, but there was no Live Aid eager to put their plight on the world's TV screens. They starved slowly, in silence.

After a three-year hiatus, Kim was succeeded by his son Kim Jong Il, who retained his father's innate distrust of reform but was forced to acknowledge that survival depended on kick-starting the stagnant economy. While his reforms were only partial and did not always succeed, they laid the groundwork and provided the legitimation for wider changes after 2010. Under Kim Jong Il, 'kiosk capitalists' began to emerge on the streets, along with embryonic multi-sectoral conglomerates in the model of those that had helped other Asian economies take off, such as Zaibatsu in Japan and Chaebol in South Korea. In Pyongyang, state-run shops started advertising medicines and motorbikes made by groups such as Pugang, Daesong, Sungri, and Rungra 88. Air Koryo moved into taxis and tinned food. The Rason Special Economic Zone and later the Kaesong Industrial Complex delivered economic paradigms and hard cash.

The fates of other leaders and countries targeted by Washington are deeply burnt into the regime's psyche. They understand the problems of Iraq, Libya, and Syria as resulting not from their possession of weapons of mass destruction but from their lack. When Libya formally renounced its nuclear programme in 2003, a sceptical North Korea rejected the invitation to give up its own nuclear ambitions and join Tripoli in the embrace of the global community of nations. Not much more than a month before Kim Jong Un succeeded his father in 2011, the video of Muammar Gaddafi's brutalisation and death was released: proof positive, from Pyongyang's perspective, of the perils of trusting the 'international community'.

The North's leadership believe that, while US hostility endures, regime survival necessitates an independent nuclear umbrella and economic growth. However, their efforts are hindered by the mutual incongruence of these goals: the first precludes the second. But the nuclear defence has other motives. Industrial and economic growth require labour power. Unlike in China, there is no vast pool of peasant labour awaiting induction into the discipline of the factory. Instead, workers have been sequestered in Pyongyang's million-strong army. This reserve army of labour needs demobilising.

Downsizing and going nuclear is a sign of weakness, not strength. North Korea has long lost the conventional arms race. Despite spending a quarter of its gross domestic product (GDP) on the military, the North is outspent by the South – which has an economy 50 times larger – by a factor of five year on year. Every time there is a naval clash along the Northern Limit Line (NLL), the disputed maritime boundary between North and South, the comparative casualty figures reflect this disparity. The gap yawns when Pyongyang's military budget is set against the combined military spending of Washington, Tokyo, and Seoul: it's barely 2 per cent of their expenditure. The nuclear deterrent thus has a double rationale, ensuring the safety of the regime and freeing labour power and resources to be decanted from the army into industrial and economic development.

Yet all of this is rendered moot by the economic embargo. Kim Jong Un has intensified and fully articulated his father's economic reforms and military developments. Early in 2013, once his authority was assured, he saw to it that the Party adopted the *byungjin* line of simultaneously developing the economy and the nuclear deterrent. Under Kim Jong Il the economy had slowly begun to open up and the first nuclear tests had taken place, but Kim Jong Un has driven both further and faster. The ride has been a rough one, but getting to the summit may just have made it all worthwhile. Now the question is whether he can barter a completed nuclear deterrent for a peace agreement and security guarantees, the lifting of sanctions, and an economic development package.

North Korea has been a 'country of concern' for almost 70 years. Initially it was one of many 'Communist' satellites, of which all but five have now crashed and burnt. Since the September 11, 2001 attacks and the ensuing 'war on terror', American foreign policy has taken on a hard unilateral edge. North Korea became a third of the 'axis of evil', a 'rogue state', and 'an outpost of tyranny', branded by the Bush administration as a clear and present danger to world peace.

Even though North Korea's last terrorist act had been in the 1980s, the US continued to classify it as a state sponsor of terror until 2008. Its reasons included an assassination attempt against President Chun Doo-hwan in October 1983. North Korean agents planted a bomb at the Martyrs' Memorial in Rangoon, Burma, that left 21 dead, including four ROK cabinet ministers. Chun escaped. Running behind schedule, he had yet to arrive when the bomb went off. The attack triggered worldwide condemnation and mass demonstrations in the South. Pyongyang had again misread public opinion. Although Chun had seized power in a military coup d'état in 1979 and was culpable of the deaths of up to 2,000 protestors in the 1980 Gwangju Massacre – as the US military watched – the population of South Korea didn't want him removed by Pyongyang.

Another reason was the Korean Air bombing. In 1987 a South Korean plane flying from Abu Dhabi to Bangkok exploded over the Andaman Sea, killing all 115 passengers and crew. The attack was designed to disrupt the preparations for the Seoul Olympics. When the two North Korean agents responsible were arrested in Bahrain, they both attempted suicide with cyanide capsules. The older male agent died, but his female partner, Kim Hyon Hui, survived. Under interrogation in Seoul, she confessed to implicating Kim Jong Il. Her death sentence was commuted and in 1993 she published a contrite memoir.

But it's a two-way street: North Korea was a victim of airline terrorism long before it became a practitioner. In 1976, a CIA-funded Cuban exile group blew up the Cubana de Aviación flight 455, killing five senior North Korean officials, including the vice-chairman of the Supreme People's Assembly's Foreign Relations Committee. Seventy-three people died in the explosion; there were no survivors. (George H.W. Bush was the director of the CIA at the time. The ringleaders were never punished.)

The US also cited North Korea's harbouring of members of the armed group Japanese Red Army. The 'terror state' designation was lifted by Barack Obama but re-instated in 2018 by Donald Trump, citing the 2017 assassination of Kim Jong Nam in Malaysia using a nerve agent.

Kim Jong Il introduced economic liberalisation out of necessity as the country's supply of energy and raw materials dried up. But it was the son who put 'the Plan' to the sword – motivated by aspiration rather than need. He wanted 'socialist enterprise management methods in which all enterprises carry out their management activities independently with initiative'.[1] In 2014 he introduced reforms allowing factory managers to set wages, hire and fire, and source spare parts and raw materials in the market. This was less than a complete success: the bottlenecks caused by erratic energy supplies and the lack of raw materials limited the beneficial impact of the reforms. Nevertheless, as Andrei Lankov argues, Kim Jong Un is 'the most pro-market leader North Korea has ever had'.[2]

Economic and social changes, catalysed by the famine at the turn of the century, accelerated under Kim Jong Un. The public distribution system (PDS), which had fed and clothed the population, still formally exists in Pyongyang but has a limited function, so inhabitants are forced to rely on the market. Elsewhere, it continues to have a limited and fitful existence. The most obvious development is the 'kiosk capitalists' who have sprung up on every street corner and the multiplication of formal markets in Pyongyang, spreading the availability of consumer goods like watches, high-heeled shoes, TVs, and smart-phones.

Pyongyang is the nation's theme park, with its stelae, monuments, and memorials paying homage to Kim Il Sung. It is the stage for military parades and civilian rallies. It is ideology in corporeal form. Since Kim Jong Un took power, a new social contract has given its inhabitants their reward. After all those touted satellite pictures of a dark North Korea at night, Pyongyang is now lit up like a Christmas tree. The capital's famously photogenic traffic women would nowadays actually have traffic to direct had they had not suffered technological redundancy at the hands of traffic lights. There are 3 million people signed up for the North's mobile network – although many have two phones, as it is cheaper to use a second phone than to recharge.

And the selfie-stick has well and truly landed.

In 2016 there was nearly 5 per cent growth, driven by trade rather than manufacture. Enterprise, rather than the Party, is increasingly

Figure 1 Traffic jams in Pyongyang.
Photo © Marialaura De Angelis.

the ticket to the future, yet Party membership remains a bonus. Amongst the entrepreneurs, the ones that endure are those sheltered in the lee of joint ventures with ministries, military units or party sections – trafficking protection for profit. *Ronin*[3] kiosk capitalists who were lucky enough a decade or so ago to get rich, and had the temerity to flaunt their wealth and engage in conspicuous consumption were brought back into line by December 2009's monetary reform, which rendered their hidden wealth worthless (even if this was not the reform's primary purpose).

Outside of Pyongyang too, in regional hubs such as Wonsan and Hamhung, living standards are creeping up. Yet a chasm remains. Outside the capital, if you're lucky, drinking water does not come through the taps but is bought for small change in 'water shops' – constructed with British and European aid – which pipe drinkable water from the mountains. Hungnam, Kimchaek, and Chongjin, cities deep in the North's 'rustbelt', remain hungry – though not starving.

The first wave of agricultural reform came in 2002, when targets for delivery to the centre were lowered and farmers allowed to sell the surplus. Within a couple of years, ministers claimed this had been more effective at boosting productivity than fertiliser. The second wave of reforms in 2012 reduced work teams to family units of four to six people and allowed farmers to retain 30 per cent of production – a variant of Deng Xiaoping's agricultural reforms of the late 1970s, when he introduced the 'household responsibility system' that effectively de-collectivised agriculture and boosted productivity by 25 per cent over a decade. Pyongyang's industrial and agricultural reforms, taken together, mean that you really don't have to be a weatherman to know which way the wind blows. It's only the interference from sanctions, floods, and drought and the myopia of Western commentators that allows reality to stay hidden.

One of the centrepieces of North Korea's search for economic success has been its special economic zones (SEZs). There were two sharply different models. The first is epitomised by Rason, an area the size of Singapore that abuts both China and Russia, with a population of around 300,000, policed and fenced off from the rest of the country. The second model is the Kaesong Industrial Complex, a joint venture with the South (detailed in chapter 5). It held around 80 companies – all small to medium-sized enterprises – and 53,000 employees commuted in daily. President Park Geun-hye of South Korea unilaterally closed it in February 2016, depriving Pyongyang of an annual bounty of US$50 million (€42 million). President Moon Jae-in promised to reopen the complex during his 2017 electoral campaign, but that waits on some settlement of the nuclear issue.

Nukes and Missiles

The regime's interest in nuclear weapons is long-standing. Kim Il Sung's initial interest was triggered by what he comprehended as a cowardly capitulation by the Soviet Union to Washington during the Cuban Missile Crisis. It also resulted in the surge in the conventional military budget that was ultimately to hollow out the North's civil economy. When the USSR disappeared almost 30 years later, Pyongyang's insecurity and paranoia became even worse.

In the early 1980s Moscow had supplied Pyongyang with nuclear technology, and the North constructed a five-megawatt Magnox reactor that went critical in 1986. Pioneered by the British, this dual-use reactor was not particularly efficient at producing electricity but rather better at generating weapons-grade plutonium. In Pyongyang's case, the absence of any reliable electricity grid indicated on which side of the fence they intended to fall. Under pressure from Moscow, Pyongyang signed the Treaty on the Non-Proliferation of Nuclear Weapons (NPT) in 1992, and consequently permitted four rounds of inspections by the International Atomic Energy Agency (IAEA). This cooperation was short-lived: it ended the moment the IAEA detected anomalies in North Korea's nuclear accounting. Under threat of preventive action from Washington, Pyongyang invoked Article X, Paragraph 1, of the NPT, which asserted a participating state's 'right to withdraw from the Treaty if it decides that extraordinary events . . . have jeopardised the supreme interests of its country'.[4] It then suspended this withdrawal in exchange for direct talks with the US. A maverick intervention by former US president Jimmy Carter led to the 1994 Agreed Framework.

Under the terms of this agreement, the Clinton administration agreed to facilitate the construction by 2003 of two 1,000-megawatt, proliferation-resistant light water reactors (LWRs); in the interim, it agreed to provide 500,000 tonnes of heavy fuel oil (HFO) per year. In return, Pyongyang promised to take its Yongbyon reactor out of service and halt construction of two new reactors at Yongbyon and Taechon.

The Agreed Framework was largely intended as a way of buying time: after the collapse of the Soviet Union, many in Washington saw North Korea as merely the last domino in the row. The domino failed to fall on cue, despite the famine of the late 1990s. By George W. Bush's inauguration in 2001, construction of the LWRs was already running almost a decade behind schedule. Then, in 2002, Bush named North Korea as part of the 'axis of evil'. In October the same year, his assistant secretary of state, James Kelly, claimed that North Korea had admitted to a secret highly enriched uranium (HEU) programme capable of producing alternative nuclear-weapons material. The agreement collapsed. (Kelly subsequently stated that Congress would have never authorised the dispatch of the necessary nuclear technology to North Korea anyway.[5])

After the 2003 invasion of Iraq, the DPRK reactivated their nuclear weapons programme. Concurrently, from 2003, Beijing brokered the Six-Party Talks, in which China, South Korea, the US, Russia, and Japan tried to persuade North Korea to give up a more advanced nuclear-weapons development programme in exchange for substantially less than had been on offer in 1994.

The process was torturous. In 2005 North Korea declared itself a nuclear state, and the following year conducted a partially successful underground nuclear test. Yet in February 2007, it agreed in Beijing to close its main nuclear reactor in exchange for $400 million (€343 million) in aid. Yongbyon's cooling tower was demolished on live TV in June the following year, as the US finally removed North

Korea from the 'terror state' list. The reconciliation didn't last. Talks broke down in December 2008, when Pyongyang refused to allow IAEA inspectors free access to nuclear facilities, all compounded by a second nuclear test in May 2009. Pyongyang finally lost patience and walked out of the talks in 2009.

Further attempts to negotiate made little progress. There was the farcical 'Leap Day' Agreement of February 2012, when Pyongyang apparently offered to renounce its missile and nuclear programmes in return for 240,000 tonnes of food aid. This lasted almost as long as it took the signatures on the agreement to dry. There was a third test in February 2013 (the first of the Kim Jong Un era). Pyongyang's problem was that its missile platforms couldn't carry the payload needed to deploy a first-generation nuclear weapon. Then, in 2015, the leadership announced their scientists and engineers had cracked the technology to miniaturise their nuclear weapons. The pace quickened. A fourth test in January 2016 was claimed as a hydrogen bomb, followed by a fifth test in September.

The summer of 2017 saw Kim Jong Un launch a bouquet of missiles, including two inter-continental ballistic missiles (ICBMs), with a threat that they could to strike 'the heart of the US'. In September, two intermediate range ballistic missiles were fired high over Japan, demonstrating a range sufficient to reach US military bases on the island of Guam. A sixth nuclear test followed. This, most observers concluded, was of a hydrogen bomb with a yield of 250 kilotons, making it 15 to 20 times more powerful than the Hiroshima bomb. On 28 November 2017 Kim launched an ICBM that demonstrated the range to hit anywhere in the mainland US and promptly announced that the DPRK now had its nuclear deterrent.

Whether Pyongyang can consummate the marriage of missile and warhead remains untested; whether it has the necessary re-entry technology also remains far from certain. Any missile launched would be a comparatively easy target even for Washington's less than fully reliable missile-defence systems, given that the payload capacity is certainly insufficient to allow for the deployment of decoys – let alone multiple independent re-entry vehicles. Yet Pyongyang's worst deficiency is its lack of sophisticated guidance systems. Washington estimates a 50 per cent chance that an ICBM launched by the DPRK would hit within 80 kilometres of its intended target. The North currently has the material to construct 15 to 25 nuclear weapons. To put that in context: one Trident submarine can fire 128 to 196 warheads. Thus Washington inflates Pyongyang's capabilities; Pyongyang exaggerates them still further.

International Relations

Conservative forces in Japan and the US have agendas. One is tempted to say that if they didn't have North Korea, they would have to invent it. But in a sense, that is exactly what they've done. They have dressed up a deeply unloved – and deservedly so – shattered remnant of world Communism, a failed state backed into a corner, as the 21st century's reincarnation of the Soviet Union at its most aggressive.

Washington

US attitudes are driven by a domestic agenda that requires an enemy in the colour and shape the DPRK is painted. Taliban terrorism and Iraqi insurgency don't justify national missile defence (NMD) or Star Wars systems; an enemy with ICBMs and nuclear weapons is a minimum requirement, even if the numbers are hundreds of times smaller and the quality barely tested. The regional arms race and the collapse of the USSR dictated that North Korea devote an ever-higher proportion of its shrinking income to military spending at the expense of consumers. Working from a position of weakness, is it any surprise Pyongyang concluded that a nuclear deterrent would be a cheap alternative to maintaining conventional forces?

The United States has directly and indirectly (through the UN Security Council) used North Korea's nuclear and missile programmes as sticks to beat it. The policy of the Obama years was 'strategic patience' but could be interpreted as 'malign neglect'; Pyongyang was under no illusion that things could get better under

Hillary Clinton, who had been a hawkish secretary of state. Trump was a wild card. In the first year of his volatile presidency his rhetoric was rancorous. In his address to the United Nations in September 2017, he graduated from earlier threats of 'fire and fury' to threaten to 'totally destroy North Korea', with Kim Jong Un as a 'Rocket Man on a suicide mission for himself and for his regime'. The US prepared for 'preventive strikes' or 'bloody nose' demonstrations – even with no imminent threat from North Korea – and for 'regime change'. These were put on hold on 8 March 2018, when Trump accepted Kim's invitation to a summit.

Seoul

Pyongyang's relations with Seoul have gone from bad to worse over the 2010s. Communications between the two were cut in 2007 when the hostile conservative Lee Myung-bak was elected president. Bad became worse when his successor Park Geun-hye closed down the Kaesong Industrial Complex. When South Korea returned a group of North Korean fishermen who had strayed into South Korean waters in autumn 2017, the only channel they had to communicate with the North was a megaphone. When Moon Jae-in won the special election in May 2017 after Park's impeachment, it was his campaign promise to reopen Kaesong and institute a new policy of engagement. It was 'four nos': no hostile policy toward North Korea; no intention to attack North Korea; no attempts to undermine or replace the North Korean government; and no efforts to hasten Korean unification artificially. The breakthrough came six months later with the offer, when Kim Jong Un, in his New Year's address, announced that the DPRK would participate in the Winter Olympics and declared a unilateral moratorium on nuclear and long-range missile tests. The North-South summit set the stage for US engagement. As for the future relationship between North and South Korea, with Pyongyang's continued embrace of a non-capitalist market economy, the best outcome for the Peninsula is likely to be 'two countries, one system' – at least for a couple of generations.

Beijing

North Korea's political relations with China – despite Trump's insistence to the contrary – are and have been toxic almost since Kim Jong Un came to power. In September 2017 Pyongyang turned down a visit by China's foreign minister, Wang Yi, while senior North Korean officials were undaunted by the prospect of military clashes with Beijing. Even when Song Tao, the international secretary of the CCP, travelled to Pyongyang in November 2017 to report the outcome of the 19th Congress to China's 'fraternal partners' in the WPK, he only got to meet his counterpart, Ri Su Yong, not Kim Jong Un.

In late March 2018 the dam broke. Early interactions between Kim Jong Un and secretary of state designate Mike Pompeo suggested Washington lacked the will to seize the offer of a grand bargain, with Pyongyang pivoting away from China to the US. If there was to be a deal at all, it was to be back to 1994's endless pettifogging over details. There were three summits with Xi in three months

Nevertheless, throughout this short decade, China remained North Korea's only serious trading partner: it effectively runs the Rason

Figure 2   A fish-processing plant in Rason.
The poster on the wall reads, 'Save Electricity.'

Special Economic Zone as a suzerainty and imports much of North Korea's raw materials. For China, the *status quo ante* with Pyongyang denuclearising is ideal. Its preference is minimum change. Beijing is convinced that it is waxing as Washington wanes: the longer any political confrontation can be put off, the better positioned China will be. From its point of view, an early economic collapse of the regime would bring serious consequences: millions of refugees flooding across its border, a possibly hostile united Korea, and the prospect of US troops patrolling the south bank of the Yalu River. A second Korean War would be infinitely worse.

Tokyo

In theory, Japan should have an important role in any diplomatic solution to the crisis. In the days when multilateral negotiations were seen as a way forward, it had been expected that Japan, alongside South Korea, would make a major contribution to the financial-aid package that would be the economic foundation on which any political settlement would be built. When Tokyo normalised relations with South Korea in 1964, it provided hundreds of millions of dollars in reparations for colonisation and a parallel payment – in present-day terms worth more than $10 billion – for the northern half of the peninsula was foreseen. But for close to fifteen years, relations with Tokyo have been poisoned by the issue of the 17 Japanese who were abducted by North Korea between 1977 and 1983; the eight abductees who are still missing have been the focus of sustained public interest in Japan. This has exacerbated hostility towards any normalisation of relations.

But this is not the sole motivation, grand strategy also plays a part. In Japan, the post-war generation, represented by prime ministers Junichiro Koizumi (2001–2006) and, more aggressively, Shinzo Abe (2006-2007 and 2012–present), have taken over. They are self-confident nationalists who want Japan, already the world's fifth-largest military spender, to become a 'normal country' by abrogating the US imposed Peace Constitution. Public-opinion polls demonstrate a majority in favour of retaining Article 9, which constrains Japan from the use of armed force in international relations and from further militarisation. Hearts and minds require kneading prior to the required referendum if Abe and his fellow neo-conservatives are to get their way. An intransigent North Korea with its nuclear deterrent, its missile tests over Japan, and the abductees, is the perfect catalyst. Japan can continue to launch its satellites from Tanegashima.

Abe, who was re-elected in November 2017, has no interest in seeking a negotiated solution, nor is he capable of delivering one. He built his political career on the abductee issue to an extent unmatched by any other politician in Japan and is now the victim of his own success in making it a *cause célèbre*. There will have to be a different prime minister in Tokyo before there is movement. Were Abe to be replaced by either the conservative Shigeru Ishiba or the more moderate former foreign minister Fumio Kishida, the prospects might be different. In the meantime, Japan will do all it can to frustrate any settlement and will only join in once it clearly no longer has a veto.

New York

The North is entangled with the United Nations, principally in relation to its nuclear programme and human-rights record – although, thanks to Trump's national security advisor, John Bolton, its missile tests are a side issue of concern. Pyongyang doesn't entirely refuse to engage with the global community on human-rights issues; rather, it spurns any involvement in what it sees as their US-driven politicisation through the 2014 Commission of Inquiry (CoI) and the consecutive appointment of rapporteurs for human rights in North Korea. The UN Commission of Inquiry took testimony from over 80 witnesses and concluded there were 'systematic, widespread, and gross human rights violations'.[6] Pyongyang ferociously rejected the report. The year the Commission reported, Pyongyang implemented 113 of the UN's Universal Periodic Review's 268 human rights recommendations in full, and more in part.

The North has also protested the Security Council's sanctions, including a ban on the import of military items and luxury goods; a ban on the export of coal, iron, and lead; and an asset ban for key North Korean figures. The DPRK has written several times asking on what legal basis these sanctions have been approved. There was no answer from Ban Ki-moon when he was secretary-general, nor will the situation change under current secretary-general António Guterres, but with Guterres it is possible that the UN could play a vital role in guaranteeing any settlement. He is keen for the UN to engage. He's already helped. He despatched Jeffrey Feltman, the under-secretary-general for political affairs, to Pyongyang in December 2017, where Feltman urged the North to use the upcoming New Year's address to confirm Kim's 28 November unilateral suspension of missile and nuclear tests.

Brussels

Pyongyang has tried to build a different relationship with the EU. In the early 2000s, *Rodong Shinmun*, the newspaper of the Party Central Committee – like *Pravda* – ran a series of editorials identifying the EU as the only hegemonic power capable of challenging the United States in the wake of a visit by the EU Troika in 2001, which established a human rights dialogue that was suspended in 2003. The EU even published a Country Strategy Paper for the period from 2001 to 2004. That potential adventurous opening to the North closed with Washington pushing hard, helped by a fifth column in Paris and London. The fitful political dialogue ground to a halt. In 2014, Pyongyang came back with an offer (which it has since repeated) to re-open the human rights dialogue. This initiative has been met with embarrassed silence. It was a demand Brussels neither expected nor wanted. Taking up the offer threatened to undermine the West's storyline.

The EU's High Representative for Foreign Affairs and Security – *de facto* foreign minister – Federica Mogherini (of the Italian Democratic Party) has a more nuanced approach and would have

Figure 3   *Rodong Shinmun* welcoming my visit to the
Mankyongdae scouts, 2016.

liked to reach out. She did so at the ASEAN Regional Forum in
Manila in August 2017, when she shook hands with DPRK foreign
minister Ri Yong Ho.[7] But back in Brussels, the Council of Ministers,
led by France, the UK, and Spain, continued proposing additional
EU sanctions. These have included banning oil exports (though
there never have been any from the EU), personally sanctioning
Kim Jong Un, and 'degrading' diplomatic relations. Meanwhile,
in 2017 the BBC launched a Korean-language radio station to be
beamed into the North – joining the dozen or so other stations
already operating – a move symptomatic of Tory pretensions and a
craven BBC. British prime minister Theresa May's government also
signed up to yet another 'coalition of the willing': in 2016 a Royal
Air Force Typhoon Squadron participated in Operation Invincible
with Washington and Seoul in South Korea. The UK has promised
continued joint military exercises.[8]

Is There a Settlement to Be Had?

Even as Pyongyang's political isolation grew in the second half of
2017, the regime fixated on the lessons of Iraq, Libya and Syria. In
2016 it had astutely put its head down and completed its nuclear
deterrent, fulfilling one of the *byungjin* line's two objectives. This
allowed the suspension of the 'active' part of the programme. A

freeze in itself might begin to ease the economic bonds binding the economy through sanctions – maybe not with votes and vetoes in the Security Council, but by pragmatic economic actors on the Sino-Korean border.

This all changed on 8 March 2018, when the director of the South Korean National Security Office, Chung Eui-yong, informed President Trump in the White House that, during his own visit to Pyongyang, Kim Jong Un had 'expressed eagerness to meet President Trump as soon as possible', coupled with a commitment to denu-clearise. Trump impetuously accepted, telling Chun to announce immediately that the two would meet in May. Chun did exactly that.

The Kim-Trump Summit was seen as a success by both sides – even if they saw very different things. Trump achieved what no American president had done before. He had made America safe again – and saved money. Afterward, the hard work started. The ultimate end of a denuclearised Peninsula was agreed but on the time-table and route the sides were far apart. Achieving this goal and the milestones en route will prove a long, drawn-out process for technical and political reasons.

Both sides need to build trust – and that takes time, effort, and commitment. Once the nukes are gone, Pyongyang is of no more interest to Washington, so all future bets are off. Pyongyang needs to keep the US's attention long enough to cement the relationship, or at least the security guarantees. The credibility gap between expecta-tions and delivery must be bridged. The most dangerous period will be the post-summit negotiations, which will expose that reality.

Even if the two sides reluctantly accept the unacceptable and forget the unforgettable, there is still the process. As we saw with the 1994 Agreed Framework – and again more recently with Iran – there are plenty of opportunities to claim cheating, ill will, and sabotage, alongside mission creep, where things not in the Agreement become points of contention. If that happens, Washington and Pyongyang abandons process and progress for more confrontation.

Any failure at the summit(s), in the detailed filling out of its heads of agreement, or in the process itself will leave the US marooned, with three hostile options that could well lead to war unless Washington accepts what was previously intolerable: a nuclear-armed North Korea. It is hard to imagine any US president, let alone Trump, being willing to endure that humiliation. Saving face may cost millions of lives. The consequences would all be bad for the Peninsula – and the rest of the world.

The first option is US-led and initiated military action. This will either be a demonstration of intent, with what Washington terms a 'bloody nose' strike: taking out missile launchers or the experimental nuclear reactor under construction or 'disappearing' a submarine. The assumption is that Kim would not respond like Saddam Hussein in Iraq, Muammar Gaddafi in Libya, or Bashar al-Assad in Syria. But that's why he would have little option. The North would be forced to respond and, not having the technology for a counterstrike against US military assets, it would have no option but to hit civilian targets in the South, with almost inevitable escalation. With no or little second-strike capability for Pyongyang, it's all or nothing. If Iraq taught Pyongyang little else, it taught them that.

A series of strikes against North Korea's nuclear and missile sites, with a simultaneous attempt to decapitate the leadership, would have the same result, but quicker. In the United Kingdom, incoming prime ministers have to write a sealed note detailing what the immediate military response should be if they are killed in a devastating pre-emptive strike. They get it back unopened on leaving office. You can be certain that Kim Jong Un's note does not read 'surrender'.

At best – if such an attack miraculously succeeded in destroying all the North's nuclear weapons – this would mean the destruction of Seoul and serious damage to other population centres in South Korea and Japan. North Korea has 14,000 pieces of artillery dug in just north of the DMZ that are capable of hitting Seoul. The ensuing war would result in millions of deaths, millions of refugees, and the collapse of North and South Korea as the Peninsula was ravaged by hunger and disease and swept by armed gangs and vigilantes. If such a preventive strike missed its target and left the North with any nuclear weapons at all, the situation would be even worse, with fallout and radiation sickness stirred into the mix.

The second option is to promote regime change – covert action by the US to destabilise the Kim regime or a 'palace coup' instituted by Washington or Beijing to replace the current regime with one more malleable to their interests. Replacing Kim Jong Un will not be easy. The prospect of such a Chinese-orchestrated intervention led to the execution of Jang Song Thaek, Kim's uncle, and the assassination of Kim Jong Nam, his half-brother. Even if Kim were toppled in a court coup, there is no guarantee that the resulting regime would be any better. Furthermore, if a coup turned out neither quick nor clean, it could lead to civil war in the North – like in Syria, except that here one side would have nuclear weapons and enemies close at hand. In this scenario, too, there would be millions of refugees on the march as the economy collapsed. It would be three or four times bigger than the Syrian exodus. A 'Magnolia Spring' sponsored by Washington would meet brutal internal repression, and outside intervention would be forcefully resisted.

The third option is a total trade embargo, which would include, crucially, oil imports. There is a real question as to whether Beijing or Moscow – even Seoul – would be willing to go along with Washington on an embargo unless Kim reactivated his nuclear and missile programmes. The US tried to push such an embargo through the Security Council in mid-September 2017, but the Russians and Chinese insisted that the ban should be partial. The non-oil-related sanctions did not prevent Pyongyang from completing its programme. Yet even with China and the Security Council on board, this is a country where millions died in the famine in the late 1990s. It won't easily be forced back to the table after a breakdown of negotiations. If and when the situation became critical, military adventurism is a far more likely response than submission. But, on the ground, it threatens to collapse into option two if Kim restrains his military. Deprivation and shortages could trigger food riots and murderous score-settling with the regime that brings on repression, intervention, and war. It's just taking the long way round.

The last, best option is a negotiated settlement, given that the other three all likely lead to war. Here Pyongyang is right to see any solution as dependent on Washington. They have no interest in resurrecting the Six-Party Talks as the principal format for negotiations: they need bilateral DPRK–USA negotiations alongside North-South talks, with a follow-on multilateral dimension to buttress and guarantee the peace agreement and security guarantees as well as fund the settlement. Their aim is a comprehensive settlement, maybe utilising elements of the mid-1970s Helsinki process's innovative political blueprint for détente between the Soviet Union and the West. Helsinki worked not by trading tit for tat but by making seemingly incommensurable concessions across different baskets, ranging from economic co-operation to human rights and security.

A new Agreed Framework, modelled on the 1994 Agreement that froze Pyongyang's nuclear ambitions, would be one option. Formal talks would follow the summit agreement to maintain the freeze on nuclear testing and the moratorium on new long-range missile development, in exchange for Trump's suspension of the joint military exercises by the US and its allies. The North could promise an early freeze on plutonium production, shut down its reactor, re-join the NPT, and open up to IAEA inspections. The spectacle of the destruction of the North's ICBMs and fabrication plant would be made for TV. The culmination of this framework – after 10 to 15 years – would see the LWRs going online and North Korea surrendering the last of its nuclear material. En route, there would be a series of intermediate steps. It may be entirely different. Trump doesn't want to repeat the mistakes of the past, so Washington may shy away from anything that could be construed as an Agreed Framework 2. Yet what is clear is that Pyongyang wants and needs a long-term relationship, not a one-night stand.

Achieving an Agreement will be hard; delivering it will be worse. When the 1994 Agreement was signed, few on the US side believed they would ever need to deliver their side of the bargain – and they didn't. The US unilaterally abrogated the deal in 2001. One lesson Pyongyang will have learnt from that experience is the need for international guarantors. Trump will be neither willing nor able to fund the final settlement, which will run into the tens of billions of dollars.

Last time, with the Agreed Framework, there were convenient cash cows to be milked: South Korea, Japan, and the EU. They paid but had no say. This time around, the bulk of the financial heavy lifting will again come from Seoul, up to 70 per cent of the costs, helped by Beijing (through an extension of its Belt and Road Initiative), possibly Tokyo (with all the reservations mentioned above), and Brussels – where German chancellor Angela Merkel has offered to contribute. This time, one assumes that they will demand a role in the decisions.

While there may be light at the end of the tunnel, there is no guarantee of a tunnel. Pyongyang could suffer the fate of Hiroshima or Baghdad. If it can escape that fate, it could turn out in the longer term to be a Beijing or Hanoi, a Tirana or Bucharest. The fate of tens of millions hangs in the balance.

Structure

This book consists of nine chapters. Chapter 2 explains the colonial history of the Korean Peninsula, its experience of the Pacific War, how it was carved up by the two superpowers, and how the two sides, north and south of the 38th parallel, left and right fought to unify the country on their own terms – a process crucial to understanding the DPRK today. The end of the Pacific War is a defining moment in Korean history, not only because of the division that followed but because it marked the end of six centuries of effective subordination to its much larger and more powerful neighbours: China, Japan, and more recently Russia.

Kim Il Sung, an anti-Japanese guerrilla fighter picked by the Soviets to help fill a political void when they occupied the North, was initially a loyal Stalinist. He sought Stalin and Mao's permission before invading the South, set on unifying the entire peninsula under the red flag. The war broke out on 25 June 1950 and quickly became internationalised. As the North pushed almost all the way down to Busan in the far south, the US joined the fray, and UN Command subsequently forced the North to retreat in places to the border with

China, at which point Beijing threw itself into the mix. Two years of stalemate ended in an armistice, which, 65 years on, has still not been turned into a peace treaty. The brutality of the war and the continuing standoff between Pyongyang and Washington continue to overshadow politics and daily life in the North.

Chapter 3 looks at post-war economic, social, and political developments under Kim Il Sung and how Kim sliced and diced the opposition, eliminating rivals outside and inside the Party to consolidate power. To legitimate and maintain his increasingly monolithic leadership, an intense personality cult developed, with autarky in economy and politics driven by Kim's notion of Juche (self-reliance). Alongside this political revolution, the North Korean economy, founded on heavy industry, experienced remarkable growth, enabling the country to quickly recover from the devastation of the war to leapfrog and race ahead of the listless economy in the South. This surge didn't last. By the time of Kim Il Sung's death in 1994, the economy was in such a fragile state that all it required was a series of natural disasters to push it into collapse.

That collapse soon came, and Chapter 4 charts the course of the North Korean famine that left millions dead and even more devastated. Refugees fled into China, while international organisations began to deliver food aid and humanitarian assistance. Kim Jong Il had blamed the famine on a series of floods and the collapse of the Soviet Union and began both to sanction economic reforms from below and institute them from above. Kim Jong Il grew his own personality cult. The chapter looks at attempts to address North Korea's human rights record and the value of the testimonies of 'defectors'.

Chapter 5 looks at the rise of the third Kim, focusing on the *byungjin* dual-track policy of economic renewal and nuclear deterrence. Since coming to power, Kim Jong Un has encouraged private markets, turning a blind eye to kiosks and market sellers. There is an added emphasis on special economic zones. Under his reign, consumer goods and Western fashions have spread in a privileged Pyongyang. Reforms of agriculture and industry continue, but the former has been more successful than the latter. Developing a nuclear deterrent was made a priority, and there was a dash to the finish line.

Chapter 6 covers daily life in the North. Despite market reforms, the political system remains as tightly controlled as ever. This chapter explores Party and Pyongyang life, education, newspapers and television, health care – both Western and traditional – and crime and punishment.

Chapter 7 further explores the nuclear weapons programme, looking at its origin and motivation, along with missile development and an overall assessment of the North's capabilities and what chemical, biological and cyber-warfare capacity it might have. It also examines previous attempts to negotiate away its nuclear programme, Pyongyang's nuclear posture, and its history of providing overseas military assistance. It concludes with a look at relations with South Korea.

Chapter 8 focuses on North Korea's foreign relations, looking at the sanctions regime and attempts during the Soviet era to find a third way. It examines relations with China (bad), the US (worse), and Japan (worst), as well as the EU and UN.

Chapter 9 concludes the book by focusing on how to resolve the crisis on the Peninsula, short of war. This will be far from easy. Good will, trust, and commitment are necessary but not sufficient. It will need an agreed framework, a detailed sequential plan for denuclearisation heavily front-end loaded with a long-tail followed by an implementation process, where ownership is as much with the international community as with the protagonists.

PART I

Roots of the Present Crisis:
Understanding North Korea's History

2
Drawing the Iron Curtain

To understand the DPRK is to appreciate its fight to survive amidst powerful and hostile neighbours. Korea, which is the size of the United Kingdom and wedged between Japan, China, and Russia, has been subject to invasion, intervention, and interference throughout its history. When Japan took over its administration in 1905, Korea was a feudal country with no experience of democracy or civic society. It remained a Japanese colony until the end of the Pacific War in 1945, when it was promptly bisected by Washington and Moscow along the 38th parallel. One occupier became two. This legacy of the Potsdam Conference agreement between Stalin and Truman (July 1945) left a 250-kilometre dividing line separating the northern, Soviet sector (55 per cent of the country) from the southern, American one (45 per cent) – an arbitrary division Washington saw as the minimum Moscow would accept.

The subsequent Korean War drew an iron curtain between North and South along the demilitarised zone (DMZ), a line roughly following the 38th parallel, a little south in the west and north in the east, reflecting the exigencies of war rather than the ruler. Over time, two sharply different countries emerged and developed separately on the peninsula.

Geography

The Korean peninsula stretches from the plains of eastern Manchuria and Siberia to within 110 kilometres of Japan's western island of Kyushu. The 1,425-kilometre border with China follows the River Amnok/Yalu, between Mount Paektu, the peninsula's highest mountain, and Sinuiju to the West Sea (Yellow Sea) and the Tumen

River to the East Sea (Sea of Japan). The source of both these rivers
is Lake Chon, the mountain's central lake. Paektu is a national icon
for both North and South, with a status similar to that of Mount
Fuji in Japan. It was at one time the subject of a border dispute with
China, but this was resolved in Pyongyang's favour. The border with
Russia has only existed since 1860, when Tsar Nicholas II acquired
the maritime territories from China. This desolate border along 19
kilometres of the Tumen River estuary has only one crossing point, a
single-track railway bridge. Large sections of the rivers forming the
Sino-Korean border can be swum or waded for most of the year or
in winter, strolled across.

Almost 80 per cent of the North is mountainous, which leaves
agricultural land at a premium. This, along with the bulk of the

Figure 4   The Chinese-Korean border, from Air Koryo.

North's 22.3 million people, is confined to narrow coastal plains in the east and wider ones in the west. This geography has moulded the country, with flooding, deforestation, and famine as its tools. North Korea's wealth of natural resources – including coal, zinc, and magnesium – underpinned the success of heavy industry in the 1960s and 1970s. The South, in comparison, is poor in minerals and rich in arable land.

Korea first emerged out of the mists of prehistory 2,500 years ago. Kingdoms waxed and waned, born of division and dying from fusion. Some, like the Koguryo Kingdom, spilled far across today's borders, deep into what is now China. These kingdoms were often semi-detached vassal states of China and in more recent times Japan, both of them all too willing to intervene when their interests were threatened. Koguryo's footprint across today's national demarcation lines excites right-wing revanchists in South Korea, who envision a Greater Korea that incorporates Manchuria's Korean-speaking majorities and minorities; some in Beijing, however, expect that, after any catastrophic collapse of the DPRK, that area would be within China rather than a Greater Korea. The long-lost kingdoms live on in the names of airlines, hotels, and restaurants.

The Yanks Arrive

Throughout the nineteenth century, Western powers attempted to use the soft seduction of Christianity to remove barriers to trade. In 1836, French Catholic priests entered Korea from China and converted an estimated 20,000 people within a quarter of a century, including the mother of King Kojong. The king's father, the Taewongun (Lord of the Great Court), sceptical of foreigners, persecuted them for undermining Confucianism. Korea's experience with China led him to believe that too much trust would lead to betrayal and foreign occupation. Foreign ships arrived and then sharply departed as the Koreans fired upon them. By the middle of the nineteenth century European nations and the United States were impatient for new trading routes in Asia.

China's position had transformed for the worse with the arrival of Western traders and gunboats, and as the First Opium War (1839–42) erupted between Britain and China, Korea slammed its doors firmly shut. This retreat into isolation was equally a retreat into denial, disguising how far behind the country's economic development and military capacity were. In 1853 Commodore Matthew Perry and his 'black ships' forcibly prised open Japan, but the gunboat USS *South America,* which anchored off Busan for ten days, received a friendlier welcome. Americans shipwrecked off Korea in 1855 and 1865 were treated well and repatriated via China, but this common courtesy and humanity were misconstrued as a willingness to open doors.

In 1866, this tension came to a head when American businessman W.B. Preston arranged for the gunboat USS *General Sherman* to sail to Korea. It steamed up the Taedong River and became beached at the islet of Turu near Pyongyang. The governor of Pyongyang sent his deputy, Lee Hyon Ik, to order the captain to leave immediately or the crew would all be killed. The Americans took Lee hostage, and four days of fighting followed. Eventually the ship was set ablaze; the remnants of the crew jumped overboard and were promptly butchered. The US returned in 1871 with a force of five ships and 650 men to establish the fate of the *General Sherman.* The resulting clashes killed 350 Koreans, but the Americans were not strong enough and did not have the authority to open Korea to trade forcibly. Nevertheless, Korea got the message. When a Japanese military expedition arrived near Seoul in 1876, Korea grudgingly signed the Treaty of Kanghwa and opened its ports. Further unequal treaties with European countries and the US followed. The Treaty of Shufeldt (1882) with the US, finally signed two years later at Chemulpo, promised mutual friendship and non-interference in missionary activity; the latter was reciprocal but, while few Confucian clerics travelled to the US to proselytise, traffic in the opposite direction was heavy.

Revolts, Riots, and Invasion

Korea suffered insurrections and food riots through much of the nineteenth century, culminating in the Tonghak Rebellion of

1894–95. Tonghak was a nativist religious movement, founded in the early 1860s in reaction to Christian evangelism and the Choson Dynasty's chronic corruption and brutality. The revolt began in the south-west but rapidly spread to the centre of the country, threatening Seoul. Desperate, the court pleaded with China to send troops to quell the rebellion. China obligingly sent an expedition. When it showed no signs of leaving, Japan responded by sending a counter-force three times larger, and the First Sino-Japanese War (1894–95) began. The Japanese promised Koreans freedom – but, like the Chinese, once there, they lingered. Next up were the Russians, whom Japan also bested. In the late 1890s China granted Russia the right to extend the Trans-Siberian Railway across Manchuria and leased them Port Arthur (now Lüshun) as a base for their naval forces in the Pacific. The line's completion would have enabled Moscow to transport troops to Manchuria and Korea swiftly. Japan – in an early rehearsal for Pearl Harbor – launched a surprise attack on Port Arthur that started the Russo-Japanese War (1904–1905). For the first time, East had defeated West.

Japanese troops occupied Seoul the day after the Russo-Japanese War started and forced the Koreans immediately to sign a protectorate treaty, effectively abrogating their sovereignty inside Japan's 'sphere of influence'. Tokyo installed a resident general (later a governor general). Violating its treaty, the US acknowledged Japan's control with the Taft-Katsura Agreement of 1905, which traded Japan's subjection of Korea for US control of the Philippines.

King Kojong declared the protectorate treaty invalid in the absence of his signature, but in 1907 he was forced to abdicate in favour of his pro-Japanese son Sunjong, who became the last Choson monarch. Popular resistance to the Japanese occupation was widespread but ineffectual, with acts of individual terror. Led by irregular forces known as the Uibyong (Righteous Army), the resistance was brutally repressed. The assassination of former resident general Ito Hirobumi in 1909 demonstrated the opposition's weakness while providing the pretext for the Japan-Korea Annexation Treaty (1910), which reduced Korea's status from protectorate to colony. Twenty thousand Uibyong died before the remainder were driven into exile.

Under these circumstances, a new nationalism emerged that rejected the restoration of the monarchy in favour of a different future. As World War I drew to a close, US president Woodrow Wilson argued for a principle of 'national self-determination'. This provided the impetus for Korean students in Japan to issue a Declaration of Independence in February 1919. Hundreds of thousands in Seoul rallied on 1 March in support. Thousands of them died when Japanese troops fired on the demonstration; tens of thousands were arrested.

Japanese repression worked, but beneath it nationalist sentiment – now known as the 1 March Movement – only grew stronger. Nationalist Korean exiles in Shanghai announced the formation of a provisional Korean government, with the conservative Syngman Rhee as president. Meanwhile, for the first time, Communism emerged inside Korea and its diaspora. At home, Communists and socialists began to organise youth and labour groups. In January 1918, just a few months after the Russian Revolution, a Korean Communist Party with a strong nationalist bent was briefly established as a section of the Soviet Communist Party. In 1925 it reformed in Seoul. One of its founders, Park Hon Yong, would become the Communist leader in the South after the division of the Peninsula in 1945. Enter two future protagonists: one stage right, the other stage left.

The Communists concentrated their activities amongst the peasantry and the vanishingly small industrial proletariat. Lenin's theory of working-class emancipation, mixed with the rurally focussed Red Peasant International (Krestintern), provided the organising framework. This appealed to their target audience, since Japanese owned both the farms and the factories. To the suppressed Koreans, pairing nationalism and Communism made an attractive amalgam. Nevertheless, by 1928, the Soviets had again grown tired of the sectarianism and squabbling of Korea's Communists. The Korean Party was dissolved and its members told to join the Party of the country where they were operating, either Japan or China. It was too late. Japan was now repressing its domestic Communists as brutally as their colonial cousins.

In 1927 the remnants of the opposition, moderate and radical, formed a united front organisation, the Singanhoe. It steadily shrank under the weight of Japanese repression, but moved left as it died. By 1931 Tokyo was in the final phase of its colonisation, with its colonies under military control. The Japanese attempted to assimilate Koreans with obligatory worship at imperial shrines, the use of Japanese in schools, restrictions on Korean script and language, and the forced adoption of Japanese names. However, peasant uprisings and labour disputes continued to grow.

Kim Enters Left

Kim's family was one of many that had fled Korea going into exile in Manchuria in 1919 and 1920. Kim Il Sung was born Kim Sung Ju on 15 April 1912, the day the *Titanic* sank. By 17, Kim had been arrested and imprisoned in China for eight months for helping to establish the South Manchurian Communist Youth Association. When he was released, he focused increasingly on agitation work, joining the Chinese Communist Party (CCP) in 1931. That year, Japan invaded Manchuria, leading to a growing armed struggle that would see more than 200,000 Chinese guerrillas and a sprinkling of Koreans – some left over from the Uibyong – fighting the Japanese. Kim Il Sung became one of them. He was fighting by 1933, and by 1935 was in the CCP's 15,000-strong North-East Anti-Japanese United Army using the pseudonym Kim Il Sung, the name of an earlier well-known resistance fighter.

Japanese attempts to suppress the guerrilla movement drove this army deep into the countryside, forcing them to abandon fixed positions and to break up into smaller mobile units. Between 1935 and 1941, Kim Il Sung rose through the ranks. His largest and most famous operation was the June 1937 attack on the Japanese garrison in the Chinese–Korean border village of Pochonbo with a company of 200 men – barely a skirmish in most wars. He was a determined, resilient patriot favoured with good luck and the Japanese singled him out as both effective and popular.

In 1941, Kim and his guerrilla band were forced to seek safety in the USSR, which was technically at peace with Japan after that April's Soviet–Japanese Neutrality Pact. In the cold harsh terrain of Siberia they were re-armed, trained, and put to study Communist orthodoxy. Kim was assigned to the Khabarovsk Infantry Services School, located close to the USSR's border with China. Soviet sources indicate that he married a fellow guerrilla fighter, Kim Jong Suk, there, and their first son, Kim Jong Il, was born. Korean history, in contrast, locates Kim's birth in a guerrilla camp on the slopes of Mount Paektu – now a place of pilgrimage'.

Kim Il Sung had effectively been in exile since the age of seven. Since his teenage years, apart from his time in the USSR, he had never lived in a town or city and had been cut off from books, newspapers, and radio. Consequently, he was ignorant of the international situation and world events. Nor is there evidence that he studied Marxism-Leninism in any sustained way, apart from a youthful reading of the *Communist Manifesto* and subsequently Stalin's 'Bible', his 1938 *Short Course of the History of the All-Russian Communist Party* (*Bolshevik*). But Kim had learnt by practice. His days as a guerrilla shaped his leadership style and moulded the future shape of the DPRK.

Colonial Consequences

Japan seized a country that was beginning to make its own way, deconstructed it, and tried to remodel, incorporate, and assimilate it. Its objectives went way beyond economic exploitation: it attempted to destroy Korean culture and society and reassemble Koreans as 'second-class' subjects of Japan's emperor. As George Orwell sarcastically reports, a Japanese radio broadcast announced, 'In order to do justice to the patriotic spirit of the Koreans, the Japanese government has decided to introduce compulsory military service in Korea'.[1]

During World War II, 2.4 million Koreans fought in the Japanese army, most by coercion. Hundreds of thousands perished.

Japanese bureaucrats and entrepreneurs took over Korea's institutions, destroying the last remnants of feudalism and bringing infrastructure, industrialisation, and rising agricultural productivity, with new planting techniques and chemical fertilisers to increase rice output. Agricultural development was concentrated in the south, with industry and mining in the north. Japan built houses and factories, roads and rail networks. It worked well: the rate of economic growth in Korea was higher than in Japan. The benefits, however, flowed not to Koreans but to Tokyo.

The Peninsula became a cog in Japan's Greater East Asia Co-Prosperity Sphere, a supplier of food, workers, war materials, and industrial production to Japan and its empire. War work was either offshored to Korea's cheap labour or the cheap labour exported to the war work in Japan – the men to the mines and factories, and the young 'comfort women' to Japanese army brothels. Seoul, using Japanese documents and statistics, claims that by 1945 more than 800,000 men and 50,000 to 70,000 women had been forcibly shipped to Japan. Pyongyang claims 2 million slave labourers.

Japan's violent and unrelenting repression, especially during the last 15 years of occupation, drove almost the entirety of the traditional nationalist leadership into exile. Away from their homeland, these would-be leaders lost touch. The transformation of Korea eluded them. They experienced neither the modernisation nor the dramatic and irreversible social changes Tokyo wrought. When the traditionalist leaders finally returned, the people had left them behind.

The Japanese occupation had produced a political vacuum in Korea – leaders without followers in exile, followers without leaders at home. It had precluded any possibility of a national capitalism run and managed by a modernising indigenous elite by refusing even to train Koreans as technicians and managers. This vacuum was filled by Communists and Communism, whose democratic centralism had a historical memory and collective will that could survive the loss of individual leaders and whose programme resonated with the post-feudal aspirations of peasants and workers.

The US victory in the Pacific theater ended the Japanese occupation. When Japan unconditionally surrendered to the Allied forces on 15 August 1945, Korean hopes for independence soared. After all, the Cairo Conference in November 1943 had stated that 'the US and its allies, mindful of the enslavement of the people of Korea, are determined that in due course Korea shall become free and independent'. But the victorious allies decided that 'in due course' was definitely not now: Franklin Roosevelt and Joseph Stalin agreed that Koreans did not have the required institutions or experience to govern themselves, being both politically immature and divided. The US proposed to place Korea under trusteeship, administered initially for five years by itself, the Soviet Union, China, and the UK (thus rewarding the latter for its role in Operation Iceberg, off the South Okinawan islands). In the end, Korea didn't achieve independence, self-government, or even trusteeship: it was just occupied.

US War Department officials proposed, a few days before the Japanese surrender, a US-Soviet joint occupation, with the 38th parallel as the dividing line. There was no political or topographical logic in Korean terms; the victors were dividing the spoils. Seoul, the capital, fell conveniently on the US side, but the deal gave Moscow enough to stop them wanting more. Stalin's indifference – at the time – to the fate of Korea was demonstrated by his acceptance of a lousy deal.

The Soviets Come and Go

Under pressure from the US and Britain the Soviets had made a secret agreement in February 1945 at the Yalta Conference that they would declare war on Japan three months after V-E Day. Moscow wanted to regain the regions lost by Tsarist Russia after the Russo-Japanese War[2] in 1905, but this was not a priority for Stalin. After all, why wait three months? An early intervention would allow the USSR to occupy not only the Korean peninsula but probably Hokkaido as well – both sideshows as far as Washington was concerned. Moscow declared war on Japan on 8 August 1945. Soviet troops entered Pyongyang on 24 August; the first US troops did not land in Incheon until more than a fortnight later.

Stalin had no clear plans for post-war government in the Soviet zone of Korea. Neither Kim nor his partisans had been seen as key players during the Pacific endgame. The Red Army had regrouped the Korean fighters, along with other remnants of the Manchurian guerrillas, in the first of four battalions forming its 88th Brigade, responsible for reconnaissance and infiltration, and made Kim Il Sung its commander. Yet the Brigade was not amongst the Soviet forces that initially entered and occupied Korea. Kim and his fellow officers only arrived six weeks later, after it was all over. Kim was presented as guerrilla hero rather than political leader.

Kim had been in exile for a quarter-century and was completely unknown outside a narrow circle of Communist crusaders. Japanese censorship had ensured that few details of the guerrillas' heroic, if limited, successes were known. The Soviets set up an interim coalition government, including a number of non-Communist parties, as per its 'people's democracy' playbook. This was achieved by taking Cho Man Sik's Preparation Committee for Korean Independence in Pyongyang and sprinkling in some Communists to act as unofficial liaisons between the Soviet high command and the local population. The government was sharply divided over Roosevelt's trusteeship proposal. The Communists, echoing Moscow's line, expressed support; the others were outraged and demanded immediate independence. Moscow moved for abandoning trusteeship, while the local commanders, impressed by Kim's dedication, discipline, and ruthlessness during these confrontations, began to promote him as 'their' leader.

On 8 February 1946, Kim became head of the Provisional People's Committee. He began the transformation. The peculiar conditions of Korea did not favour a vanguard proletarian Communist Party: there were no industrial workers. Instead, what was required was a mass party mobilising small farmers. In the North, alongside social and economic change came political consolidation. Kim's key strength was his relationship with the Soviet administration. Under the Soviet umbrella, he welded together a coalition of domestic Communists (many of whom had fled to the North from the American-occupied South), Chinese Koreans who had fought with Mao Zedong's Communist forces, Soviet Koreans, and his own small but cohesive group of partisan fighters.

Kim and his allies took control and began to systematically side-line and eliminate the opposition and arrest non-Communist leaders, such as Cho Man Sik. Long before 1949, when the North Korean Workers' Party merged with the South Korean Workers' Party to form the Workers' Party of Korea (WPK), it was obvious which was the horse and which the rider. Kim Il Sung became chairman and the South's leader became vice-chairman. It was a 'Russified' Korean from the diaspora, Ho Ka I, who copied and pasted the structure and organisation of the Soviet Communist Party onto Korea. The Party inducted tens of thousands of poor peasants into its ranks and embarked on the road of popular reform. The mass mobilisation of women and youth changed forever Korea's patriarchal, deferential society. As Suzy Kim argues, from the end of the Japanese occupation to the Korean War, a period she terms a 'liberatory space', North Korea was filled with potential.[3] For the first time, women came out of the kitchen and onto the front lines. A mass literacy campaign was launched to educate the 80 per cent of Koreans who had never received schooling; by March 1948, 92 per cent of peasants had learnt to read and write, and the number continued to creep upwards. Land reform redistributed land to the peasants, resulting in a sharp rise in productivity. In August, nationalisation gave the state control of 90 per cent of what little industry there was.[4] The economy, replicating Moscow's model, gave priority to heavy industry over agriculture. The Soviets provided loans totalling 212 million roubles ($7.5 million, or €6.1 million) to smooth the process. The North's gross national product doubled between 1946 and 1949. With Moscow running political interference and providing hard cash, Kim had strong popular support and a loyal following amongst militant nationalists and former guerrilla fighters.

Both the US and the USSR initially worked within the administrative architecture put in place by the Japanese. Nationwide, almost all significant enterprises were the property of Japanese colonists who had fled back to their devastated homeland, leaving Korean collaborators in charge. Kim's nationalisation of industry changed that in the North. But retaining these quislings in the South did not endear the US to those who had suffered under the occupation. The People's Committees in the South organised huge popular protests against the US military government in Korea. With the consolidation of political power and a growing economy, it was time to turn to unfinished business.

Gerrymandered Elections

The division of the Peninsula had been intended as a temporary measure, like in Austria. The US and the Soviet Union were to organise nationwide elections to enable a single Korean Government to be established. But the US–Soviet Joint Commission on Korea failed to agree. Elections frightened Washington, for while the South had almost twice the North's population, there was enormous enthusiasm and support for left and progressive parties. Anything close to 'free and fair' elections would have had only one result: a landslide victory for Kim and his left coalition. The Communists and their left allies were widely perceived as having led the struggle against the Japanese; more importantly, they espoused a package of populist and popular policies.

In Pyongyang's local elections in 1946 and 1947, the North Korean Workers Party had been the biggest winners, with over 30 per cent of the seats; another 20 per cent was split between the anti-Western nationalism/nativism of the Chondogyo Young Friends Party and the Democratic Party, with 50 per cent going to independents. A year later, in the People's Assembly elections, the figures for those elected were 36 per cent Workers Party, 13 per cent Chondoists, 13 per cent Democratic Party, and 38 per cent independents.

The US turned to the United Nations. In September 1947, a General Assembly resolution proposed a plebiscite, under a UN guarantee. The Soviets regarded the UN as a wholly owned US subsidiary and rejected the proposal arguing that the US's surrogate candidate would inevitably be declared the 'winner'. The plebiscite went ahead in the US zone alone.

The US chose Syngman Rhee, a graduate of Princeton University and the first Korean to receive a doctorate from an American university, as its surrogate. He had been hand-delivered to Seoul on 16 October 1945 on General Douglas MacArthur's personal plane. Rhee's fierce anti-Communism and his long exile in the States were decisive, but he had little if any credibility or support inside Korea. Few remembered his spell in 1920 as president of the Shanghai-based provisional Korean government in exile. Nevertheless, he had the backing of powerful US patrons who saw him as a malleable tool. They badly misjudged him. Rhee would prove to be almost impossible to manage, and even less grateful to Washington than Kim Il Sung would be to Moscow.

Pyongyang countered deceit with 'democracy'. Local elections had been held in 1946 and 1947. The North Korean Workers Party were the biggest winners with over 30 per cent of the seats. The DPRK was born on 9 September 1948. With Moscow's support, Kim Il Sung set up a parallel state north of the demarcation line. The North-South border was closed. Neither government recognised its counterpart; both claimed to represent the entire nation. Seoul left one-third of its seats in the National Assembly empty for future members from the North, while Pyongyang claimed that 360 of its 572 assembly members had been elected in 'secret' balloting in the South. Pyongyang 'demanded' the withdrawal of US and Soviet troops. Moscow's troops departed the following month, leaving behind old weapons and new arms factories. Belatedly, driven by US public opinion, US forces withdrew in June 1949, leaving behind 500 'military advisors'. With both governments completely at odds and pledging to reunify the whole country by any means, the question was not whether there would be war, but when and where.

Figure 5   A Party poster from the mid- to late-1940s.
It reads: 'All hail the establishment of the North Korean
Workers' Party/Workers unite with the Party'.

Pre-War War

The US military government, under the command of General John R. Hodge, had strict instructions to prevent a Communist takeover in the South. It watched placidly as the regime murderously suppressed popular protest as well as Communist insurgency, with mass arrests of 'suspects' and the complete suppression of the People's Committees. In 1946, the South Korean Workers Party (SKWP) instigated the failed Autumn Harvest Uprising. By December, when the disturbances had been contained, hundreds had been killed and thousands jailed. Sporadic violence continued until the spring of 1948, when it exploded into armed struggle and guerrilla warfare on Cheju Island.

Cheju was followed in October 1948 by a mutiny of the 14th Regiment of the South Korean Army in Yosu-Sunchon. In putting down this mutiny, troops loyal to Rhee killed 2,000 alleged participants. Park Chung-Hee, the ROK's future right-wing dictator, was sentenced to life imprisonment for his part in the rebellion. The increasingly dictatorial Syngman Rhee had to cleanse the South of Communists and Communism if he was to impose himself on a reluctant population that had a sneaking sympathy and admiration for Kim Il Sung and his patriots, who had fought their war rather than spectating from the comfort of US exile. By 1949, 100,000 political prisoners were crowded into Rhee's jails. The number of civilian deaths in the South had reached at least 200,000 – some claim as many as 800,000 – before the Korean War even started.

Cornelius Osgood, an American anthropologist living on Kanghwa Island, summed up the situation:

'Communist' has become a strange word in our time and it may refer to a political philosopher, a Russian spy, a member of any other political party, a labour organiser, a traitor to one's own country, or someone who happened to be regarded as an enemy. On Ganghwa (now Kanghwa) it seemed to mean just 'any young man of a village'.[5]

The inevitable civil war followed. Both sides were driven by the feeling that the country's arbitrary division was deeply unjust; North and South wanted one Korea. Rhee's slogan 'March North' and Kim's 'Fatherland Liberation' were both calls to arms. Border clashes and conflicts, largely provoked by the South, started in May 1949 and died down by December, after the North came off distinctly better in the exchanges. Kim was waiting to be let off his leash. When the US withdrew its troops in June 1949, not trusting Rhee and reluctant to be drawn into any major conflict by Rhee's military adventurism,[6] the US limited his ambitions by leaving the ROK army bereft of heavy weapons.

Kim's ambitions were reinforced by US Secretary of State Dean Acheson's speech to the National Press Club on 12 January 1950.

There he defined the US 'perimeter of defence' in Asia to include Japan and the Philippines but not south Korea or Taiwan.[7] His failure to put the South inside the US's circle of wagons was read as a clear sign that if the South was attacked, the US would not intervene. Acheson added a prescient addendum: 'Should such an attack occur . . . the initial reliance must be on the people attacked to resist it and then upon the commitments of the entire civilised world under the Charter of the United Nations'. Kim saw a window of opportunity for the North. He had reasons and resources for war: his Korean People's Army (KPA) had tens of thousands of battle-hardened troops who had fought with Mao in China, plus a smaller number trained by the Soviets in the early 1940s.

Rhee, meanwhile, was desperately trying to persuade Washington of the Soviet threat. He was partly successful. In March 1950, Congress voted an extra $11 million (€8.9 million) of military aid to the ROK. The idea was to leave Rhee strong enough to put down internal unrest but incapable of conducting an aggressive war. The vote pushed up the date of Kim's attack.

In March 1949, Kim Il Sung had gone to Moscow to attempt to secure backing from Stalin for a fight. He argued that the North would quickly subdue the South. Stalin refused to endorse Kim's plans; his focus was on Europe, not Asia, and he wanted to avoid a direct clash with Washington. To compensate, Stalin agreed to provide some limited material assistance to the KPA. A second attempt in August to persuade Stalin that the North was capable of a swift victory also failed. He was unaware of the full extent of KPA's successes in armed clashes along the 38th parallel, because the Soviet ambassador in Pyongyang had failed to report them fully to Moscow. This omission cost Kim dearly. Had Stalin known and given his backing, an earlier invasion would have favoured Kim.

After collaborating against the Japanese in the 1930s and 1940s, the Chinese and Korean Communists had a close relationship. There were particularly strong links in Manchuria, where Kim Il Sung had fought with the North-East Anti-Japanese Army as a member of the CCP. Tens of thousands of ethnic Koreans from both sides of the

Yalu and Tumen Rivers had fought the Japanese. After August 1945, many had continued the fight as part of Mao's People's Liberation Army against Chiang Kai-shek's nationalist Kuomintang in China's resuscitated civil war. Kim Il Sung supplied aid, assistance, and volunteers. When the forces of Mao's commander Lin Biao fell back at the end of 1946, the North provided refuge for soldiers and their families fleeing South Manchuria.

Mao's victory on the mainland and the founding of the People's Republic of China encouraged Kim. In May 1949 Mao had returned to Kim two Korean divisions of 14,000 soldiers who had fought in the civil war. With Stalin's April agreement in his pocket, Kim Il Sung travelled to Beijing the following month to secure more military assistance. Mao, entering the endgame of the Chinese civil war, was initially reluctant to become embroiled in another war, especially one where the US might intervene. Yet he wanted Stalin's help with the invasion of Taiwan.

On 14 February 1950, the People's Republic of China and the Soviet Union signed a Treaty of Friendship, Alliance, and Mutual Assistance. The treaty eased Stalin's mistrust of Mao and made Communist revolutions in Asia a Chinese franchise. Stalin had decided that there were advantages to opening a surrogate second front in Asia, drawing US resources away from the Cold War stand-off in Europe. China was to be that subcontractor and proxy partner. In April 1950, after Acheson had apparently disavowed Korea, Stalin did not deny Kim thrice. He gave war his imprimatur, along with an early dispatch of weapons and equipment. Mao begrudgingly agreed to Kim's attack. This was secured by the South's Communist leader Park Hon Yong's personal assurances that the population would immediately rise in support if the North marched south.

But Park was wrong. At best, the Communists were welcomed from the balconies rather than the barricades. The massive rebellions in the South before the war had involved a united front of progressives, socialists, and Communists opposed to Rhee's growing authoritarianism. When Kim invaded and people were forced to take sides, there was no automatic left turn. It was no longer 1945. A degree of separation had taken place as Communists and capitalists passed each other, going in opposite directions across the demarcation line. Most importantly, the remaining Communists and other progressives had been savagely repressed and all but eliminated as a mass movement. When Park assured Kim that tens of thousands of Southern Communists would give their lives in the battle for national liberation, he failed to appreciate that the majority already had. Two years earlier, the Southern Communists would have been a fifth column at the heart of the country, ready to fight and die. Kim invaded too late. By 1950, almost all were dead or had fled.

Kim factored in Southern support and factored out American intervention. Far from alone amongst Communist leaders, he judged Acheson's statement to mean that the US did not see Korea as vital to their interests and therefore would not intervene, as they had not intervened to stop China falling into the hands of the Communists in 1949. Neither miscalculation alone would necessarily have stopped Kim, but the conjunction proved fatal. There has been continuing debate as to who started the Korean War. Kim Il Sung claimed it was an attack from the South on 25 June 1950. If it had been the South that launched a pre-emptive strike, their subsequent collapse and headlong retreat suggests their generals had all the tactical skill of General Custer at the Battle of Little Big Horn. In reality, there is little doubt it was Kim who initiated the invasion of the South on 25 June. The more interesting question is: when did the Korean War start? There was an inevitability stretching back almost to the initial division: it was dead peace walking. Were its origins back in December 1946 with the General Strike and riots, with Pak Hon Yong's guerrilla warfare in defence of parts of the population in 1948 in Cheju, or with Yosu in the prolonged 1949 skirmishes between North and South? When did escalation build to inevitability?

From Civil War to Cold War

At 04.00 on 25 June 1950, 90,000 North Korean troops equipped with Soviet weapons and tanks crossed the 38th parallel. Ongoing manoeuvres turned into war. Korea invaded Korea. Left fought right. North swept South. Within four days, Kim's troops had seized Seoul; within a month, they had reached the foot of the Peninsula. Only a small pocket around the south-eastern port of Busan, known as the Busan Perimeter, continued to resist. The ground invasion had been accompanied by a series of landings on the east coast. A North Korean ship carrying 600 troops, who could have easily occupied a defenceless Busan, was serendipitously intercepted by the South Korean navy and sank, an incident that may have shaped the outcome.[8]

Civil war turned into clash of civilisations, as it became a global conflict from every continent. Korea was the first proxy war of the Cold War era and the UN's first – and last – military engagement. The world divided along ideological lines with the West fighting or supporting the UN and the South. The Soviet Bloc and China provided the North with material aid and assistance. Moscow provided fighter planes and pilots and Beijing landing strips to the north of the Yalu. When the North started to buckle and break under the weight of the US counter-attack China added more than a million troops.

International reaction was swift. The UN Security Council passed a resolution the same day calling for 'immediate cessation of hostilities' and for 'North Korean authorities to withdraw forthwith their armed forces to the 38th parallel'. The Security Council requested that UN member states 'refrain from giving assistance to the North Korean authorities'. A second resolution two days later added that member states should provide 'assistance to the ROK as may be necessary to repel the armed attack and to restore international peace and security in the area'.[9] The Soviet Union, which was boycotting the UN over its refusal to recognise the People's Republic of China in place of Taiwan, lost the opportunity to veto UN intervention. Not that that would have stopped the US:[10] Washington had troops on the ground before UN Command was established.

The US used its control of the UN to internationalise the conflict. The civil war became a global conflict involving 25 countries. It was the first proxy war of the Cold War and the UN's first – and last – military engagement. The world divided along ideological lines, with the West fighting or supporting the UN and the South and the Soviet bloc and China providing the North with material aid. Moscow provided fighter planes and pilots, Beijing landing strips to the north of the Yalu. Communist Parties around the world backed the North, but with the onset of the Cold War the mainstream left was more equivocal.

The US response reflected domestic politics. The Communist victory in China had come as a profound shock to Washington, particularly in the wake of the 'Iron Curtain' descending across Eastern Europe. Obsessed by fear of Communism at home – the 'Red Scare' and McCarthyism – and abroad, the US felt the need to stop a Soviet Communist takeover of Korea. According to early versions of 'domino theory', Japan, which had the world's largest Communist Party outside the Soviet bloc, would be the next to fall. Now was the last best opportunity to fight.

The US was no longer alone in holding the secrets of fission. The Soviet Union had tested its first atomic bomb in 1949, and the US hoped to take it on, or at least a proxy partner, before it became an order of magnitude more dangerous. The US wildly over-estimated the threat. In mid-1950 the CIA estimated the Soviet nuclear stockpile at 10 to 20 bombs and predicted it would have as many as 135 by mid-1953. Yet it was not until December 1951 that the USSR's Avangard Electromechanical Plant produced its first operational weapon. To organise the US's response, President Truman immediately assigned General MacArthur to lead the US forces in the Far East as well as the South Korean Army.

The first US troops landed on 1 July 1950, pre-empting formal UN approval to intervene by a third Security Council resolution on 7 July 1950, which established the United Nations Command (UNC) and a UN intervention force under MacArthur. The US's 'coalition of the willing' was Australia, New Zealand, Britain, France, Canada, South Africa, Turkey, Thailand, Greece, the Netherlands, Ethiopia, Colombia, the Philippines, Belgium, and Luxembourg. Denmark,

Sweden, Norway, India, and Italy provided hospitals and medical personnel. Of the 342,000 UN troops, 300,000 were from the US, and 92 per cent of those who fought were American or British, with the rest sending token detachments.

When the US arrived, it took control of the air. The North's few antiquated planes were swept from the skies in the first weeks of the war. After that they had only 'MiG Alley' in the north-west where Soviet planes, flying out of Chinese airbases, protected the Yalu River bridges.[11] The first non-US troops did not arrive until 29 August. The US and South Korea were in dire straits, trapped in the Busan Perimeter, until on 15 September an amphibious landing by US troops behind enemy lines at Inchon, a port directly west of Seoul, proved a breakthrough. Within a fortnight, UN forces had recaptured Seoul and KPA forces had retreated north of the 38th parallel. The US saw and seized the opportunity.

Containment became rollback. US government lawyers were soon advising that the (previously inviolable) border at the 38th parallel had 'no legal basis'. Benegal Rau, one of the rotating presidents of the UN Security Council and India's representative, urged the UNC not to try to reunify Korea by force; after all, UN troops had been dispatched to stop exactly that from happening. But the US had its way. Now the war was for one Korea. News dispatches now talked of 'liberated areas'. Pyongyang fell. The UNC encountered little resistance with the collapse of the North's forces and moved rapidly to occupy almost the entire Peninsula.

Washington wanted a decisive victory over Communism. If it failed to crush Kim totally, the North would reform, regroup, and try again. But the US misread Beijing as badly as Kim had misread Washington. The Americans were convinced that China would not enter the conflict, as it was only just beginning to recover from its not-quite-concluded civil war. President Truman and General MacArthur discussed the prospect of Chinese intervention on 15 October. MacArthur reassured the president that the superiority of US air cover would deter China from intervening, and that if Beijing did, he could counter the attack. MacArthur advanced forces to the

Chinese border on the Amnok (Yalu) River, while continuing to bomb Chinese and Russian targets in the borderland.

The US's aggressive approach proved counterproductive. The Chinese believed war with the US was inevitable and chose to fight on Korean territory rather than on their own.[12] More than a quarter of a million troops from the Chinese People's Volunteers (CPV, though 'volunteers' was a misnomer) were ordered to cross the border, which they did undetected on 26 October 1950, within ten days of Beijing sending 30,000 troops into Tibet. MacArthur only became aware of the Chinese intervention when CPV soldiers began to sweep down in human waves on his front line. The UN forces, overwhelmed, broke in disarray. They found it impossible to regroup and stabilise the front, split as they were between the east and west coasts by the inhospitable central mountains.

The heaviest fighting of the war was during the exceptionally cold winter of 1950. Kim Il Sung and his comrades were holed up in Kanggye, near the Chinese border, after fleeing Pyongyang. The US

人民踴躍支援前綫

Figure 6 Chinese poster celebrating the dispatching of the Chinese People's Volunteers, 1950.

made an early attempt to eliminate him with a series of five-tonne 'bunker buster' Tarzon bombs. They failed, but with the Chinese intervention, Kim had other problems. Criticism of his handling of the war rose sharply. In December 1950, a Party plenum in Kanggye forced him to purge a number of his leading critics. Kim explained:

> A war presupposes both attack and retreat. This can be likened to a football match. In this game, if one side gets off balance, being hard pressed by the opposing team, it falls back to recoup and then presses forward by seizing upon a favourable chance.[13]

The UN forces suffered devastating defeat after defeat, virtually collapsing as they fled south. The US evacuated 100,000 troops and the same number of civilians from the port of Hungnam. (Among those evacuated were the future parents of current ROK president Moon Jae-in.) Communist forces captured Seoul for the second and last time on 4 January 1951, but the Chinese and what remained of the North Korean forces were overextended, with weak supply lines. When the UNC launched a counter-attack, Seoul changed hands for the fourth time on 15 March and the Communists were pushed north of the 38th parallel once more. By late spring, the conflict had reached a stalemate. Both sides had suffered heavy losses, though the Chinese troops, with no proper winter equipment, fared worse.

MacArthur, determined, requested authorisation to send US planes across the border to attack Chinese bases in a public expansion of the war. The request was officially refused – Truman was wary of starting World War III – but 'hot pursuit' continued. MacArthur challenged Truman publicly and was relieved of command on 11 April 1951. He was replaced by General Matthew Ridgway, who was prepared to obey his president and fight a war limited to Korea – which made it unwinnable.

The war was brutal on both sides. Besides the deaths in action and collateral damage, there were mass killings and mass graves. Neither South Korean government officials nor Communist cadres were spared. With both sides occupying virtually the whole of the Peninsula and sweeping across much of the country twice, the opposition was culled and many tens of thousands executed. Credible reports have the North executing prisoners in Seoul's jails prior to their second withdrawal. UNC soldiers were killed to prevent them from being freed by advancing forces. There were reports of Chinese troops looting and raping. The victims were not always the enemy. Yet, with these significant exceptions, both North and South Korean forces normally treated their fellow countrymen as exactly that. Both were fighting to reunite a single country and a single people.

This was not always the case with the US troops.[14] The Army, Air Force, and Navy frequently strafed refugees as they attempted to cross UN lines. (The strafing was depicted as early as 1952 in Tay Garnett's *One Minute to Zero,* starring Robert Mitchum, which showed retreating civilians and North Korean infiltrators being shelled by US artillery. The film was banned by the US military.[15]) The US carpet-bombed and more or less levelled the North. The eastern port of Wonsan endured 861 straight days of naval shelling. More bombs were dropped on the North than on Germany in World War II, with 600,000 tonnes of bombs razing cities, towns, and villages. The bombers ran out of targets and were left to rearrange rubble. Many of the bombs contained napalm, used here as a weapon of mass destruction for the first time: the liquid petroleum jelly stuck

Figure 7 The window sticker reads, 'Visit to Sinchon Museum' (2011).

like glue and burnt its victims alive. Oceans of petrol were poured over the civilian population, incinerating them in the tens of thousands.

Around Sinchon, from mid-October to the beginning of December 1950, tens of thousands of Koreans were massacred. Pyongyang claims the perpetrators were US troops, and there is a grisly Sinchon Museum of American War Atrocities; South Korea's Truth and Reconciliation Commission accepted that mass killings had taken place but argued that right-wing militias carried them out with the knowledge of the UNC. In recent years, additional reports of US atrocities have surfaced. In the summer of 1950, US military forces opened fire on a large group of South Korean refugees at a railway bridge and killed as many as 400, mainly women and children. Retreating US commanders had issued orders to shoot approaching civilians, to guard against North Korean infiltrators amongst refugee columns.[16]

Both during the war and after, famine stalked the land, driven by economic collapse and natural and unnatural disasters as the US destroyed hydroelectric power stations and dams. Typhus and cholera, meningitis and tuberculosis revisited the North. In the last six months of the war, more soldiers died of tuberculosis than died at the front. By the end of the war, 250,000 surviving soldiers had contracted the disease, one in six Koreans was dead, and the North had been destroyed as an industrial society. All four horsemen of the apocalypse had done their worst.

Five years after the US military's anti-Japanese racism during World War II, it viewed Koreans just as badly. The anti-Asian racism was supplemented by Jim Crow: while President Truman had ordered desegregation of the military in 1948, the last all-Black unit was not disbanded until September 1954. In Korea, African Americans got the dirty and dangerous jobs.

Neither total defeat nor total victory was possible any longer for either side. In November 1950, President Truman stated that he would not rule out the use of nuclear weapons. In Britain, the Labour Party were outraged. Under pressure from Labour prime minister Clement Attlee, Truman was forced to clarify his position: he would authorise the use of nuclear bombs only to prevent a forced evacuation of the Peninsula or a military disaster. (It was this threat that would push China to begin its own nuclear-weapons programme in 1955.)

The US and UN needed a negotiated solution. The UN's first secretary-general, Trygve Lie, urged Moscow to intervene to promote armistice talks. On 23 June 1951, Soviet ambassador Yakov Malik announced, 'The Soviet people believe that, as the first step, discussions should begin between the belligerents for a cease-fire and an armistice providing for the mutual withdrawal of forces from the 38th parallel'.[17] Beijing concurred; truce talks opened on 10 July 1951. Negotiations dragged out over two years. The first round stalled after six weeks and only resumed on 25 October. Between 1951 and 1953, the two sides talked their soldiers to death, first at Kaesong then at Panmunjom, the 'truce village', which now straddles the border between North and South in the middle of the DMZ. Ground fighting continued on both sides, bombing on one. Lives were squandered in the ground war, for little territorial gain, the bloody nature of these battles epitomised in names like Heartbreak Ridge, Punchbowl, and Pork Chop Hill.

The Chinese and North Korean negotiators were formally led by the North's Lieutenant General Nam Il, the US and UNC by Vice Admiral C. Turner Joy. Allowing Kaesong to be chosen as the venue, formerly in the South but now held by the North, was a tactical mistake by the US. Initially the US had wanted to hold the talks on a Danish hospital ship but Pyongyang refused. Instead, the North offered Kaesong. The public in the US had lost any appetite they had for war, so Washington acquiesced. The result was that the immediate vicinity of Kaesong was out of bounds to military action. It gave the North home advantage for the talks, a quiet ride in a potentially difficult military area, and a strategic advantage in any future conflict.

The two main issues at stake were the demarcation line between the two sides and the fate of the prisoners of war (POWs). The UNC wanted the military demarcation line at the current Line of Control, while the North demanded the 38th parallel, which it said was 'recognised by the whole world' since it had been the dividing line before the conflict erupted. The UNC, abandoning any lingering pretence that the UN's intervention was to force a return to the *status quo ante*, turned the argument around, asserting that the conflict was precisely what showed the vulnerability of the line. In the end, the UNC got its way.

However, the maritime boundary was left unresolved. The UNC unilaterally set it between the mainland portion of Kyonggi Province and the island just off its shore, the former under North Korean control and the latter South Korean. Later, Seoul single-handedly demarcated a Northern Limit Line (NLL), but Pyongyang refused (and still refuses) to accept a straight extrapolation of the land border as the basis for the Maritime Demarcation Line. Ever since, the NLL has continued to cause clashes between North and South naval units. (The South's determination is so distinctly partisan that even Washington has reservations; the UN Convention on the Law of the Sea, which both sides signed in the 1980s, would push the line well south of the NLL.)

The Chinese and North Koreans demanded the repatriation of all POWs, in line with custom and practice and the Geneva Convention. However, the US refused to abide by the Geneva Convention, adopting instead the principle of 'voluntary repatriation': that no POWs should be returned without their agreement. This blocked negotiations while the killing continued. While voluntary repatriation became almost an article of faith for some Americans, others were more sceptical. Admiral Joy wrote later:

> Voluntary repatriation put the welfare of ex-Communists soldiers above that of our own United Nations Command personnel in Communist prison camps, and . . . still on the battle line in Korea. I wanted our own men back as soon as we could get them. Since we were not allowed to achieve a victory, I wanted the war halted. Voluntary repatriation cost us over a year of war, and cost our United Nations Command prisoners in prison camps a year of captivity. The United Nations Command suffered at least 50,000

casualties in the continuing Korean War while we argued to protect a lesser number of ex-Communists who did not wish to return to Communism.[18]

The pressure on POWs in the South was enormous. Chinese novelist Ha Jin, in *War Trash*,[19] a thinly disguised biography of his father, writes about the fate of Chinese soldiers who spent years in South Korean POW camps. For the Chinese POWs, the choice was to be China or Taiwan and for the Koreans, North or South. The third option of a neutral country existed, but few knew of it and even fewer chose it, though handfuls of Communist POWs ended up in India and Brazil. Former Kuomintang troops, who had been forced to fight with the Chinese Volunteers and the Taiwan regime, worked together to ensure a 'Hobson's choice' for many. Within the camps rival gangs of POWs fought for or against repatriation, with camp guards complicit with the anti-Communist groups. Many wanting to return to China or the North were forcibly tattooed with 'death to Mao' or 'death to Kim Il Sung'.

The North's POWs had their leadership strengthened when a senior KPA general was ordered to let himself be captured so he could take command of the North's POWs. Manipulation and coercion were used freely by both sides; hundreds of POWs died in a series of riots.[20] Britain's *Daily Mail*, on 18 December 1952 demonstrated the absurdity of the position: 'The United Nations refuse to return captives who would almost certainly be shot when they got home.... but the effect of this humanitarian policy will be weakened by continual shooting of prisoners, even in self-defence'.

The Never-Ending End

Dwight Eisenhower's promise to end the war helped get him elected in 1952 as the first Republican president since 1928. Final agreement, however came from a change of leadership not in Washington but in Moscow. Upon the death of Stalin in March 1953, Vyacheslav

Molotov was re-instated as foreign minister. He and his Chinese counterpart, Zhou Enlai, conceded on 'voluntary repatriation' on 8 June 1953. Each side was given the opportunity to persuade recalcitrant POWs who had refused repatriation to change their minds. Few did; months and years of intimidation and indoctrination were not to be overturned in a five-minute interview. Almost two-thirds of the 21,374 Chinese prisoners chose to go to Taiwan and a substantial number of North Koreans chose to stay South. Captured South Korean soldiers were given the option of joining the KPA or going home. Some 50,000 chose to remain. Amongst the UNC's foreign troops, 21 US POWs chose to stay in North Korea or go to China; one British marine, Andrew Condron, went with them.[21]

Not all the returnees were who they seemed. By 1959, the US claimed to have identified 75 former POWs as Soviet agents, including the most notorious, George Blake, who became a spy in the British Foreign Office. Washington was incredulous that Americans could voluntarily convert to Communism. They found their *deus ex machina* in brainwashing and hypnotism.[22] Just how many North Koreans and Chinese went the other way, as spies for the US, will probably never be known.

Syngman Rhee, who wanted to use the UNC to unify the Peninsula by force, rejected the armistice negotiations and did everything he could to wreck them. He attempted to sabotage the last stage of negotiations on 18 June by releasing 27,000 North Korean POWs to remain in the South. This united Washington and Pyongyang in fury, but by then everybody had had enough. The armistice agreement was signed in Rhee's absence, on 27 July 1953 at Panmunjom, by the chief negotiators of the UNC, North Korea, and China.

The armistice never became a peace treaty. The US and North Korea are still at war, as of the time of writing. The armistice established a two-kilometre DMZ on either side of the Line of Control and a Military Armistice Commission (MAC) to monitor compliance with the agreement. Two UNC positions on the MAC were allocated for South Korea, one for the US and the UK, and the final one on a rotational basis among the other members of the

UNC. The MAC kept a channel of communication open between the two Koreas in the darkest days of the Cold War.

Without US intervention, the war would have been over in six weeks and Korea would have been unified at a cost of 50,000 lives rather than 5 million – but 'better dead than red'. The human cost was enormous: 4 million Korean military and civilian casualties, a million Chinese troops, 144,000 US soldiers, and 14,000 from the rest of the coalition. The lives of all the survivors were devastated, with half of industry and a third of all houses destroyed. Countless civilians, including the maimed and scarred, war orphans, and napalm victims, roamed the rubble in hunger and despair. Eleven million Korean families were separated and remain so 70 years on.[23] Worst, the war created a fear and hostility that poisoned North and South relations for decades, turning them into mirror images of each other.

What did North and South Korea gain? As John Halliday and Bruce Cumings put it, 'Each side proclaims that it won, yet each actually seems to feel that it has lost'.[24] Viewed from the North, the situation was dire. The whole country had been destroyed, and Kim's promise to Stalin and Mao of a swift and easy victory lay buried in the battlefields – along with Mao's son Mao Anying, killed in an American bombing raid on Pyongyang while serving with the CPV.

Kim portrayed the end of the war as North Korea's victory, but it just didn't feel like that. Although he had failed to take over the South and reunite the Korean peninsula, he claimed political legitimacy from direct negotiations with the US and forcing them to beg for peace. Not all his Communist colleagues were as impressed. Kim was in trouble and he knew it.

There were few winners. The North had lost and so had the South. As Chuck Downs puts it: 'Limited war led to limited objectives and produced limited results'.[25] The South was bitter, having gained nothing apart from heavily reinforced anti-Communist authoritarianism. Syngman Rhee was 're-elected' in 1952. When it became clear that the National Assembly would not re-elect him, he sought instead a constitutional amendment to elect the president by direct popular vote. When that was rejected, he had dissenting National Assembly members arrested for their alleged Communist links. Those who remained voted in his favour the next time. Rhee manipulated the law and arrested those who threatened him. Anti-Communism became the excuse for, rather than the cause of, decades of political repression.

Of the interventionists, Beijing had the most reason to be pleased. China had fought US-led UN troops to a standstill, proving that its military was capable of holding its own with the West. Within the Communist camp, the USSR was the biggest loser in the long term. Korea gave the US's military-industrial complex the green light for re-armament. Moscow had no choice but to follow where Washington led, and for 40 years military necessity starved the Soviet civil economy of scarce resources its people desperately needed.

Washington had suffered its first defeat in a major war and had failed to convince the American people of its purpose and mission. It had fought the Communists to a standstill but could not deliver final victory at a price its people were prepared to pay. Korea became the first domestically 'unpopular war', prefiguring the conflict in Vietnam. Korea fuelled the rising intolerance and paranoia of McCarthyism; US Communists were persecuted, but so too were thousands who had done little more than attend a meeting or donate a few dollars to some organisation Joe McCarthy later decided was a 'Communist front'.

The US increased its national defence budget by a factor of five and established a global network of military bases. In Western Europe the effect was the same, with new military build-ups. Winston Churchill said, 'Korea does not really matter now. I'd never heard of the bloody place until I was 74. Its importance lies in the fact that it has led to the re-arming of America'.[26] The US increased its commitment to the North Atlantic Treaty Organisation, established in April 1949 as a counter-weight to the Soviet threat in Europe.

The country that gained the most was one that did not fight: Japan. The US, forced to take the lead role in North-East Asia, decided it needed Japanese help. Japan's economy took off with American aid, trade, and financial assistance to rebuild its industry and fill enormous orders for materials to support the war effort. By 1952, with the San Francisco Peace Treaty, the US occupation of Japan was more or less over – except Okinawa, never really fully part of Japan, and the remaining US bases – and it was independent again, save for its US-imposed constitution. The Korean War flipped Japan from US enemy to US ally.

More than 65 years since the armistice, there are few surviving Korean War veterans. Americans call it 'the forgotten war'. This twisted partial perception explains the US failure on the Peninsula: it is certainly not forgotten in Korea, where North and South continue to live with its consequences on a daily basis.

How would things have turned out if the Korean War had unfolded differently? It is impossible to tell, but what is clear is that it reinforced and consolidated the Cold War and superpower standoff. Today, the division of Korea is the last dangerous remnant of a period rapidly passing into history.

3
Kim's Korea

At the end of the war, Kim needed to consolidate his position quickly. He choreographed his survival elegantly, on two separate fronts: the ideological front and the struggle inside the Party. These were the foundations of an operation that was to put him in total control within six years.

Kim transmuted doctrine from Stalinist orthodoxy to a Confucian Communism that resonated more with the pre-war Japanese emperor cult than with Marxism-Leninism. He stood on its head the 'inexorable' economic determinism read into Marx by early commentators: Humanity makes the world, rather than the world making humanity. In its 'hard' form, economic determinism was disarming, threatening to turn revolutionary into spectator – after all, one could just sit on the side-lines cheering the inevitable, awaiting the chrysalis of history to crack open and let tomorrow be born.

Despite the disproportionate devastation, the North's economy bounced back more quickly than the South's. Aid poured in from the USSR, China, and the Eastern Bloc, covering over a third of the budget in 1954. Throughout the 1950s, North Korea could boast one of the fastest-growing economies in the world.

Divide and Rule: The Intra-Party Struggle

As early as the 1920s, the Soviets had despaired of the factionalism of the Korean Communists. Moscow was prescient. Korean sectarianism was resurrected in the wake of victory. The Soviets may have initially selected Kim Il Sung as a less-than-ideal option, but he quickly rose to the position of 'first amongst equals' in the swirling dance of parties and factions vying for power and influence in the

aftermath of liberation. They were all leftist and progressive organisations; the Soviets would have tolerated no other.

In Manchuria, two main Communist guerrilla groups operated,
both ultimately under the leadership of the CCP. Kim's group had
fought in the North-East Anti-Japanese Army, while the other group
had fought with the Chinese Eighth Route Army and New Fourth
Army and were closer to Mao. This latter group were the basis of the
Yan'an Faction. Immediately after liberation, they formed the New
People's Party (NPP), under their leader Kim Tu Bong. In August
1946 the NPP merged with Kim's North Korean Communist Party
to create the North Korean Workers' Party, which three years later
merged with the South Korean Workers' Party (SKWP) to become
the Workers' Party of Korea (WPK).

By 1949 the WPK had four main factions. First was the Domestic
Faction, comprising those who had remained in Korea, generally in
jail or in hiding, during the Japanese occupation. They were split
between North and South, but predominately came from within the
SKWP. Second, the Yan'an Faction, from the NPP, was under the
indirect patronage of Mao. Third, the Kapsan (Partisan) Faction,
led by Kim Il Sung, comprised those who had fought in China and
retreated with him to the Soviet Union. Finally, the Soviet Faction
consisted of second- and third-generation Koreans drawn from the
diaspora that was then in Kazakhstan and Uzbekistan to the Soviet
military and military academies,[1] then sent by Moscow to Korea.

Before joining the intra-Party struggle, it was necessary for Kim
to dispense with the petit bourgeois and nationalist parties. The
progressive nationalists, an eclectic group, were organised around
two main parties: the Korean Democratic Party (KDP), set up in
November 1945 and led by Cho Man Sik, and the Party of Young
Friends of the Celestial Way (or Chondoist Chongu Party) established in February 1946 by followers of the Chondoist religion,
an anti-Western nativist movement with its roots amongst the
peasantry in the late nineteenth century. The Soviets had done the
early winnowing, arresting Cho Man Sik and other KDP leaders in
January 1946, because of their opposition to trusteeship. In contrast,

in July 1946 the Chondoist Party had allowed itself to be forcefully assimilated into the Popular Front government, modelled on the Soviet empire's 'people's democracies'. The WPK was in control, buttressed by house-trained partners. (Even today, two other parties are represented in the North's Supreme People's Assembly, or SPA: the Chondoists and the Social Democrats.)

Figure 8   'All Out to Vote, 2014'.

While Kim had the advantage of early Soviet sponsorship, it was by no means inevitable that he would be the last man standing. In the late summer of 1953 his position was perilous, but he proved a master of Party infighting, setting group against group and individual against individual. Divide and rule proved an effective strategy, and power eventually rested in a single pair of hands: Kim's.

The war had cost millions of lives and devastated the country, all for nothing. No territory had been gained; indeed, some had been lost. Syngman Rhee's weak position had been consolidated, and Washington was in the South to stay. During the war, the WPK lost up to half its 700,000 members through death, desertion, and expulsion. Kim rapidly enrolled almost half a million new members – mainly peasants, loyal to him because of land reform – to dilute the influence of the Soviet Koreans. Nevertheless, he needed a scapegoat in a hurry.

One was available. Park Hon Yong, leader of the Domestic Faction, had personally assured Mao and Kim that the South would rise in support of the initial onslaught. Park paid the penalty for his misleading optimism. He was arrested in August 1953 and executed in December 1955, after a show trial in which he confessed all that was necessary. Kim branded him 'a spy on the payroll of the American scoundrels, [who] bragged that South Korea had 200,000 Party members and that in Seoul alone there were as many as 60,000. But, in actual fact, this rascal, in league with the Yankees, totally destroyed our Party in South Korea'.[2] There is no evidence that Park was guilty of anything, apart from refusing to face reality. His now-leaderless faction collapsed in disarray. The other factions got off lightly. The Yan'an Faction's military leader, Choi Chang, was dismissed; a prominent member of the Soviet Faction, Ho Ka I, committed suicide.

Even after the sacrifice of Park, Kim's responsibility for the war was not forgotten or forgiven; the remaining opposition harboured a growing resentment of his burgeoning personality cult. But the next battle was to be over economics. On this there was no Party consensus. Polemics went back and forth in the pages of *Rodong Shinmun* ('The Workers' Paper') and the Party's theoretical journal, *Kulloja* ('Labourer').[3] The question was how to apply the principles of Marxism-Leninism to the realities of Korea. Kim Il Sung and his supporters advocated a forced march towards post-war reconstruction by means of an almost exclusive emphasis on heavy industry. Others argued for more balanced development. It was an echo of the Stalin-Bukharin struggle in the Soviet Union of the late 1920s, and a rehearsal of Mao-Liu Shaoqi in the 1960s. As in Moscow and Beijing, red triumphed over expert.

In February 1956, the secretary of the Communist Party of the Soviet Union (CPSU), Nikita Khrushchev, denounced Stalin and Stalinism at the CPSU's 20th Congress. In North Korea, Politburo members affiliated with both the Soviet and Yan'an Factions responded by attacking Kim. The August meeting of the WPK's Central Committee brought matters to a head. They mocked Kim as Korea's Stalin, with a hand-me-down personality cult and industrial policy. Deputy Prime Minister Choi Chang Ik, leader of the Soviet Faction, and Commerce Minister Yun Kong Hum, from the Yan'an Faction, castigated Kim for his authoritarianism and for continuing to promote heavy industry at the cost of widespread starvation.

The Soviet Faction, working with the Soviet ambassador, attempted to orchestrate a coup. However, they were betrayed by a Kim loyalist they had recruited to the conspiracy, and Kim pre-empted the coup.[4] He purged Choi and sent a series of senior figures from the Yan'an Faction, including Yun, into internal exile with minor provincial posts – shades of Trotsky's exile to Almaty – or stripped them of power entirely. Some sought refuge in China. The Party leadership was cowed, then culled. Kim Tu Bong, leader of the Yan'an Faction and the North's largely ceremonial president, who was not initially associated with the failed coup, hung on until 1958, when Kim retrospectively labelled him the plot's 'mastermind' and purged him. By then it was all over. Kim and his partisans were in total command. *Rodong Shinmun*'s days of debate were over; it shrunk to become the journal of record and Party noticeboard. Politics had withdrawn from the public arena and were now relegated to a shadow world of hint, nuance, and nepotism.

Khrushchev's denunciation of Stalin's terror, cult, and economic policy opened a Sino-Soviet rift, which Kim was left to straddle. Korea could become an adjunct of China or the Soviet Union, or risk walking a political tightrope between the two. He chose the latter, re-launching himself and his politics in a new paradigm of independence, nationalism, and autarky.

The Kim Cult

The 1960s were the era of the partisan generals. But autocracy had its price; North Korea was left increasingly isolated. Kim turned necessity into virtue and promulgated independence, self-reliance, and a personality cult. Here he was far from alone – yet, compared to those of Stalin, Mao, and Ceausescu, Kim's cult was exceptional in its scope, intensity, and longevity.

Kim became the father of the nation and orthodox Communism left asunder his beatification began. Korean history became a family affair. His parents were rediscovered as exemplary revolutionaries. His father, Kim Hyong Jik, who had run a small store selling traditional medicines, became an indefatigable revolutionary fighter in the vanguard of the movement. Kim's mother, Kang Bang Sok, became both a revolutionary fighter and the leader of the Korean women's-liberation movement. His late wife and Kim Jong Il's mother, Kim Jong Suk, was the venerable mother of the nation. Even Kim's great-grandfather, Kim Ung U, turned out to have led the destruction of the *General Sherman*.

Kim was omnipotent and omniscient. Like all religious prophets, he – and later Kim Jong Il – became synonymous with miracles. Legend held that he had won a hundred thousand battles and could turn sand into rice and cross rivers on leaves or pieces of paper. Kim Jong Il's birth on Mount Paektu was accompanied by thunder and lightning that shattered the caldera lake's ice, resulting in spectacular double rainbows. When Kim, at the age of four, smeared ink across a map of Japan, he created violent storms there. Once, the Korean Central News Agency (KCNA) even reported a rainbow over Kim Jong Il's car that seemingly followed him for miles.

The cult penetrates every aspect of society even today. The North Korean calendar counts up from the year of Kim Il Sung's birth (in Japan, it's from the year of the emperor's accession). Pictures and plaques, busts and badges of the 'Great Leader' Kim Il Sung – increasingly in tandem with 'Dear Leader' Kim Jong Il – are everywhere. Excerpts from the Kims' writings are featured daily on radio and TV. Their *Collected Works* and Kim Il Sung's autobiography, *With the Century* – new volumes of which continued to appear for a dozen years after his death – are prominently displayed in every bookshop, library, workplace and school, and come pre-installed on the North's Android tablet, Samjiyon. Even the North's literary works, especially

Figure 9   The two Kims, and one of the last
remnants of Communist orthodoxy. The slogan
on the monument says, 'All hail to the . . .
banner of Marxism-Leninism'.

after the early seventies, revolve around Kim as the nation's father
and supreme sacred being.[5] From nursery to university, all classrooms
are decked out with pictures of the Kims, as are all homes and even
the carriages on the underground. Inside, the two portraits hang side
by side. Outside, propaganda posters are interspersed with scenic
views of Korea, wall murals, statues, plaques, and 'shrines'.

The ubiquitous Kim badges pinned to the lapel of every adult exist in a variety of styles and sizes. The claim that they are sophisticated indications of status doesn't ring true, although senior Party members have the more elegant smaller badges in their collections. Students at Kim Il Sung University sport their own special badge. In 40 years at the helm, Kim managed to visit almost every farm and factory in the country, providing 'on-the-spot guidance' and leaving in his wake a trail of holy relics. Chairs he sat on are roped off, papers he signed framed, photos of the visit mounted, and his words memorised. Kim Jong Il carried on the tradition, as does Kim Jong Un. After Kim Jong Un's accession a substantial number of retrospective visits appeared on the record.

Other personality cults wither and die with their subjects; the tombs of Lenin, Mao, and Ho Chi Minh are more tourist attractions than sanctuaries. In contrast, the Kim cult survived and thrived. After Kim's death in 1994, his presidential office was turned into a mausoleum (reportedly at a cost of $650 million, or €600 million) and his body was embalmed and displayed in a clear glass sarcophagus. In 2012 he was joined by Kim Jong Il in the renamed Kumsusan Palace of the Sun, a place of pilgrimage where tens of thousands file slowly by every week as they circle the coffins, bowing three times to each. Groups from the outer provinces can wait years to be allocated a visiting slot. To be included in such a group is seen as a sign of merit. To the tune of 'When the Carnival Is Over', women cry and men look stern. Select groups are taken off to view the two Kims' trains, the elder Kim's V12 600SEL Mercedes, and the younger Kim's yacht, plus galleries displaying their hundreds of honours and academic awards from around the world.

According to *With the Century*, Kim considered himself a Communist from his teenage years, yet rejected the sectarianism and opportunism of the Chinese groups. Many argue that he fell into that very trap after 1956, when WPK ideology veered off the path laid down by Marx and Lenin.

Marxism-Leninism, from its inception, had its schisms and its heretics. Trotsky and Bukharin were two early examples, along with

English Communist J.T. Murphy, who had moved for Trotsky's expulsion from the Comintern in 1927, only to be expelled himself five years later from the Central Committee of the Communist Party of Great Britain on charges of Trotskyism. More successfully, after World War II, Albania's Enver Hoxha, Yugoslavia's Josip Broz Tito, and Romania's Nikolae Ceauşescu never entirely followed Moscow's dictates with their own variant national Communisms – to Stalin's fury. Kim was to go further.

Kim's challenge to the old order was a speech to the Propaganda and Agitation Unit of the WPK on 28 December 1955, titled 'On Eliminating Dogmatism and Formalism and Establishing Juche in Carrying Out Ideological Projects'. Juche's full articulation followed rather than preceded Khrushchev's iconoclasm. Kim emphasised that 'Marxism-Leninism is not a dogma, but a creative theory and guide to action' – a clear sign that the stink of heresy was in the air.

The word *juche* is a combination of two Korean letters, *ju* 'master' and *che* 'oneself', thus literally meaning 'master of oneself'. The term's meaning has been malleable over time, indicating varied amalgams of national identity, self-reliance, patriotism, and national assertiveness. In the 1960s, Juche's four theses were identity in ideology, independence in politics, self-sufficiency in economy, and reliance on Korea's own forces in national defence. These principles legitimised the state and its polities. In a 1972 interview with Japan's *Mainichi Shimbun*, Kim defined Juche as

> the idea ... that the masters of the revolution and construction are the masses of the people and that they are also a motive force of the revolution and construction. In other words, it is an idea that one is responsible for one's own destiny and that one has also the capacity for hewing out one's own destiny.[6]

The word *juche* is carelessly translated in the West as 'self-reliance' and then further misread as autarky. This is only true in the sense of intellectual and spiritual independence. In this sense it came to permeate every aspect of society and provided guidance – often from

Kim himself – for everything from film-making to potato farming, manufacturing to martial arts.

Juche was a direct challenge to Marxist economic determinism, which argues that society reflects technology – the water mill feudalism, the steam mill capitalism. Or, as Lenin said, 'Communism is Soviet power plus the electrification of the whole country'.[7] Koreans' will and leadership would override technology and economics, as Kim put it: 'Man is master of all things and decides everything, and man is capable of anything, unrestrained by the narrow realities of the world'. This idea was indispensable in the North's situation – how else would one explain true Communism in a small, backwards country on the periphery of global economic activity?

Figure 10   'Juche' spirits, one with an adder's head.

If Stalin's 'socialism in one country' was seen as an absurd betrayal of Marx, then how much more so to attempt it in a country a hundred times smaller, with less than a sixth of the population? Juche cut the Gordian knot of choosing between the Soviet Union and China. Juche evolved. Initially a national patina on a universal Marxism-Leninism, in the 1960s and 1970s it began to represent a stronger challenge to the orthodoxy. In 1967 Kim wrote, 'Juche ideology refers to the most correct Marxism-Leninism oriented philosophy designed to carry out our revolution and construction'.[8] The North's 1972 constitution, in Article 4, added that Juche was a creative application of Marxism-Leninism to Korean reality'. References to Marx in Party publications began to fade and vanish; the 1992 constitution eliminated them completely.[9] While the commitment to socialism remained, it was no longer phrased in traditional terminology. Juche and the revolutionary thought of Kim Il Sung were the sole guides. A heresy had superseded the old religion and broken with its past as the Soviet church collapsed into history.

North Korea is the only Communist state that metamorphosed into a theocracy. It has its messiah who works miracles and a church of the elect, with an internally coherent set of ideas that explain the world and its works. They are imbued with a missionary zeal to spread the gospel, with sparsely attended Juche Study Groups littering the world and a self-discipline that requires no sanctions. There is holy scripture that merits constant study and unconditional faith. There was a period in the 1970s where prizes were awarded for those who most successfully memorised hundreds of pages of Kim's writings, speeches, New Year greetings, and Party Congress reports.[10] The theological college of Juche is the Party School in Pyongyang, near the Juche Tower, which holds periodic re-induction courses for the church's rising stars. There is no escape even for transport workers, who are – or were – educated by the Railway University of Communism. There are millions of worshippers. The mass grief at the funerals of Kim Il Sung in July 1994 and Kim Jong Il in December 2011 was genuine. It explains the deep and sincere condolences I was offered by North Korean officials over the death of Princess Diana when I visited Pyongyang for the first time in autumn 1997. It came naturally to them to empathise with those they imagined must be overwhelmed by the death of a beloved national idol.

The Economy Takes Off

Kim Il Sung's formal training in Marxism-Leninism started with Stalin's *Short Course of the History of the All-Russian Communist Party (Bolshevik)* (only 392 pages) and the trilogy: centralisation, collectivisation, and the Plan. The North replicated Stalin's economic model of state ownership and control. It re-ran the tape of Soviet history on fast-forward. The first stage to be implemented after liberation, in 1946, was the state or collective ownership of industry. Korea prior to 1910 had been a feudal economy and during Japan's occupation the mines and factories were under Japanese ownership. After their surrender those Japanese that could flee did so and those who remained had other things on their mind than claims of ownership or for compensation. Disgruntled Korean capitalists (and there were few) whose factories, workshops, and shops had been seized could flee south. Thus the North could nationalise industry smoothly, with little resistance. Indeed, the line was porous even up to the start of the Korean War. By 1947, private companies that had initially been transformed into co-operatives were converted into centrally or locally owned enterprises. The public sector accounted for 72.4 per cent of industrial production in 1946 and 99.9 per cent in 1958.

The North had inherited the heavy industry and power plants that the Japanese had constructed during the occupation, topped up by substantial economic and technical assistance from the Soviet Union.[11] This aid, however, paled in comparison with what Washington provided to the South. Figures vary, but a reasonable estimate is of grants and loans from the Soviet bloc equivalent to $3.5 billion (€2.6 billion) between 1946 and 1984. As Table 3.1 shows, about 45 per cent of that assistance came from the Soviet Union, 18 per cent from China, and the rest from the German Democratic Republic and Eastern Europe.

Table 1   Economic Assistance from the Communist Countries (Unit: $M)

	1945–49	1950–60	1961–69	1970–76	1978–84
Soviet Union	53 (Loans)	515 (Grants) 199 (Loans)	197 (Loans)	906 (Loans)	0
China	0	336 (Grants) 173 (Loans)	105 (Loans)	2 (Loans)	259 (Grants)
East Germany	0	101 (Grants)	35 (Loans)	0	0
Other Eastern Europe	0	326 (Grants) 4 (Loans)	0	0	0
Total	53 (Loans)	1,278 (Grants) 376 (Loans)	337 (Loans)	908 (Loans)	259 (Grants)

Source: ROK National Unification Board, *Statistics of North Korean Economy* (Seoul: 1986).

In 1946 Kim concentrated on land reform, breaking up large farms and redistributing the land to the peasant sharecroppers, who were able to farm their own land for the first time. This created massive support for Kim and the WPK, making it possible for him to side-line the left nationalist opposition and then other factions within the Party. After the war, phase two began. Individual plots were subsumed in a growing number of collective farms, which swelled in size as demands for increased productivity drove attempts to deliver greater and greater economies of scale. It worked for a time, allowing a rapidly shrinking number of agricultural workers to maintain and improve production. The millions released from agriculture moved from farm to factory as living standards gently rose.

After the armistice in 1953, progress followed the 'Plan'. The Three-Year Plan (1954–56) rebuilt the country's shattered infrastructure, followed by a foreshortened Five-Year Plan (1957–60) that laid the foundations for heavy industry, rebuilt the housing stock, and brought the North close to self-sufficiency in food production. By 1958, when Kim's control was complete, the state owned and managed everything.

North Korea achieved 'Asian Tiger' growth rates, with mass mobilisation and appeals to good practice and patriotism. In 1956, during a visit to the Kangsong Steel Works, Kim stated that rising productivity was a pre-condition for the advance of socialism. This speech, along with a follow-up visit in 1957, was the launch pad for the Chollima movement. Named after Korea's legendary flying horse, the campaign was a nationwide exhortation to work harder and improve productivity. The Chollima statue on Mansu Hill, overlooking Pyongyang, embodies the continuous advance of the workers under socialism. A worker spurs the horse forward, holding the hammer, sickle, and calligraphy-brush symbol of the WPK; a young woman follows behind bearing a sheaf of rice.

In 1960 Chollima was augmented by the Chongsanri campaign, named after a co-operative farm where Kim Il Sung's 'on-the-spot guidance' had married the usual exhortations to work harder with the idea that productivity gains could come from drawing on craft practice and local knowledge through direct dialogue between workers and farm managers. This state version of syndicalism – or, at least, workers' control – proved effective, driven by the incentive that agricultural labourers, unlike workers in heavy industry, got to share the 'profits' from increased production. This was extended to manufacturing: the Taean work system applied bottom-up management techniques to industry by encouraging high-level Party officials to learn both from middle management and shop-floor workers. One catalyst for success was, again, the introduction of material incentives for the workers.

These campaigns shared the exhortation elements of China's mass led 'Great Leap Forward' (1958-60) and the individualism of the Soviet Stakhanovite movement of the mid-1930s when heroic workers set new productivity records, thus by example driving up output and allowing the early fulfilment of the Plan. The 'heroes' gained certificates, medals, and the loathing of their fellow workers.

(This approach has continued into recent years: there were 'speed battles' in 1980, 1988, 2009, and 2016 to boost production in advance of major national events. In December 1998, with snow on the ground, tens of thousands of workers seconded from Pyongyang's offices began construction of the Pyongyang-Nampo motorway. Construction was by hand, with almost no mechanical assistance aside from a couple of lorries and two mechanical diggers. In contrast Korean Central Television that evening, showed heroic workers labouring under waving red banners, with stirring martial music and juddering earth-moving equipment. The road was finished ahead of time. But as early as summer 2003, it was showing signs of flawed construction, with the sparse traffic zigzagging around patches of subsidence.)

The results were remarkable. Annual economic growth rates of 20 per cent or more throughout the 1950s and early 1960s made the North one of the fastest-growing economies in the world. By 1960, aid was down to less than 2.5 per cent of GDP as the economy massively outperformed the basket-case South. There was a shortage of skilled labour, so 65,000 stateless Koreans who had been marooned in Japan since 1945 were pushed by Tokyo and pulled by Pyongyang into returning 'home' between 1959 and 1970. Hundreds of Japanese wives came with them. (No husbands are mentioned.)[12]

However, continuing imbalances in the industrial sectors contained the germ of what was ultimately to undermine the economy. But those who had earlier debated in *Kulloja* and warned of the consequences of over-emphasising heavy industry in the early and mid-fifties had been silenced by the purges. There was no one left to protest.

The slow Seven-Year Plan (1961–70)[13] re-emphasised the priority of heavy industry, especially the machine-tool sector. Kim Il Sung reiterated in 1965 that 'the keystone of socialist industrialisation lies in the priority development of heavy industry. Only with the establishment of a powerful industry is it possible to ensure the development of all industries, transport and agriculture, and the victory of the socialist system'.[14] But, by then, men and material were being drained away to the defence sector in response to the military regime in the South, the widening Sino-Soviet split, Moscow's cowardice over Cuba, and (slightly later) the US invasion of Vietnam.

The machine-building and metal-working industries' share of gross industrial output rose from 1.6 per cent in 1944 to 17.3 per cent in 1950, 21.3 per cent in 1960, and 31.4 per cent in 1967.[15] The economy had been transformed from rural to urban, from agricultural to industrial, and from underdeveloped to developed. In 1946, industrial and agricultural outputs had been 16.8 per cent and 63.5 per cent of GNP, respectively. By 1970 this was reversed, with 57.3 per cent for industry and 21.5 per cent[16] for agriculture.

Nevertheless, in sharp contrast to the rapid and uninterrupted growth of earlier plans, 1961's Seven-Year Plan limped for nine years to the finish post. Economic growth, for the first time, began to stutter and slow. Growth based on continued capital construction, rather than rising productivity led by technical innovation, had reached its limit. With Soviet and Chinese technical assistance at a post-war low (see Table 1) and 'speed battle' following 'speed battle', the workforce was increasingly exhausted. Agriculture and light industry were both suffering from a serious lack of investment and, as a result, the production of consumer goods slowed down. Even when heavy industry shrank from 55 per cent of output in 1963 to 51 per cent two years later, this indicated not a change of direction but fresh problems, as material inputs temporarily dried up. The problem was that the North's engineers and technicians had been so well schooled in how to manage and run heavy industry that they were incapable of thinking any other way. They over-performed, consuming a disproportionate share of scarce resources, thus increasingly starving light industry and agriculture and further exaggerating the economy's asymmetry. By 1970, heavy industry accounted for 62 per cent of total industrial output.

In recognition of the previous Plan's overambitious targets, those of the Six-Year Plan (1971–76) were substantially scaled down. The Plan implicitly acknowledged earlier failings with more emphasis on technical change, greater self-sufficiency in raw materials, improved product quality, and further development of the power and extractive industries. It also attempted to shift some resources into light industry.[17] This was paralleled by yet another attempt at mass mobilisation with the Three Revolutions Campaign (technical, cultural, and ideological). The ideological and cultural revolutions were intended to raise the political consciousness of the workforce, driving them to yet higher levels of effort, while the technological revolution was to modernise process and product.

For Kim, economic independence was the key to national independence. As he wrote in 1971:

> Only when a nation builds an independent national economy can it secure political independence. . . . A country which is economically dependent on outside forces becomes a political satellite of other countries. . . . Without building an independent national economy it is impossible to establish material and technological foundations for socialism, or build socialism and Communism successfully.[18]

Thus Kim resented the growing pressure from Moscow to join the Council for Mutual Economic Assistance (COMECON), with its policy of industrial integration across the Empire, inevitably creating dependence on the Soviet Union for technologically advanced products. He rightly regarded it as an attempt to lock the North into the Soviet sphere of influence, undermining and restricting its autonomy.

Initially established in 1949 by the USSR, COMECON was the Communist version of the Common Market: an integrated economic area would 'allow' each country to specialise in producing the raw material and products it did best – or was allocated in the great Plan – and rely on others for the rest of its needs. It was an economic trap. The Soviet Union was the core and the remainder the periphery. Once inside the system, a country's dependency increased year by year. Kim rejected all attempts to incorporate the North, claiming (rather disingenuously) that economic self-reliance aided rather than impaired socialist solidarity:

> Only by building an independent national economy can we meet each other's economic need with fraternal countries, ensure more effective mutual cooperation and division of labour with them on principles of proletarian internationalism and of complete equality

and mutual benefit, and contribute to the strengthening of the entire socialist camp.[19]

Kim acknowledged the need to import raw materials not available domestically and to purchase advanced technology. The ideology of self-reliance was a catechism. Imports were to be kept to a minimum. The Plan called for a self-sufficiency rate of 60 to 70 per cent in all industrial sectors through increased import substitution – replacing imported materials with alternative domestic ones wherever possible – and through adapting processes and products to reduce import demand. The new, innovative technology would deskill processes, enabling unskilled workers to bridge the shortage of skilled workers.[20] To meet the future manpower and technological requirements of the Three Revolutions economy, the education sector needed to train more and better technicians and to expand the number of specialists, particularly in fuel, mechanical, electronic, and automation engineering.[21]

The subsequent Plan followed the same logic. Aiming at mechanising and automating industry using modern production and management techniques, the second Seven-Year Plan (1978–84) urged yet further self-reliance, alongside modernisation and 'scientification' of the economy. It was an echo of the previous Plan. The emphasis on import substitution became more shrilly imperative, reflecting that outside capital and resources were becoming impossible to obtain. This was a result of the financial fiasco that followed the North's venture into borrowing from the West, and its consequent default in 1976.

The debt originated with massive purchases of capital goods, such as machinery and equipment, from Western countries in the early 1970s, at the start of the Six-Year Plan. These loans were to be repaid by increased export earnings and new short-term credits, neither of which were possible in the aftermath of the 1973 global oil crisis. Pyongyang suspended payments, then rescheduled them, but its debts and unpaid interest spiralled upwards. The North's inability to pay its debts destroyed its financial credibility and any possibility of future loans. The Plan failed. Its predecessor had underachieved, but here the production target was only met in a single consumer sector – textiles. Even heavy industry was in the doldrums, with a static 62 per cent of production. An economy once seen as a model for the non-aligned world was exhibiting signs of systemic failure.

Growth slowed year on year before finally grinding to a halt in 1990. Previous targets were rolled over in the stillborn third Seven-Year Plan (1987–93), in which targets were once again adjusted downwards, with more emphasis on light industry and consumer goods. The North's industrial collapse was almost as swift as its rise. By the end of 1998, the economy had recorded a negative growth rate for nine straight years, with some years showing double-digit declines.[22]

Diverting substantial resources into the military was probably a Hobson's choice. Nevertheless, its failure to invest – or to find investment – to substitute for the reallocated funds, plus its initial refusal, and later inability, to turn away from heavy industry towards light, together cost the economy all its forward momentum.

To make matters worse, the collapse of the Soviet empire in 1989 stripped Pyongyang of one of its last remaining benefactors – and its bargaining power. The natural disasters of the mid-nineties were the final straw. Communism's former economic poster child became a failed industrial state. With Kim's death in 1994, the economy and society were left paralysed by indecision and indifference, famine and isolation. North Korea waited on a new leader and a new millennium. Prompted by the emergence of a market economy from below, the North attempted to skirt its problems with patchy economic reforms – a shortcut to market Leninism. Only with the new century did the North's economy start to bounce back and slowly start to grow again, from a dramatically reduced base.

The Welfare State

Post-war industrialisation and economic growth had brought improved living standards, modernisation, and urbanisation. After 35 years of colonial rule and centuries of feudalism, Communism had – albeit slowly – delivered material well-being. The state provided housing, health care, education, employment, maternity benefits, and pensions. The public distribution system (PDS) provided basic foodstuffs and household goods. It was possible to live without money. Cash was only used for life's little luxuries. There were special allocations to officials: for example, Zebi beer was exclusively reserved for the Party.

In 1950, seven years' compulsory education was introduced. Everything was provided, from schoolbooks to board and lodging. During the colonial period, the majority of adults had been illiterate

Figure 11 Pyongyang tenement.

and barely a third of children in primary school;[23] within a decade, the literacy rate was close to 100 per cent. Nor did education end with school: there were adult learning programmes and on-the-job training.

Education and industrialisation reconstructed the country's demographics and social architecture. Farmers went from being three-quarters of the workforce in 1946 to a third 40 years on. In

Table 2 Political Classification System in North Korea by Social Origin

Categories	Sub-Categories	Treatment
'Friendly' (28%)	1. workers from working families 2. former farmhands 3. former poor peasants 4. staff members of state organisations 5. WPK members 6. family members of deceased revolutionaries 7. family members of participants in the revolutionary and national liberation movements 8. revolutionary intelligentsia (that is, those who received their education after liberation) 9. families of civilians killed during the Korean War 10. families of soldiers killed during the Korean War 11. families of servicemen 12. war heroes 13. families of the socialist patriotic victims	• Qualified to become cadres in the Party, government, or military • Privileged treatment in food and necessities, promotion, housing, medical care, etc.
'Neutral' (45%)	1. former small vendors 2. former medium-sized traders 3. former independent craftspeople 4. former owners of small enterprises 5. former owners of small service businesses 6. former owners of medium service businesses 7. families of people of good social origin who went to the South but did not actively oppose the North Korean regime 8. former middle peasants 9. returnees from China and Japan 10. old intelligentsia who received their education before liberation 11. those who studied abroad 12. people prone to hooliganism 13. 'suspicious women' – former *mudang* (shamans), *kisaeng* (courtesans), and the like 14. people from the South who did not participate in 'factional activities' (that is, did not relate to the Communist movement in South Korea) 15. the wealthy in small villages	• Qualified to become low-ranking officials or engineers • A limited chance to be reclassified as friendly

'Hostile' (27%)	1. workers who became workers after liberation, but had formerly been entrepreneurs or officials	• Forced labour in remote places
	2. former rich peasants	
	3. former traders who represented small and medium capital	• Disqualified from Party membership and colleges
	4. former landlords	
	5. people who participated in pro-Japanese or pro-American activities	• Forced to move to
	6. former officials in the Japanese colonial administration	remote areas, or segregation
	7. families of people of 'bad origin' who fled to the South during the war	
	8. Protestants and people observing Protestant rituals	• Constant surveillance
	9. Buddhists and people observing Buddhist rituals	
	10. Catholics and people observing Catholic rituals	• Limited chance to be reclassified into the 'wavering' stratum
	11. Confucian scholars	
	12. people expelled from the WPK	
	13. former Party cadres fired from their posts	
	14. people who served in the police and state apparatus of the South during the occupation of North Korea	
	15. families of prisoners	
	16. people involved in espionage and their families	
	17. anti-Party and counter-revolutionary elements, as well as members of various factions	
	18. families of people punished for political crimes	
	19. people released after serving prison terms for political crimes	
	20. people released after serving prison terms for stealing, embezzlement, or other non-political crimes	
	21. former members of the Party of Young Friends of the Celestial Way	
	22. former members of the Democratic Party	
	23. former capitalists	

Sources: Adapted from the '3 class, 51 group' classification system in H.J. Chon (2004), 51–52, Tables 7 and 8. Detailed discussion of social classification structure can be found in Oh and Hassig (2000), 133–35.

contrast, over the same period, factory workers jumped from 12 to 57 per cent.[24] Industrialisation drove urbanisation. From 1953 to 1960, the urban population grew between 12 and 20 per cent yearly, with one in nine of the population living in Pyongyang.[25] By 1987, 60 per cent lived in cities, making North Korea at the time one of the world's most urban economies.[26]

Starting in 1958, the whole population was placed into three broad categories: 'friendly' (*hacksim kyech'ng*, literally 'main class'), 'neutral' (*tonyou kyech'ng*, 'wavering class'), and 'hostile' (*chuktae kyech'ng*, 'hostile class').[27] The political history of three generations, including in-laws and relatives, was factored in. Those placed in the 'friendly' class were either active members of the regime or fully supportive of it, including former revolutionaries and families who had lost members during the Korean War. 'Hostile' was reserved for families of bourgeois landowners, defectors, and collaborators with the Japanese and US. Former prostitutes were 'wavering'. Those who had lost out in the inner-Party faction fights were 'hostile'. It was possible to escape one's lot in life by meritorious actions or through political re-education, but relegation was always easier than promotion. In 1967 the three classes were presented with 51 sub-categories. Social status determined a person's education, occupation, residence, and ability to travel at home and abroad. Kim Il Sung stood capitalism on its head: superior living standards and opportunities were now the preserve of the children of the working class and the Party.

Alone Abroad

Rejecting the poisoned chalice of COMECON affected Pyong-yang's foreign relations particularly, after Khrushchev denounced Stalin in 1956. Initially Kim had been close to the Soviet Union – the country responsible for his military training and the rise of his nation – but it was Mao, not Stalin, who had come to his rescue in 1950. Soviet support did flow after the armistice with $650 million (€600 million) in grants and loans to help reconstruct the devastated economy. Yet Beijing, despite having its own reconstruction to do less than four years after the end of the civil war on the mainland, nearly matched Moscow, with $500 million (€376 million). North Korea owed its survival to its two Communist neighbours, who became its major – in fact, almost its only – trading partners and its sources of oil and military equipment at 'friendship' prices.

After the Sino-Soviet rift, Pyongyang opted for independence over alignment and skilfully juggled relations between the two. In July 1961, North Korea signed Treaties of Friendship, Cooperation, and Mutual Assistance with the Soviet Union and then China, seeing these as guaranteeing support for the North as a check to US military adventurism. Yet Kim was almost as worried about Moscow and Beijing as about Washington. The treaties served as a barrier to any attempt by either to swallow the North. Kim strengthened his links with the Communist Parties of Japan, Vietnam, and Indonesia.[28] By 1963, he was arrogant and angry enough to complain that:

> certain persons propagandise as though a certain country's armed forces alone were defending the entire socialist camp, as though the latest military technique of a certain country alone were maintaining the security of the socialist camp and world peace. They make light of the role of the other fraternal countries in the defence of the socialist camp and neglect their due cooperation in strengthening the defence power of these countries. All who are truly concerned about the security of the socialist camp and world peace cannot agree to such a stand.[29]

It was a blunt rejoinder to Moscow's rejection of his request for nuclear weapons.

The North was left with little choice but to develop a powerful independent military capability. In Kim's view, this necessity was only reinforced by Khrushchev's appeasement of the US, with his policy of peaceful coexistence, and Park Chung-hee's 1961 coup in Seoul. Military government in South Korea meant Park was off to the races, and Pyongyang was forced to follow, in case Park decided the Peninsula problem had a military solution. In December 1962, Kim launched a campaign of 'Equal Emphasis', balancing the commitment to continued economic growth with accelerated indigenous weapons production. The inexorable logic of doing it alone meant year-on-year increases in the defence budget and the consolidation of the North's military-industrial complex.[30]

When the Soviet Union backed down during the Cuban Missile Crisis of October 1962, China denounced it. In private, Cuba concurred. Kim agreed. In response to China's earlier denunciations of 'socialist imperialists', Khrushchev had cancelled China's aid package and backed India's provocations en route to the 1962

Sino-Indian border war, so China's denunciation should not have come as any great surprise. Kim felt similarly betrayed and – temporarily – leant towards Beijing and away from Moscow. But he didn't lean quite far enough. Kim's failure to endorse China's denunciation of the Soviets for unilaterally claiming the leadership of world Communism irritated Beijing. By 1964 Kim had leant further. *Rodong Shinmun* castigated Moscow, arguing that 'their anti-China campaign which has been whipped into a new frenzy recently and their noisy clamour about the so-called "collective measure" show that they are sinking deeper into splittism'.[31] During the Cultural Revolution, Kim straightened his stance with the Red Guards, who labelled him 'Korea's Khrushchev' and worse. Growing tension between the two big Communist powers made Pyongyang's position increasingly cramped as the sixties progressed. Kim's condemnations of Soviet imperialism and Chinese dogmatism amused neither.

By 1966, Kim was proclaiming revolutionary independence. Empathising with the Communist Parties of other contested parts of the Soviet empire, Kim reflected: 'Our Party, too, has had the bitter experience of interference by great-power chauvinists in its internal affairs. Needless to say, those great-power chauvinists met with rejection they 'deserved'. In October 1966 he proclaimed self-reliance in national defence with the Four Military Lines policy: 'Make our army a cadre army, modernise it, arm all the people and turn the whole country into a fortress'.[32] Military expenditure soared from 10 per cent of GNP in 1966 to 30.4 per cent in 1967.[33] The civil economy began to live the lie. That lie would kill Soviet Communism in 1989 and more than a million Koreans a decade later.

For most of the seventies, relations with the Soviet Union remained cool, while relations with China warmed up once the frictions of the Cultural Revolution had been oiled. Zhou Enlai went to Pyongyang in 1970 and four years later Kim went to Beijing despite, or maybe because, of the shock of US president Richard Nixon's 1972 visit. China had, for the moment, replaced the Soviet Union as the Pyongyang's leading supplier of military hardware. This would end once China signed the Sino-Japanese Treaty of Peace and Friendship in

September 1978 and normalised relations with Washington four months later.

When Deng Xiaoping came to power in China in 1978, his economic pragmatism and advocacy of market reform were encapsulated in the adage 'White cat, black cat – who cares as long as it catches mice?' The CCP's new direction emphasised modernisation and economic reform at the expense of revolution and ideology. The market continued to gain ground throughout the 1980s. China and North Korea made reciprocal high-level visits early in the decade. The North had little option. Friendly relations were a necessity for economic and military reasons.

Moscow, like Pyongyang, did not welcome the US–China rapprochement.[34] The Soviets saw it as a betrayal. Their relations with Washington had been severely compromised with the USSR's 1979 intervention in Afghanistan. Ties with the North were restored, especially after Yuri Andropov replaced Leonid Brezhnev as Soviet leader in November 1982. North Korea's foreign trade, which had in the late 1970s been split evenly between the USSR, China, Africa, and Europe, thus swung back towards Russia, propelled by the consequences of the 1983 'oil shock', the 1976 default on European loans, and the reconciliation with the Soviets. By 1985, nearly half of the North's trade was with Moscow. Kim visited Moscow in 1984; two years later, Soviet foreign minister Eduard Shevardnadze returned the visit. The two countries consolidated and strengthened their military cooperation, holding annual joint naval and air force exercises between 1986 and 1990.

But the end of the decade brought a fundamental change in relations. Mikhail Gorbachev, elected general secretary of the Soviet Communist Party in March 1985, began to pursue domestic economic and political reforms, including *perestroika* (transformation) and *glasnost* (openness), shifting the emphasis of Soviet foreign policy to favour economic development over Great Power rivalry. Gorbachev continued to engage with Pyongyang, but the consequences of reform swept all before it. This 30-year waxing and waning of Moscow and Beijing's sway is colourfully illustrated in the

North's postage stamps, in which Russian and Chinese themes chop and change across the decades.[35]

Any final faith died in 1990 when the USSR, on its deathbed, established diplomatic relations with Seoul. Beijing's betrayal came only two years later.

The Third Way

Kim explored a 'Third Way' in the mid-seventies with the Non-Aligned Movement (NAM), whose 'neither Moscow nor Washington' rhetoric appealed as his own relations with the Soviet Union and – to a lesser extent – with China deteriorated. The NAM had its origins in the 1955 Bandung Conference in Indonesia. It was a meeting of Asian and African states, mostly newly independent, that condemned colonialism – including its Soviet variant. It was formally established in Yugoslavia in 1961 to group together Third World states experiencing 'similar problems of resisting the pressures of the major powers, maintaining their independence, and opposing colonialism and neo-colonialism, especially Western domination'.[36] The NAM refused to take sides in the East-West ideological conflict, seeing them as two sides of the same coin.

Kim wanted support to underpin his struggle against the US and help win the diplomatic battle with the South. The NAM seemed a perfect forum for him to promote his own particular vision of the Third Way and himself as a Third World leader. Initially, it proved highly successful. North Korea began to rapidly expand its diplomatic relations with Third World countries, but did not formally join NAM until August 1975, along with North Vietnam and the Palestine Liberation Organisation.

The North's accredited diplomatic partners jumped decade on decade, from nine at the end of the 1940s to 113 by the turn of the millennium. In the interim, Pyongyang filled the gaps with ambassadors and embassies accredited to UN agencies that issued visas and wandered far from their formal remit. In Rome it worked through the Food and Agriculture Organisation (FAO), in Paris the

United Nations Education, Scientific and Cultural Organisation (UNESCO), and in London the International Maritime Organisation. Italy and the UK established diplomatic relations with North Korea in 2000; only UNESCO in Paris still has an accredited ambassador, although the FAO still has a permanent representative from Pyongyang.

Kim's first success was to see South Korea's bid for NAM membership rejected in 1975 as the North was admitted. South Korea was rejected because the massive and continued US military presence made any claim to non-alignment farcical. Kim's smugness was short-lived. Pyongyang's lobbying led to a series of pro-North resolutions but turned counterproductive as member states reacted against Pyongyang's excessive pressure. The North's argued support for international terrorism, Kim's growing personality cult, and the 'miracle on the Han River' (of the South's economy taking off) didn't help. NAM resolutions about the Korean peninsula began to favour Seoul. Kim found the Third Way a dead end; the NAM disappeared into ineffectiveness and obscurity, destroyed by its own internal conflicts.

The main vestiges of this period include a special relationship between Pyongyang and Jakarta and an unfortunate flower. During Kim's tour of the Bogor Botanical Gardens in 1965, Indonesia's President Sukarno named an orchid *Kimilsungia*. While the national flower is the magnolia now, every year, for the Day of the Sun (15 April, Kim Il Sung's birthday), thousands upon thousands of *Kimilsungia* are displayed despite freezing temperatures. There is also a *Kimjongilia*, which – thankfully for Korea's horticulturalists – is a mere begonia, even if his birthday on 16 February is less than ideal. While his father was getting his flower, Kim Jong Il, at 24, was spending time with the Sukarno's 18-year-old daughter, Megawati Sukarnoputri. They were reunited in 2002, during her state visit to the North as Indonesian president.

Aside from the NAM, Pyongyang was putting itself about in Africa. North Korean troops and military advisors were spread throughout Africa in the 1970s. In Ethiopia, they helped Mengistu

Haile Mariam, leader of the Communist military junta, in the Ogaden War with Somalia and the unsuccessful fight to crush the insurgent Eritrean People's Liberation Front. In Angola, they sided with the People's Movement for the Liberation of Angola and sent troops to fight alongside the Cubans in the civil war and against the South Africans. As late as 1985 they still had a thousand troops stationed there. In 1976, Madagascar president Didier Ratsiraka hosted a conference on Juche.

They also had quirky relations with Forbes Burnham's Guyana and Dom Mintoff's Malta, where Kim Jong Il spend 1983 (not) learning English. Party-to-party relations included German Trotskyists, Brazilian and Belgian Communists, French socialists, and the US's Black Panther Party. Panther activist Eldridge Cleaver visited the North in 1969 and 1970 and subsequently peppered *The Black Panther* with articles about Kim, showing the logic of 'the enemy of your enemy is your friend'. In 1972 he published a foreword to the English translation *Juche! The Speeches and Writings of Kim Il Sung*.[37]

Most intriguing – and most bizarre – was the February 1981 visit by French presidential candidate François Mitterrand and his top two aides, who would in a few months become prime minister Pierre Mauroy and incoming Socialist Party first secretary Lionel Jospin. Thus barely three months before being elected president, Mitterrand travelled halfway around the world to meet Kim Il Sung and his houseguest, the Cambodian leader in exile Norodom Sihanouk,[38] without even stopping in Beijing to meet Chinese leader Deng Xiaoping. Pyongyang's only reward after Mitterrand's election was that its embassy to UNESCO in Paris got double-hatted as its Délégation Générale to France, putting the North on par with the Walloons, Quebeçois, and Palestinians.

Japanese colonialism and the US role in the Korean War left an intense antipathy that continues today. North Korea's animosity towards Japan is two-fold. Japan has not only chosen to ally itself with the US but remains unapologetic about its colonial past. As many as 2.5 million ethnic Koreans were there at the end of World War II. Initially a few came in the early years to study or work; later more, were sent as willing or unwilling guest workers. After 1937 the majority were coerced. The bulk of them were able to return at the end of the war, but hundreds of thousands were left behind. An additional tranche returned voluntarily to the North in the sixties. Today, around 600,000 ethnic Koreans live in Japan.

Overseas Koreans in Japan divided on left-right rather than North-South lines. The organisation Chosen Soren (General Association of Korean Residents in Japan), established in 1955, was a front for Pyongyang that represented the large majority of those remaining. It founded schools and a university with North Korean curricula (all wonderfully described by Sonia Ryang, a former pupil, in *North Koreans in Japan*[39]). Initially the North extended generous financial aid, substantially greater than Seoul afforded its counterpart group, Mindan (Korean Residents Union in Japan). As the DPRK economy collapsed, however, Chosen Soren turned from recipient to donor, with its leadership continuing to act as de facto spokespeople and diplomats on behalf of Pyongyang. More recently, the organisation, under pressure from the Japanese authorities, has begun to take a marginally more independent line. Some members have broken with the organisation over the DPRK's treatment of those who were repatriated in the sixties.

With its intervention in Korea's civil war, the US overtook Japan as 'enemy number one', becoming the prime target of Pyongyang's anti-imperialist rhetoric. A particularly sore point is the continued US military presence in the South. Since 1970 the total number of US troops has been below 50,000; as of 2018 it is currently 37,500.

The goal of reunification was, at least until recently, a given for North and South. Kim laid out his reunification road map. First, the removal of US troops was imperative:

At present the root cause of our country's division and of all misfortunes and sufferings of the people in South Korea lies in the occupation of South Korea by the US Army and the aggressive policy of the Americans. As long as the US Army is stationed in South Korea, it is impossible to accomplish the peaceful unification of the country, and the South Korean people cannot extricate themselves from the present miserable plight.[40]

Second, Kim proposed 'institutionalisation of a Confederation of North and South'.[41] Pyongyang's focus was ending the inter-Korean armed confrontation, securing the withdrawal of US troops, and stopping the military build-up by both sides. Confederation was 'unity in diversity': a 'one country, two systems' solution to ending division.

In contrast, Seoul wanted peaceful coexistence. 'Peace first, unification later', with mutual recognition and economic cooperation. The two sides were miles apart. The situation changed when Nixon went for détente in Asia with the rapprochement with Beijing. After the lesson of Vietnam, he declared, in 1969, that Asian nations had to be responsible for their own security. The 'Nixon doctrine' paved the way for a partial wind-down of US engagement in Korea. Nixon announced troop withdrawals: from 1969 to 1971, troop numbers fell from 66,000 to 40,000.

Neither North nor South was happy. In 1971 the two Red Cross societies were the vehicle for initiating inter-Korean talks, ostensibly around the issue of family reunions. These behind-the-scenes contacts led to a joint communiqué on 4 July 1972 declaring that both sides accepted three principles: that unification should be achieved independently, without external interference; that it should be achieved by peaceful means; and that 'great national unity' should be achieved by 'transcending differences in ideas, ideologies, and systems'. Both agreed to refrain from slandering and defaming one another, and a South-North Coordinating Committee (SNCC) was established. The SNCC held its first and third meetings in Seoul in November–December 1972 and June 1973, with a second in Pyongyang in March.

It was a first attempt to ease tension and foster mutual trust after 20 years of unrelenting hostility. Negotiations floundered. North Korea failed to convene the fourth SNCC meeting scheduled for August 1973 in Pyongyang. It refused to negotiate with the head of the Korean Central Intelligence Agency (KCIA), Lee Hu Rak, because of his responsibility for the abduction and attempted assassination of opposition presidential candidate Kim Dae-jung in Tokyo.[42] An additional reason given was Seoul's merciless repression of Christians!

Kim Il Sung's attempt to unify the country by force proved both destructive and counterproductive. It consolidated Rhee's regime and kept US troops in the South for more than 70 years. But that didn't stop attempts to destabilise both regimes. From the time of the armistice on, there were border incidents and cease-fire violations. These escalated after Kim's new line in 1966, with both sides infiltrating agents and making commando raids over the next three years. For some, this period in the late sixties was effectively a second Korean War.[43]

Serial violations of the armistice along the DMZ (and further) were common to both sides, but it was the US intervention in Vietnam that gave the opportunity for a proxy fight. The ROK sent 300,000 troops to Vietnam between 1964 and 1973. The estimated 560 captured by the North Vietnamese were 'repatriated' to the North. Pyongyang, in response, provided economic assistance and provided places for thousands of Vietnamese students to study. The KPA provided military advisors to Hanoi, and in 1966 the North Korean chief of the general staff, Choi Kwang, offered 'volunteers' to pilot MiG-17s and MiG-21s, along with ground personnel and anti-aircraft artillery regiments. These were all accepted by Hanoi. More than 200 pilots served in 1967 and 1968. The attrition rate was high, and 21 pilots who died in Vietnam are commemorated with a plaque in Pyongyang's Victorious Fatherland Liberation War Museum. North Korea also sent about 100 tunnel-warfare experts to Vietnam to help dig the 250 kilometres of tunnels that the North Vietnamese and Viet Cong used to infiltrate the South. It also sent psychological warfare units to target the South's troops, while front-line observers monitored fighting tactics, combat readiness, and morale. Relations soured with the opening of the Paris peace negotiations. North Korea was close to the Khmer Rouge regime of

Pol Pot, through its links with Norodom Sihanouk. When Vietnam invaded Cambodia, Pyongyang – like Washington – sided with Pol Pot and denounced Hanoi.

Nearer to home, in January 1968, the North captured the US National Security Agency (NSA) spy ship USS *Pueblo*. The North's navy boarded and seized the vessel, claiming it had violated their territorial waters; whether or not that was true, it was certainly spying. The seizure was a huge embarrassment for Washington. The US suffered more humiliation when it was forced to apologise to the North to secure the return of its 83 officers and men. A sailor had been killed. A year later, the US Navy reconnaissance plane EC-121, with Russian and Korean linguists on board, was shot down close to the North Korean coast by two MiG-21s. There were no survivors and there was no apology. Instead, nuclear-capable B-52s flew up and down the DMZ. Until 1998, the *Pueblo* was moored in Wonsan harbour, where it was captured. Kim Jong Il decided it should be moved to the capital. The *Pueblo* was camouflaged and sailed under cover from Wonsan around the southern tip of the Korean peninsula and up the Taedong River to Pyongyang. Concerns that the US would attempt to seize the vessel proved groundless. Either the NSA and its satellite spy partner, the National Reconnaissance Office, didn't even see it coming, despite their billion-dollar budgets, or they were warned off. In Pyongyang, the ship was restored to its original condition and opened for business in October 1999. It has since been moved again, into the grounds of the Victorious Fatherland Liberation War Museum, and is proudly on view to tourists, with the original NSA equipment and documents still intact.

In 1966 the South Koreans retaliated, raiding a North Korean divisional headquarters. Kim was trying – unsuccessfully – to replicate the North Vietnamese insurrectionary model. Its limited success was down to the fact that the US didn't want to start a second war, with Vietnam already on its plate. Armed resistance didn't work in the absence of both sanctuary and popular support, although it did help Hanoi, as Park was forced temporarily, at least, to restrict South Korean troop deployments to Vietnam.

The casualty rate on both sides was extremely high. Around 7,000 agents and infiltrators went north and probably half that number of trained guerrillas came south. Those captured by the South were held incommunicado for decades. Some were released after Kim Dae-jung's election in 1998. Each side tried to assassinate the other's leader. An unsuccessful attempt was made on Park Chung-hee's life in 1968[44] and another two years later. The third attempt, in 1974, killed Yuk Young-soo, the president's wife and future president Park Geun-hye's mother.

Seoul's contribution was to establish Unit 684, where a group that included convicted criminals was recruited for a commando operation to blow up the Kumgang Palace and kill Kim Il Sung. They were trained on the remote island of Silmi and mutinied when a rapprochement between North and South in the early 1970s led to the mission being aborted. The revolt was suppressed, with no survivors, and is dramatically portrayed in the film *Silmido* (2003).

The late sixties and early seventies saw agitators substitute for guerrillas in the infiltration of the South. The Underground Revolutionary Party (1969–72) aimed at fomenting civil unrest. They had their own radio station broadcasting from the North. This was no more successful than the armed struggle. Those arrested received the same treatment as the guerrillas.

Another very public clash was the 1976 'axe murder' of two US servicemen pruning a poplar tree that was blocking the view from a UNC observation post in Panmunjom. The tree was in the neutral zone, where no weapons are allowed. The US did not inform or seek the approval of their counterparts on the other side of the DMZ. Consequently, the North ordered a group of soldiers to stop the operation. One seized an axe being used for the pruning and killed two US soldiers with it. As with the EC-121, the US dispatched B-52s to flirt close to North Korean airspace, while President Gerald Ford instructed that the tree be removed once and for all. Three days later it was chopped down, with US fighters flying overhead. The axe is currently on display in the North Korean Peace Museum adjacent to the DMZ, where the armistice was signed.

In the late 1970s, there were further failed attempts to revive a dialogue. In 1980, the WPK's Sixth Congress adopted a less confrontational notion of unification, though this did not prevent its assassination attempt against President Chun Doo-hwan in October 1983. Still, reconciliation came sooner than expected. In September 1984, when there was serious flooding in the South, the North offered aid and assistance. After some hesitation, Seoul accepted, unfreezing North-South relations. The dialogue resumed, but ended in January 1986 with Seoul and Washington's Team Spirit joint military exercise. Such exercises were not only threatening for Pyongyang but cost them dearly. Mobilising their forces in response costs the North 6 to 7 per cent of its GNP, deliberately timed as they are to clash with the planting and harvesting seasons.

The next round of negotiations awaited President Roh Tae-woo and his *Nordpolitik* ('Northern policy'), designed to establish and improve diplomatic and economic ties with the crumbling Soviet bloc. Lim Dong Won, Roh's advisor and later the architect of Kim Dae-jung's 'Sunshine Policy', got the North back to the negotiating table in exchange for the cancellation of 1992's Team Spirit exercises. Two agreements came out of the talks: first an Agreement on Reconciliation, Non-Aggression, Exchanges and Cooperation; second, a Joint Declaration on the Denuclearisation of the Korean Peninsula. The agreements were never fully implemented. Lim's efforts were undermined by the US commander in South Korea pre-emptively announcing the resumption of Team Spirit and by hard-liners within the former KCIA – renamed the Agency for National Security Planning – intercepting and delaying Lim's message from Pyongyang seeking Roh's approval for the deal. In the end it was too late. Presidential elections were looming. Roh was out of time.

Kim Young-sam succeeded Roh in December 1992. His initial stance towards Pyongyang was hard-line despite, or perhaps because of, his perceived progressive leanings. It became more uncompromising with tensions rising over the North's nuclear-weapons programme. Nevertheless, when former president Jimmy Carter freelanced his way to Pyongyang in a successful attempt to head off

Figure 12 A poster from the Kim Jong Il era showing a North Korean soldier crushing a US soldier.

a preventive strike by Washington, he took with him an invitation from Kim Young-sam for a North-South summit. Kim Il Sung accepted. The summit was scheduled for 25 July 1994, but it was not to be. Kim Il Sung died of a heart attack on 8 July, and 20 years of stop-start negotiations with four different administrations in the South went nowhere. While in Pyongyang, Carter made a series of attempts to meet putative heir Kim Jong Il, but was unsuccessful. The younger Kim thought his father was being far too accommodating to Washington.

Kim's Legacy

The hereditary succession – a challenge more to Marx than to Juche – was to preserve Kim's legacy. He had seen how Stalin and Mao had been betrayed. That was not to be his fate. In the process of grooming his son as a successor, Kim Il Sung arranged for his friend Dom Mintoff, the prime minister of Malta from 1971 to 1974, to host and guard Kim Jong Il at a specially built, secluded country house on the island. Kim spent more than a year learning English and familiaris- ing himself with Western music and European ways. After his return to Pyongyang in 1973, he was made Party Secretary in charge of Organisation and Propaganda. Here he promoted, systematised, and consolidated his father's personality cult, a job he was prepared for by his previous work promoting films and operas glorifying Kim Il Sung's role in the struggle against Japan. He also managed the 'Three Revolutions' campaign, which dispatched teams across the country to preach the merits of the political, ideological, and cultural revolu- tions. Their activities enabled Kim to bypass the WPK's bureaucracy, get a feel for the country, and build his own reputation and support base. He was an enthusiastic – if rather obsessive – writer on Juche, with 400 articles to his name.

Just when Kim Jong Il got the final nod is not known. There was a long lead time. From 1975, official sources began rather enigmatically to refer to the 'Party Centre'. It was revealed that this had in fact been Kim. Initially, some had seen Kim Il Sung's younger brother, Kim Young Ju, as heir apparent. Between 1975 and 1977, those opposing or even sceptical of Kim Jong Il were purged from Party, state, and military.[45] Kim Young Ju himself vanished from public life in 1976 (he reappeared in 1993, elected to the Party Central Committee). The survivors learnt to read the writing on the wall.

A decade later, one of Kim Jong Il's half-brothers, Kim Pyong Il (born in 1954), was seen as another prospect, with his mother, Kim Song Ae, promoting his cause. He was a Military Academy graduate with support within the army. At one time Kim Il Sung was thought to have had a plan for Kim Jong Il to be the Party Centre and Kim

Pyong Il the Military Centre. It never happened. There was no love lost between Kim Jong Il and his stepmother or her children, and Kim made it clear that you were for him or against him. There was no middle way. Despite his wife's entreaties, Kim Il Sung decided – if he had ever thought differently – that shared leadership was not an option. Kim Pyong Il was exiled to Hungary as ambassador in 1988. Further postings followed in Bulgaria, Finland, and Poland. Kim Il Sung wanted no confusion about his intentions and placed his other son out of harm's way.

The Sixth Congress of the Korean Workers' Party met in October 1980. The new members of the Central Committee were all Kim Jong Il loyalists. Apart from softening the line on unification, the Party platform was revised to give Kim Jong Il control of the Party, the administration, and the military. He moved from being the power behind the throne to the front row. He was elected a full member of the Politburo, the Military Commission, and all the Party's key committees. Throughout the 1980s he played an ever more prominent role in the WPK, and the North Korean people became acquainted with their future leader. The transfer of power from Kim to Kim continued unchallenged.

Compared to China and the Soviet Union, where there was significant turnover and diversification in the top ranks of the Party in the 1980s, North Korea showed stability and continuity – at the expense of almost all else. The ruling elite shrank in the 1990s, becoming more exclusive and more homogenous, its members intricately linked by a nexus of personal and educational ties.[46] They emerged as loyal supporters of Kim Jong Il, the old guard, the second revolutionary generation, and military elite speaking with a single voice. The dynamics of politics and decision-making within the leadership mitigated against division and dissent. There had been no factions since the late 1950s, a credit to Party management.

By the early 1990s, Kim Jong Il was in complete control of the state and Party, subject only to his father's restraining oversight. In 1992, despite his lack of military experience, he assumed the top two military posts: Supreme Commander of the KPA and Chairman of the National Defence Committee (NDC). When Kim Il Sung, 'Liberator of the Fatherland' and 'Great Leader', died on 8 July 1994, all was ready for the dynastic succession.

Kim was dead. Long live Kim.

4

Famine, Markets, Refugees, and Human Rights: The Kim Jong Il Era

A series of domestic and international events during the 1990s left North Korea struggling for survival. These included the collapse of the Soviet Union and its empire, the US–DPRK nuclear crisis, the death of Kim Il Sung, and the ensuing leadership vacuum before Kim Jong Il formally took power. These events were compounded by a series of natural disasters and consequent socio-economic problems, all culminating in a vicious famine, which eventually saw humanitarian aid flowing in and refugees spilling out, contributing to a growing concern on human rights in the North. The regime weathered the storm. The price was the markets. Yet North Korea's hidden strength lies in its history and culture, facets absent from the 'imposed regimes' of Eastern Europe. They continue to sustain the regime to this day.

The single most important cause of the economic meltdown and all that ensued was the collapse of the Soviet Union, which – overnight – ended decades of generous assistance and subsidies in the guise of 'friendship prices' for oil and raw materials. By 1993, Russian imports were only 10 per cent of what they had been from 1987 to 1990.[1] It was all made worse by the North's obstinate attachment to a command economy obsessed with heavy industry. This had worked miracles in the initial phases of development, but for a decade or more had been dysfunctional, distorting the economy and driving standards of living down, with a privileged call on state resources and consequent failure to shift towards consumer-oriented light industry.

All this was further compounded by the regime's inability to boost exports, attract investors, or secure loans – factors emphasised by Stephen Haggard and Marcus Noland in *Famine in North Korea*.[2]

Figure 13   The African Renaissance Monument in Senegal, inaugurated
in 2010 in the presence of DPRK head of state Kim Young Nam.

They point out that not only was the quality of the North's exports
poor, but that the regime's 'unrelenting emphasis on autarky and
self-reliance' meant that 'the political leadership seemed strangely
unable to grasp the epochal nature of the changes around it'. This
meant that, although the proximate cause of the famine was drought
followed by floods in 1995, in reality the North was an economic train
crash just waiting to happen. When the crash came, failure to reform
and then failure to lead resulted in millions dying of starvation and
tens of thousands crossing into China's Jilin Province, with its ethnic
Korean majority, to seek relatives or refuge.

In retrospect, the famine served as the tipping point for the North, providing the imperative for economic and social change and shepherding the country to the market. Kim Jong Il, when he finally picked up the baton, started – not without opposition – to pave the way. The rhetoric of 'building a powerful and prosperous country' followed.

The famine also exposed the country in an unprecedented way to the West. North Korea opened up to Western non-governmental organisations (NGOs) and governments bringing humanitarian aid. In the aftermath of the famine, coaxed by South Korean president Kim Dae-jung, a score of new countries established diplomatic relations with Pyongyang. EU member states took the lead: Italy and the United Kingdom in 2000, then Germany, Greece, the Netherlands, Belgium, Luxembourg, and Spain in 2001. In July 2001, Britain became the first Western permanent member of the UN Security Council to have an embassy in Pyongyang. This opened a window into the North. Meanwhile, the testimony of refugees – real, rehearsed, and recalled – led to growing concerns regarding human rights in North Korea.

The Famine

Mountainous North Korea has limited fertile land and its climate is prone to drought, which is compounded by deforestation and flooding. Food shortages and even famines punctuate Korean history, including in the aftermath of liberation and the armistice. The North is only self-sufficient in basic foodstuffs when it has an exceptional harvest. Under Kim Il Sung, Juche had worked in the fields. In the drive to maximise production, farming had been mechanised and irrigation extended, and fertilisers and pesticides carpeted the soil and crops.

The industrial stagnation of the 1980s inevitably extended to agriculture. Spare parts were not to be found, the machines stopped, and factories idled. Pesticides and fertilisers vanished. The attendant poorer harvests could no longer be efficiently gathered in, nor flood waters pumped from the fields. With both machinery and the workforce exhausted, the 1991 'Let's eat two meals a day' campaign left many wishing that they could be so lucky. Foreign inputs were no longer available, with importers demanding payments up front and in hard currency. The collapse of the Soviet Union and China's market reforms made a bad situation worse.

Pyongyang publicly pinned blame for the food crisis on a series of natural disasters – floods, hurricanes, and drought – that struck the country in 1995 and 1996. The economic situation was already at a crisis point, but these events turned crisis to disaster. Bridges were swept away, mines flooded, and tens of thousands of acres of good farming land sterilised by saltwater. Millions of tonnes of cereals withered on the stalk, resulting in catastrophic food shortages. Two-thirds of the North's electricity came from hydroelectric power, and the floods damaged and destroyed many plants while the drought starved the surviving turbines of water. Industrial production ground to a halt in the absence of power and raw materials. Slogans from a similar period of adversity, Kim Il Sung's 'Resistance against the Japanese' campaign, were recycled. The Arduous March for Socialism and March Under Trial saw workers, soldiers, and children leaving the factories, barracks, and schools for the fields.

By 1995, the grain ration for farming families had shrunk from 167 kilograms per person per year to 107 kilograms, not enough to live on.[3] The harvest was barely 40 per cent of what was needed; staple foods like rice were only fitfully available, and at times ran out completely. Those most at risk were not in Pyongyang or the countryside but North Hamgyong Province and the remote industrial cities of the far north-east, where the large manufacturing complexes were rusting and the narrow coastal plains abutting the central mountains left little room for agriculture. Although the sinews of society just about held together, many of the young, the old, and the vulnerable died premature deaths. Slow starvation and wasting meant that opportunistic diseases killed the majority before malnutrition had time to do its worst. The World Food Programme's (WFP's) 1998 nutritional survey found that one in six North Korean children had brain damage from chronic hunger, with a further 50 per cent permanently stunted. The FAO estimated that 13.2 million people, or 57 per cent of the population, were malnourished in mid-2002.[4] Between 1995 and 1999, somewhere between 800,000 and 3 million died.

They died amidst a conspiracy of silence. The North was not telling – it was hardly an advert for the system – and those in US intelligence who knew felt no need to offer help. After more than a year of anguished internal debate between Ministry of Foreign Affairs, military, and Party, the silence was broken. The Ministry issued an international appeal for emergency food aid in 1995. The appeal had a limited response, overshadowed as it was by the nuclear crisis. This was compounded by the North's lack of diplomatic relations with the West, its earlier reneging on its debt repayments, and its long history of providing military training and aid to the 'wrong side' in Third World conflicts. When asked for money to feed the North's hungry, and consequently sustain the regime, the West was slow to respond.

However, after the FAO and WFP visits, which reported 2.1 million children and up to 500,000 pregnant women near starvation,[5] the UN and NGOs sprang into action. The WFP, along with the United Nations Development Programme (UNDP) and United Nations Children's Emergency Fund (UNICEF), began delivering food aid. Between 1995 and 2005, the WFP alone provided North Korea with nearly 4 million tonnes of food worth $1.7 billion (€1.6 billion), helping to feed 6.5 million people a year – more than a quarter of the population. Direct emergency food aid from individual governments and NGOs followed. In 1995 alone, South Korea provided 150,000 tonnes gratis. Japan provided 300,000 tonnes, half gratis and half at subsidised prices. Between 1995 and 1998 Seoul provided $316 million (€298 million), a third of the North's total aid. China had its own bilateral assistance programme, which Beijing claimed constituted 80 per cent of its total overseas aid budget. Other assistance was largely channelled through UN agencies. The US contribution was funnelled through the UN, but clearly labelled with its point of origin. Haggard and Nolan say the US was 'North Korea's largest benefactor'; between 1995 and 2005, it donated over $1 billion (€950 million) in aid.[6]

As a member of the European Parliament (MEP), I had a visit in Brussels from North Korean diplomats based at the embassy to UNESCO in Paris during the late spring of 1997. They described the dire situation on the ground and stated that they were desperately seeking EU assistance but had no idea how to proceed. In the absence of formal relations with the EU, they had no access to or communication with the European Commission, and therefore no knowledge of mechanisms to access European aid directly. At that time, Commission officials were forbidden even to speak to North Korean diplomats. This was just when 'mad cow' disease was revealed to have crossed over to humans in Europe, with all the restrictions that followed: Pyongyang asked to take the potentially affected meat.

I asked to see the situation on the ground for myself and travelled to North Korea in October 1997 with two fellow Labour MEPs, Clive Needle and David Thomas. We met with the vice minister for foreign affairs responsible for North America and Europe at the time, Choe Su Hon, as well as with international NGOs and the Flood Damage Rehabilitation Committee, and visited children's centres, hospitals, and PDS distribution centres around the country. The situation was grim.

Back in the European Parliament, we proposed a resolution (passed the same month) on the desperate situation that included a paragraph demanding the EP be allowed to send an official delegation to Pyongyang.[7] A further resolution on the food crisis in North Korea passed the following March, asking the European Commission and member states to provide additional humanitarian aid, conditional on monitoring its distribution.[8] The first official delegation from the European Parliament went to North Korea in December 1998. It was led by former Belgian prime minister Leo Tindemans, future Dutch agriculture minister Laurence Jan Brinkhorst, and me.[9]

I visited the Huichon Children's Hospital, the only hospital in this city 200 kilometres north of Pyongyang.[10]

It was cold and damp. They had had no heating since the floods in 1995, which ruined the boiler. There was no medicine and no food. Huddled listlessly in the small communal rooms that serve as wards were groups of mothers with their thin, emaciated children in advanced stages of malnutrition, too weak to cry, too strong yet to die. Nearby, on the other side of the river that divides the town – and brought its destruction – was the local People's Distribution Centre. The cupboard was bare: there was literally nothing there. Children received an allocation for 33 days; teachers, nurses, and doctors 16 days; and the rest of the population 11 days. But the daily allocation was only 250 grams, far short of the UN recommended minimum of 700 grams for long-term survival. All around, the last of the harvest was being gathered. An expected 3.8 million tonnes of cereals had slimmed down to 3.2 million tonnes. In Huichon, Chinese cabbage was being harvested, the central component of *kimchi*, the spicy vegetable dish that forms the basis of Korean cuisine. Men, women, young children, and the army were systematically stripping fields and piling small trucks full of vegetables. These were dragged along by hand to the nearby river for washing, and onward for pickling and storage. Traditionally kept in pots underground for two to three years to ferment, this latest batch probably did not last longer than two or three months.

That month the EU opened, for the first time, an informal political dialogue with Pyongyang. This led to a European Parliament resolution calling for the establishment of diplomatic relations, a dialogue on human rights, and the extension of assistance beyond food aid.[11] In April 1999, the EP received a return visit from a delegation led by Vice-Foreign Minister Choe Su Hon, who became the first North Korean to face the EP's Foreign Affairs Committee.

The EU's engagement with North Korea began with providing aid and humanitarian assistance targeting those at particular risk – children under seven and pregnant women. The aid was provided through the European Commission's Humanitarian Aid Office, and for the period from 1995 to 2005 it amounted to over €344 million ($430 million). The EU, despite a slow start, was the largest and most consistent donor, apart from the US, South Korea, and China. During the famine, others – Japan in particular – tended to use humanitarian aid as a political football, giving it and taking it away to match the changing political environment, a practice that subsequently proved contagious. On top of emergency food aid, the EU later supplied fertiliser and technical assistance to improve crop yields and undertook a series of health care, water, and sanitation projects. In June 2005, despite the nuclear crisis, the European Commission allocated €10.7 million ($13.5 million) for medicines and equipment.

Some questioned the value and use of the aid. In 1998, Médecins Sans Frontières (MSF – Doctors Without Borders) claimed that the PDS's food distribution was discriminatory, with rations determined by political loyalty instead of aid-agency criteria such as gender and age. (UN special rapporteur Vitit Muntarbhorn would later specifically reject this allegation.) Those counties closed to the WFP and NGOs for security reasons received no food distribution.

MSF moved its operations to the Chinese side of the Sino-Korean border, providing shelter, clothing, food, and medical care for refugees. They reported that the refugees they came across there painted an even bleaker picture of the famine than MSF staff had observed for themselves, and claimed that the large majority had received no aid from international donors. It was all perfectly logical. Most of the counties without WFP access, and where MSF argued no food aid should be provided, were located in the north central regions. These militarily sensitive areas adjacent to the Chinese border were where the bulk of the refugees the MSF was interrogating had originated. It was the very absence of assistance that helped create the refugee flow.

In February 2003, WFP director James Morris testified to the US's House Committee on Foreign Relations, reiterating that WFP staff had access to 85 per cent of the population and noting the WFP's belief 'that most food is getting through to the women and children who need it'. The WFP reported a marked improvement in children's health, with the virtual elimination of acute malnutrition. Moreover, attendance in primary schools had risen from 75 to 95 per cent with the introduction of WFP biscuit distribution in schools. This was confirmed by a UNICEF study that reported food aid was reaching the most vulnerable and that between 1998 and 2002 the number of underweight children had dropped by two-thirds, while acute malnutrition had been cut almost in half, with chronic malnutrition down by a third.[12]

In reality, the vast bulk of aid was provided through the machinery of the UN, with NGOs providing only 2 per cent of the total. The WFP did not pretend to have perfect control of every single bag of food, but it claimed to have a 'reasonable degree of assurance that the food provided through WFP gets to those who need it'. Furthermore, it refuted claims from US intelligence that food was being diverted to the military. With Chinese and South Korean aid unmonitored, the North could, if necessary, feed the military without WFP supplies.

The famine was easing, but hunger remained. The WFP's 2004 assessment estimated that, even with the best harvest since 1995/1996, 37 per cent of young children were still suffering from chronic malnutrition. Yet Pyongyang announced in August 2005 that it no longer required food assistance from the WFP and other aid groups and that aid agencies involved in humanitarian work should leave by the end of December 2005, except for those finishing ongoing development projects.

With the immediate crisis mitigated, Pyongyang wanted to move away from long-term dependence and towards capacity building. They had announced in September 2004 that 'although there is still a need for humanitarian aid', they would 'welcome in the future more technical assistance and more development-oriented support'.[13] This would focus on infrastructure rehabilitation, such as irrigation systems and road repairs, to allow farmers to raise production and transport their crops. A sound strategy, yet a bridge too far for many donors. Another factor was political, as Pyongyang saw a link between the passage of human rights resolutions in the UN condemning Pyongyang and Washington using humanitarian assistance as an element of its regime-change agenda.

The EU was worried about the impact of an abrupt termination of aid on the most vulnerable and argued for a continuation.

Pyongyang, having made its point, gave permission for European NGOs to continue their activities under the umbrella of the EU, with the NGOs re-organised as units of the European Commission. They arranged a two-year operation to combat nutritional deficiencies and boost grassroots food security amongst 1.9 million of the most vulnerable women and young children. The operation was to provide vitamin- and mineral-enriched foods, processed at local factories supported by WFP, to young children and pregnant and nursing women. Additionally, cereal rations were to be provided to under-employed workers through food-for-work schemes on community development projects aimed at rehabilitating agricultural and other community infrastructure. The EU, which claimed to have provided a total of €500 million ($630 million) of humanitarian assistance to the DPRK in the decade up to 2010, gave a further €10 million ($13 million) in emergency aid in 2011 to relieve the consequences of the previous year's dire harvest.[14]

The Emergence of Markets

The famine devastated the lives of North Koreans. When the PDS collapsed, people struggled to feed themselves. They abandoned homes, jobs, and families to search for food. The black market flourished. The sharp decrease in rations in 1995 meant that farmers, who could no longer rely on their basic needs being supplied by the state, gave priority to their own survival. They started to divert production in order to build up their own stocks and spent increasing amounts of time growing crops on their own private (and often illegal) plots outside of the collective. The scale of diversion reached a level where the military was sent to protect the fields from illegal pre-harvesting and, in some cases, to work fields deserted by farmers. Kim Jong Il was forced to appeal to the farming community:

> If we cannot give them [the military] rice then when the Yankees invade us we cannot defeat them and your sons and daughters will become imperialist slaves once more. . . . It is this logic that must

be used to persuade those who hide and smuggle food to regain their conscience.[15]

Another consequence of food diversion and moonlighting was the spread of farmers' markets. Initially barely tolerated, the state was forced to turn a blind eye as other sources of food dried up. Toleration turned into grudging acceptance. The PDS's inability to deliver sufficient rations (or sometimes anything at all) left no alternatives but forage, barter, and the market. Farmers' markets became permanent features of suburbs, towns, and cities, with non-agricultural products increasingly available. Now they are just 'markets'.

The food crisis was the motor of reform. Markets meant money. In March and July 2002, measures were announced 'to improve the management of the socialist economy'. The State Price Control Bureau introduced price and wage systems, endorsed 'markets', and granted greater autonomy to farmers and enterprises. It set new low targets for delivery to the state, with the surplus for sale. Monetary

Figure 14   Orphans in a children's centre near Hamhung, 2011.

reform devalued the won to a fortieth of its former value. Salaries were increased by a factor of 18 and food by a factor of 26, with the exchange rate for the euro – at the time Pyongyang's currency for foreign exchange – rising by a factor of 70. Until then, Pyongyang had favoured numerology over macroeconomic stability, fixing the won-dollar rate at 2.16 in homage to Kim Jong Il's birthday – 16 February.

Legalisation swelled markets in size and numbers. Initially they had been rudimentary assemblages of open-air stalls enclosed by make-shift fencing, strictly off limits to foreigners. They evolved into large, covered, state-regulated markets, complete with foreign-exchange facilities at 'grey' rates substantially better than those offered at banks or hotels – although only sporadically available to foreign visitors. They began to stock a wide variety of both domestic and imported consumer goods as well as food. In Pyongyang, the Tong-il (Uni-fication) Market was thronged with thousands haggling, selling, and buying goods at free-floating prices. On display was a broad array of products: fresh meat and dried fish, Spanish oranges and North African dates, clothes, shoes, cosmetics, and a range of elec-trical goods, from lightbulbs to computer parts – plus, of course, the ever-present alcohol and tobacco. The range of imported products showed the emergence of a middle class with money to spend.

The emergence of markets drove up productivity. In the agricul-tural sector, farms and co-operatives' commitment to the central government was now the delivery of a readily achievable cereal quota. The surplus above target could be sold. They showed productivity increases far above those procured with the mere application of fertiliser. For those with capital and enterprise, the emerging market economy has enormous benefits. Small informal co-operatives appeared, making and selling handicrafts and snacks or repairing shoes or bicycles.[16] Some got rich from market trading. More than a decade ago I saw an ice-cream maker – identical to a machine on sale for the equivalent of more than two years' wages in Tong-il Market – perched on the pavement next to a block of flats, where an electric cable was connected through a hole in the wall and an orderly queue was waiting to buy. Street vendors litter the landscape. Urban centres are awash with kiosks, and alongside rural roads pedlars colourfully punctuate the passing landscape.

Pyongyang next went a step further in industrial reform, acknowledging the death of central planning for all but the most vital industrial sectors. This coincided with the end of the state's ability to supply the raw materials needed. In 2004, the state plan was thus officially abandoned, allowing most factories to fire and hire at will and choose their own products and processes. The results for industry were disappointing in comparison to agriculture. In the manufacturing sector, the means of production were outdated and at times archaic. On the land, physical labour is the main factor of production. However dedicated a factory team may be, in the absence of energy and raw materials, the only option is to continue to produce nothing, with the new rich's demands satisfied by sucking in imports.

These reforms came with a cost. Inflation shot up to more than 30 per cent. The ostensive gains from wage reform were swiftly eroded. Three to four million people fell into hunger, not earning enough to feed themselves. Month on month, prices ticked steadily upwards, creating hundreds of thousands of new poor in an underclass dependent on family plots, connections, or humanitarian aid. Finally, in 2005, the PDS was partly revived. Cereals, including rice, were taken off the market and PDS deliveries partly restored.

These were the first steps of a long march to a market economy. North Korea wanted to learn from the West and the rest. In 2004 and 2005 the European Commission, together with the Ministry of Foreign Affairs, organised two workshops on economic reform in Pyongyang. European experts presented lessons from other economic transitions and argued the need to improve the climate for inward investment. The third seminar, scheduled for November 2006, was postponed in response to Pyongyang's opening nuclear-weapons test – perversely punishing Pyongyang's bad behaviour by refusing to teach it better. The country came to terms with the arrival of millions of tonnes of food aid labelled a 'gift' from the EU, USA, South Korea, and Japan. Principle and convention gave way to pragmatism in a country forced to seek a new accommodation and enact reforms that dared not speak their names. Change needed a neutral catchphrase.

Initially Pyongyang emphasised the difference with 'socialism in our own style' (*urisik sahuijuyui*), setting North Korea's socialist system apart from those of a failed Soviet Union and a revisionist China. Kim Jong Il blamed the collapse of the Soviet Union and Eastern Europe on weak leadership, poor decision-making, and loss of faith. Back home, unity was to be maintained through stronger social and ideological integration.

Facing a changed world, the regime's first reaction was to dig in. In a speech to Central Committee officials in January 1992, Kim Jong Il pointed to 'socialist ills', surmising:

> After adopting revisionism, socialism in the former Soviet Union and the East European countries has collapsed one by one. . . . The imperialists are attempting to infiltrate bourgeois culture into the socialist world [and] thus to paralyse the revolutionary spirit of the people there. . . . If the masses are equipped with a firm ideology, then they will be victorious, but if they are ideologically ill, then socialism will face ruin because the superiority of socialist society over capitalist society can be represented by ideological superiority.[17]

The threat was cultural and ideological pollution. Capitalism was a drug that led to addiction and destruction. The job of the Party was to keep the 'pushers' out and to 'save the masses from the danger of being exposed to the evil drug'.[18] People were to 'live according to our own style, rejecting ideological and cultural infiltration of capitalism'. This anti-capitalist campaign was supported by films, pictures, and posters illustrated with stills of former Russian officers selling hot dogs on the street and the unemployed and the homeless struggling to survive.[19] I have a poster from the time showing a determined steelworker stoking the furnaces with porn videos and copies of *Penthouse*. Capitalism was said to breed greed, poverty, and crime.

Unfortunately, 'our own style' of socialism and segregation proved an economic disaster. If the collapse of the Soviet empire vindicated Kim Il Sung's political choice, it damned his economic one. As the trajectory of *glasnost* and *perestroika* led to collapse of the Soviet 'utopia' and the birth of crony capitalism in Russia, the situation turned sour on the Peninsula as the economic consequences finally broke the back of the North's faltering economy. And then, amidst the nuclear crisis and rising tension between the DPRK and the US, Kim Il Sung died on 8 July 1994.

Kim Jong Il Steps Up

Kim did not formally succeed his father until three years later, on 8 October 1997, with the long interregnum billed as a period of mourning on the Confucian model. He remained, throughout the interregnum, the KPA's Supreme Commander and Chairman of the NDC, but it wasn't until the mourning period was exhausted that he took on the mantle of Party general secretary. He took his time, but when he finally arrived at centre stage and the country was beginning its long slow climb back to any kind of normality, he grasped the opportunity, faced down the disgruntled opposition, and started to do what needed to be done.

Nevertheless, the succession was not without its critics. Former ideology secretary Hwang Jang Yop had escaped to Seoul earlier in the year, making him the highest-ranking North Korean ever to defect, and complained of Kim's over-centralised and autocratic style compared to his father. When I interviewed him in 1999, he was still a true believer. For him, Kim Jong Il was the heretic Pope, 'betraying Juche and building feudalism instead of socialism'.

Hereditary succession as part of 'our style of socialism' implies no gaps or pauses but an immediate transition. Yet it was not a good time to be in charge: the country was enduring its worst decade since the Korean War. Kim Jong Il was pre-emptive in his own defence, saying in December 1996, 'If I concentrated only on the economy, there would be irrevocable damage to the revolution. The Great

Leader told me when he was alive never to be involved in economic projects, just concentrate on the military and the Party and leave economics to Party functionaries'.[20] The country was left without leadership during its most challenging period.

Kim Il Sung's death strengthened the military's role in state affairs. Kim Jong Il was rarely seen or pictured other than with senior military figures. Along with the military's growing representation in the ruling elite came concepts such as 'military-oriented thought' and 'military-first politics', shuffling Juche aside. For the moment, military requirements took priority over all else. For a country with no unemployment, the military was the reserve army of labour. Soldiers had long brought in the harvest and undertaken public works. The five-year construction of the West Sea Barrage near Nampo, to provide port facilities and control flooding, had been a military operation. Now the military moved from labour to management, navigating the political, economic, and security storms.

In September 1998, the 10th SPA amended the constitution, elevating Kim Il Sung posthumously to 'Eternal President'. Kim Jong Il was re-elected as chairman of the NDC, with the position enshrined in the new constitution as the state's most senior post. He was officially back in charge, though still running shy of economic affairs. Cabinet government left the prime minister and his ministers with this poisoned chalice. Kim warned that 'those who have stood with folded arms during this hard time will have to account for their actions in the future'. One who was judged to have stood with arms crossed was WPK agriculture secretary Suh Gwan Hee, publicly executed in Pyongyang in 1998 as an 'American spy and saboteur'. The restructuring of North Korea's political architecture centralised power, divested responsibility, and strengthened the hand of the military. 'Meeting and greeting' was transferred to Kim Young Nam, president of the SPA and now – if in protocol terms only – head of state.

With Kim embedded, by the end of 1998 the political emphasis was readjusted, with the slogan *kangsong daeguk* ('a powerful and prosperous nation') balancing military strength with economic prosperity and foreshadowing economic reform to follow. The slogan's first appearance was in a September 1998 *Rodong Shinmun* editorial titled 'Let's Construct *Kangsong Daeguk* as Led by the Great Leadership of the Party' that explained how the North was to be built into an ideologically, economically, and militarily strong country. No U-turn, but a sharp change in direction.

With the new millennium, the past was laid to rest. *Rodong Shinmun's* 9 January 2001 editorial argued that

> we should transcend the old working style and fixed economic framework of other countries in old times . . . it is impossible to advance the revolution even a step further if we should get complacent with our past achievements or be enslaved to outdated ideas and stick to the outmoded style and attitude in our work.[21]

Economic reform 'in our own style' had replaced socialism, while Juche had passed the parcel to *kangsong daeguk*.

The English-language *China Daily*, which in the post-Deng era normally extolled the virtues of the market, privatisation, and profit, ran a series of articles in September 1998 laden with arcane Marxist jargon and saluting Kim's leadership. They were not written for domestic consumption – few readers would have struggled beyond the opening paragraphs – but as tribute, sign of fraternal solidarity, and quarry for quotes for the KCNA and *Rodong Shinmun*.

Kim Jong Il's bold changes of policy and rhetoric were too fast for some. There followed a major restructuring and reshuffling of the WPK for the first time since his father's death. Kim Jong Il abolished the Bureaus of Military Affairs, Economic Policy, and Agricultural Affairs, and reassigned 40 per cent of the Secretariat. Jang Song Thaek, Kim's brother-in-law – considered by some to be North Korea's effective number two – and his two brothers, who were prominent in the military, used their positions to try to undermine Park Pong Ju, the premier responsible for economic reform. Jang and his coterie were all dismissed from their Party posts. Kim's purge, and the restructuring, removed the Party's ability to interfere. Military matters would be under the sole purview of Kim and the NDC, while the cabinet was given licence to continue the economic, industrial, and agricultural reforms.

Jang, newly penitent, seemingly took heed and was rapidly reha-bilitated, re-emerging as the first director of the WPK's Department of Working People's Organisation and Capital Construction, then took responsibility for the economy after the death of Prime Minister Yon Hyong Muk in 2005. One can only wonder whether Jang would have so easily been allowed back into the fold without his sister's entreaties. In March 2006 Jang led a 30-strong delegation on an 11-day visit to Wuhan, Guangzhou, and Shenzhen, tasked with drawing lessons from China's reform process.

Seoul's and Washington's media spent 2004 speculating on the stability of the regime. Apart from Jang's removal, the Agency for National Security Planning (South Korea's equivalent of the CIA) claimed to have identified an assassination attempt against Kim that May. The chemical signature of a devastating explosion in Ryongchon, close to the border with China, contradicted Pyong-yang's claim that a train laden with chemicals had accidentally hit a power line, causing the explosion, and that it was merely coincidental that Kim Jong Il had passed through the same station that morning, eight hours earlier than scheduled, on his way back from a trip to China.

November saw the *New York Times* (Nov 22) speculate on Kim's health, and on the unsubstantiated claims of anti-Kim protests in the North. They also reported the removal of Kim Jong Il's portrait from the meeting room during the first EU-DPRK workshop on economic reform, speculating that this was a sign of rising opposition, sabotage, Kim's imminent demise, or worse. There was a frenzy of media speculation as to the North's imminent collapse. Yet having marched Korea-watchers up to the top of the hill, the media then marched them down again. Kim was declared safe, with no evidence he had ever been in danger, apart from possibly at Ryongchon.

With Kim Jong Il turning 65 in 2007, the question of the succession reappeared. Few speculated it was to be other than a family affair. There had been some who thought the position could go to Jang Song Thaek, but he was only four years younger than Kim. Moving to the next generation left a limited selection. Eldest son Kim Jong Nam was effectively sidelined after a 2001 fiasco in which he attempted a trip to Tokyo Disneyland on a false passport and was arrested by Japanese police. Any possible reconsideration was negated by his cheap playboy lifestyle.

Speculation moved on to the two sons of Kim Jong Il's late wife, Ko Young Hee. Kim Jong Chol and Kim Jong Un were both in their 20s and working in the WPK's Organisation and Guidance Department. Kim Jong Chol was the elder and would have been the obvious choice for any early transition. His devotion to the music of English rock guitarist Eric Clapton was less dysfunctional than his elder half-brother's enthusiasm for Disneyland. The deciding factor in the end was that, despite his age advantage, he was the weaker personality. In the meantime, Kim Jong Il had other issues to deal with, including the flow of economic refugees crossing over to China and growing international concern as to the human rights situation.

Defectors, Refugees, or Migrants?

During the height of the famine, the normal to and from of Chinese and Koreans across the border turned into a flood of refugees into China. Some NGOs claimed there were up to 300,000. These claims were difficult to sustain. Certainly there were tens of thousands. Yanji in Jilin Province, on the border, has a population of 350,000, of whom 210,000 are ethnic Koreans; 300,000 would have been the equivalent of the population of the largest city in the region. The reality is that many crossed on a temporary basis to visit relatives, buy and sell goods, or search for food. The Tumen River serves as the border for hundreds of kilometres, and a drive along the road paralleling its Chinese bank shows all too well that, despite recent increased security on both banks, it is no formidable barrier, with water shallow enough to wade across in summer. In the early 1960s, with the famine in China following the disaster of the Great Leap

Forward, the traffic had been the other way, with the North receiving and feeding tens of thousands of starving Chinese.

Famine drove the first refugees, but afterwards more were pulled by China's growing prosperity. The bulk were no longer refugees but economic migrants. There are an estimated 25,000 to 50,000 indentured labourers on local farms in that part of China who lack access to even basic health care and education, but still live in better conditions than the rural fastness they come from south of the Tumen River. The shortage of women in rural China (owing to the now-abandoned one-child policy and to women migrating to urban centres) means that young Korean women are particularly welcome. Up to 70 per cent of young women are trafficked into the Chinese sex trade.

Mixed up amongst these illegal economic migrants and short-term visitors are refugees and defectors. Definitions are not easy: terms like *defector*, *asylum-seeker*, *refugee*, and *economic migrant* are all beset with ambiguity. Politics play an important role in the choice of language: one person's defector is another person's economic migrant. 'Returning illegal immigrants to their country of origin' has a very different sound from 'deporting defectors to their death'. Noting that grey areas exist, the terms here are used broadly as follows: a *defector* is someone in a senior position of responsibility in the North who is attempting to flee to South Korea for political reasons; a *refugee* is someone who has fled a natural or man-made catastrophe, in this case famine; an *asylum-seeker* is someone who has fled to a third country and has a 'well-founded fear of persecution'; and an *economic migrant* is someone who has moved to improve their living standards.[22]

Many of the North Koreans Barbara Demick interviewed for her award-winning book *Nothing to Envy* (2009) – the best popular account of the famine – left the North for purely economic or individual reasons. One family left to inform their South Korean relatives of the death of their father; a doctor fled because she learnt she would not be allowed to join the WPK; and a third fled after early release 20 months into a three-year sentence for black marketing. If they had been sub-Saharan Africans instead of North

Koreans, all three would have struggled to get asylum in the EU on these grounds.

A complication specific to North Korea is that economic migrants metamorphose into refugees. Economic migrants are not refugees when they set off, but they are when they arrive. They are *refugees sur place,* meaning people whose need for protection has arisen after they have left their own country. This transformation occurs because North Korea punishes those repatriated by China (or Russia). The Chinese authorities carry out sweeps from time to time to round up the more obvious immigrants and return them to the North. There is a degree of tolerance for local communities going back and forth, as they have done for decades. This, however, very definitely does not extend to senior Party members and officials suspected of trying to defect. Equally, repeat offenders accused of smuggling, associating with South Koreans, or religious proselytising can and will be sent to the camps.

The lucky ones end up in the South. All North Koreans are automatically South Korean citizens. In the early days of the famine, before the Chinese tightened security, refugees travelled to Beijing to seek asylum in foreign embassies before generally moving on to the South. It worked for a while. Now embassies in Beijing are fenced off from the street and surrounded by guard-posts manned by Chinese police.

Currently, a wide variety of alternatives are available. A business-class 'defection', at around $10,000 (€8.500), involves a chauffeur-driven car to the border, being carried across the Tumen River by a KPA soldier, a false passport, and a plane direct to Seoul. Economy class, in contrast, can involve ten hours a day of reciting and copying the Bible for months on end under the tutelage of Korea's evangelical Christian sects, followed by a long and dangerous hike over the Laos, Cambodia, or Thailand borders en route to Seoul. A typical 'defector' is a middle-aged female farmworker from a border county. Until 2004, South Korea paid a resettlement payment of $24,000 (€20,000) to each 'defector' arriving from the North. The growing numbers arriving as the operation was industrialised saw

Seoul slash the bounty to $8,000 (€6,800). (Those with 'high-level intelligence' could get ten times that; in March 2017 this jackpot was upped to $860,000, or €730,000.) Cutting the settlement grant by two-thirds was done to discourage criminal gangs and those purely in it for the money. Gangs smuggle the refugees across China into South Korea, often via a third country, in exchange for cash from the resettlement money. Much of the rest is taken as a down payment on smuggling the next member of the family chain out, repeating the process *ad infinitum*. The evangelicals do the same for souls.

In comparative terms, the numbers are small. In the last 65 years, just over 31,000 'defectors' have arrived in the South. The comparable rate from East Germany, from the construction of the Berlin Wall until its collapse in 1988, was 30 times higher. In 2016, West Germany received more Syrian refugees in a single weekend than South Korea's total for the whole post-war period.

Upon arrival, 'defectors' are housed in *hanawon* (hostels) for three months for resettlement training, education, and interrogation. The interrogations are conducted by the intelligence services and the police to weed out imposters. These include Chinese ethnic Koreans piggybacking on the South's largesse, who are inspected for dental work and the ability to sing 'Song of the Dear General', and Pyongyang's double agents. The latter are sent in to assassinate high-level defectors, such as Hwang Jang Yop and Thae Yong Ho, a minister in the London embassy who defected in 2016, and to intimidate the lower ranks working in the 'defector industry'. Those seriously thought to be under threat are given special watches that, when triggered, bring armed police units within three minutes. (One can only presume North Korean assassins are slow on the draw.) In addition to Seoul, New Malden in Surrey, England, is the home of 600 North Korean 'defectors', the largest concentration in Europe. The UK Border Agency is less astute at separating Chinese 'sheep' from Korean 'goats'.

NGOs and aid agencies rightly criticise Pyongyang for its treatment of those returned from China, as well as China for its refusal to grant refugee status. For the NGOs they are all refugees;

for Beijing they are all economic migrants. The reality is somewhere in between. The large majority, with the effective end of the famine a decade and a half ago, are economic migrants. Nevertheless, some have a 'well-founded fear of persecution' – and worse – should they be returned. Under the Geneva Convention, this group should be granted asylum. But Beijing makes no distinction between those who will spend a few days or weeks in detention and those who will be incarcerated for years or worse.

Yet the real barrier to North Korean refugees is Seoul. Yanji Airport has six airlines with direct flights to Seoul. The ROK could, if it wished, permit all who wanted to do so to travel south, asking Beijing to take the attitude of Hungary immediately prior to the collapse of the Berlin Wall in 1989 (when the Hungarians allowed East Germans free passage into Austria and on to West Germany). Yet this prospect horrifies Seoul. They neither want to turn the current trickle into a flood nor to threaten to precipitate the North's collapse. Neither the government nor the public is prepared for the social, political, and financial burdens that would inflict. Individual South Koreans might want their own relatives out, but they certainly don't want everyone else's.

Many South Koreans view North Koreans in the same way that some West Germans viewed their Eastern compatriots – 'feckless and idle'. North Korean immigrants find it extremely hard to adjust to the South's complex, competitive, and individualistic society. Some, persuaded to come south by those preying or praying on them in Jilin, end up feeling it was all a terrible mistake. Suicide rates are high, and a small number re-defect back to the North. One new danger Seoul now faces is that, if the situation in the North seriously deteriorates and the refugee camps near the Chinese border start to fill up, the Chinese will expect South Korea to allow them in.

The North's prison camps are real and reasonably documented, and tens of thousands are incarcerated there, suffering appalling deprivation. The worst camps are reserved for the victims of the Party's own cannibalism. Those on the wrong side of Party history end up in the ninth circle of hell, from which it is impossible to escape, while more mundane offences lead to temporary detention. Nevertheless, to believe some reports is not to believe all.

The majority of those who flee the North lie low. In the South, a Northern accent or evidence of Northern origin invites ostracism and discrimination. A minority turn it into a cause and career, with NGOs running competing campaigns and a cacophony of radio stations. They smuggle in missionaries, money, and USB sticks loaded with the Bible, porn, or South Korean soap operas and in return bring out reports and refugees.[23] Out of this competitive whirlwind, a few emerge as serious players. Others, like the North Korean People's Liberation Front, who dress in uniforms and dark sunglasses almost identical to those of North Korea's Special Forces, could have stepped straight out of an ill-conceived fancy-dress party.

A career as a professional defector brings cash. In the 1990s a nominal payment of 'inconvenience money' of $30 (€28) was expected for an interview with a defector. More recently there has been sharp inflation, with payments of $50 to $500 (€42 to €420) an hour the norm. Some now travel the West retelling their stories. The quality varies: most are embroidered, some have fictive elements, others are pure fantasy. It doesn't pay to tell the truth.

To take one example, Kang Chol Hwan, the author of *The Aquariums of Pyongyang: Ten Years in the North Korean Gulag* (2000), was imprisoned in Yodok Camp from the age of nine. His parents were wealthy Koreans living in Japan. They owned a pachinko parlour in Kyoto and provided substantial financial support to Chosen Soren. The whole family joined the exodus back to the North in the 1960s. Initially, because of his mother's contacts in the Party, they had a privileged existence in Pyongyang, even having their own car – almost unheard of at the time. It all ended when his grandfather was arrested for treason. The whole family was sent to Yodok and only released a decade later. While Kang was in Yodok he reported meeting Park Seung Jin, a member of the squad of North Korean football squad that came to England for the 1966 World Cup, in 1978. He claimed that the whole team had been sent to the camps. Park had been in Yodok for 12 years and was severely weakened and appeared to be dying, according to Kang's account. Yet, in 2002, Park appeared in the film documentary *The Game of Their Lives*,[24] which featured the surviving members of the team returning to Middlesbrough, the scene of their famous victory, 36 years later.

Kang did not escape from hell direct to the South. He spent five years in the North after his release in 1987 before opting to become an economic migrant. After his release he found a job at the local PDS, moved on to become a student at the University of Light Industry in Hamhung, then dropped out and finally made his way to China. Eventually, in 1992, he went to South Korea and later was invited to visit President George W. Bush's office as a prominent defector.[25] His co-author, Pierre Rigoulot, is a neo-conservative activist on the French extreme right.

Another famous memoir is Blaine Harden's *Escape from Camp 14: One Man's Remarkable Odyssey from North Korea to Freedom in the West*,[26] the biography of Shin Dong Hyuk, whom of the UN's Commission of Inquiry described as the 'single strongest voice' from its hearings.[27] After arriving in the South, Shin was fast-tracked by the Korean National Intelligence Service into becoming a career witness. Barely a year after he arrived, his book was published, emblazoned with the claim, 'No one born in Camp 14. . . . has escaped. No one except Shin'. In 2015 Shin recanted. He now claims to have escaped not from Camp 14 but from Camp 18, which had a milder regime. That has not, however, stopped Harden from republishing the book with the same title, prefaced by an apologia in a new foreword. Pierre Rigoulot wrote the afterword for an earlier French edition of the book.[28]

Similarly, in 2014, a refugee called Park Yeonmi had audiences in tears with her stories of brutalities in the North. No doubt her life had not been easy. Yet when an Australian journalist investigated, she discovered Park's tales to be riddled with inconsistencies, contradictions, and straightforward lies. Yeonmi works with a for-profit libertarian organisation in Seoul called Freedom Factory.[29]

Likewise, Lee Soon Ok, who claimed to be a former general manager of the Onsung County Officers' Distribution Material

Centre and a senior member of the Party, authored the evangelical Christian memoir *Eyes of the Tailless Animals: Prison Memoirs of a North Korean Woman*, detailing her seven years in Camp 14 between 1987 and 1993, before she defected to the South on her release. She testified before the US House of Representatives and the UN Commission of Inquiry, just as Shin had. In her memoir she reports torture, public executions, and biochemical-weapons testing on the prisoners. On a visit to the European Parliament during the famine, Lee argued that the EU should stop sending food and send Bibles instead.

In February 2004 a BBC documentary echoed Lee's claims of biochemical weapons testing on prisoners, this time in Camp 22.[30] The claims came from Kwon Hyuk, whom the BBC claimed had been head of camp security. Kwon's story was that he defected whilst posted as military attaché to the Beijing embassy. His key evidence was a copy of a letter stating, 'The above person is transferred from . . . camp number 22 for the purpose of human experimentation of liquid gas for chemical weapons'. Kwon's story quickly unravelled. No one of that name had ever been military attaché in Beijing, and South Korean Intelligence identified the letter as a forgery, as it used neither the language nor the seals nor the paper type of the North. When questioned, Olenka Frenkiel, who produced the documentary, said that while she had not seen the gas chambers or prisons, 'the next best thing you have is testimony and what documentary evidence you can find'. It turned out Lee Soon Ok was little better: she was not a political prisoner but had been convicted of forgery. The stories she had recounted in Congress of Christians being killed with molten iron were untrue.

The problem is that all of this makes a difference to how the North is perceived by the West. Congress passed the North Korean Human Rights Act on the basis of such testimony. No one argues – or should argue – that there are not very serious and large-scale human rights problems in the North. Nevertheless, both the US and the UN have taken action against the North on the basis of flawed and mendacious testimony, in some cases 25 to 30 years out of date. The most extreme claims were exported globally by US think tanks and lobbies financed by Christian fundamentalist groups, by the right-wing Heritage Foundation, and by monies made available by the North Korean Human Rights Act (2004). This act, in turn, was pushed through Congress by a Republican right bent on regime change.

The 2004 act was a more elaborate version of the 2003 North Korean Freedom Act, which aimed to make it easier for the US to assist North Korean refugees by providing humanitarian assistance to North Koreans inside North Korea; to provide grants to private, non-profit organisations to promote human rights, democracy, rule of law, and the development of a market economy; to increase the availability of information inside North Korea; and to provide humanitarian or legal assistance to North Koreans who have fled the country. The act assigned an initial budget of $124 million (€98 million) a year and made North Koreans eligible for political asylum in the US. Freedom House, a neo-con organisation (see above), scooped the funding pool.

The 'most effective witness' of the UN Commission of Inquiry was a liar promoted by South Korea's equivalent of the CIA. Friends of Shin Dong Hyuk who were aware of his plans to recant in late 2014 pressured him not to go public until after the Security Council had approved the General Assembly's resolution to refer North Korea to the International Criminal Court in December 2014. Yet the resolution originated with the Commission of Inquiry, whose chair had been so impressed with Shin's testimony.

Politics, like nature, abhors a vacuum, and this is what happens in the absence of credible reports from Amnesty International and others as to the situation in the North. Pyongyang should allow monitoring on the ground. It should provide access to the UN special rapporteur, Tomás Ojea Quintana. It should also publicise its response to the UN Human Rights Council's Universal Periodic Review of Human Rights, where it accepted 81 of 167 recommendations in whole and 6 in part, noted 15, and rejected 65. Any reports produced by Amnesty International and the UN would no doubt be highly critical, but almost certainly better than the image Pyongyang allows to fester and grow in the West.

By contrast, the EU's response to human rights concerns has taken a different form. In May 2001 the EU Troika visited Pyongyang and raised human rights, amongst other issues, directly with Kim Jong Il. He agreed to establish a formal Human Rights Dialogue with the EU, modelled on the EU–China human rights dialogue established in 1997. The first dialogue took place in June 2001 and the second a year later. Pyongyang officials argued that they had their own standards and their priorities were the rights to subsistence, development, and equality. Nevertheless, the talks resulted in the North Korean authorities giving a partial breakdown of figures of those held in 're-education camps' and proposing to amend the Criminal Code to reflect international standards. The EU voiced its concerns at the lack of access by UN human rights rapporteurs and NGOs, as well as the absence of any official statistics on human rights issues. Pyongyang responded by expressing reservations about such visits due to previous 'bad' experiences. Its defensive line was that 'arbitrarily assessing human rights in other countries and imposing one's will on others is an infringement on their sovereignty and interference in their internal affairs'.[31] The EU seemed to be the exception to this rule.

Before a third round could be held, however, the process was derailed within the EU, as the different institutions contradicted and opposed each other, aided by the activities of US right-wing lobbyists. In 2003, France slid through the European Council of Ministers a proposal to sponsor a resolution on human rights in North Korea at the UN Commission on Human Rights meeting in Geneva, with no discussion of the consequences and without informing Pyongyang. The result was all too predictable. Pyongyang announced in December 2003 that it was suspending the dialogue, expressing regret that the EU's sponsorship of the resolution had placed those who advocated and participated in the dialogue in a very difficult position. Pyongyang claimed it would have accepted the EU voting for a resolution sponsored by someone else, but the EU as sponsor was just too much.

In April 2005 the EU sponsored a second resolution jointly with Japan. In preparatory meetings – with Heritage Foundation staff hovering on the fringes – they used the catch-22 argument that a second resolution was needed because there was no dialogue, conveniently forgetting that the reason there was no dialogue was because of the previous resolution. The DPRK dialogue was at the time part of the EU's broader commitment to promoting universal human rights and democratisation in Third World countries.[32] When the European Parliament delegation raised human rights issues, their North Korean interlocutors were partially disarmed by them passing around copies of two of the Parliament's Annual Human Rights Reports: the first on the EU itself and the second on human rights around the world.

It was more than a decade before Pyongyang signalled that it was prepared to re-open the dialogue. In autumn 2014, the international secretary of the WPK, Kang Suk Ju, visited Brussels and met with Stavros Lambrinidis, EU Special Representative for Human Rights, and invited him to Pyongyang. The North's ambassador to the EU, Hyon Hak Bong, formally confirmed the offer a few weeks later. Subsequently it was re-confirmed for a third time in early 2017 by the current vice-chairman of the WPK and head of the international department, Ri Su Yong. Despite global demands for a dialogue on human rights, the EU has studiously and capriciously ignored Pyongyang's offer.

While North Korean defectors emphasise the dark side (and there certainly is one), during the era of Kim Jong Il, visitors to North Korea were seeing a changing country. The emerging 'markets' in the grassroots economy 15 years ago were a revelation.[33] Members of a US delegation as early as 2004 confessed that they found considerable evidence that the North was moving towards a market economy.[34] The journey continues. China's and Vietnam's success in marrying market reform and regime stability provided an alternative to the Soviet vision. The system had to change radically. With the state unable to deliver the daily necessities sufficient for survival, there was no alternative. Goods started to appear on shop shelves, and the restaurants on Changgwang Street were open and serving. Billboards sprang up in Pyongyang proudly advertising cars produced in Nampo by PyongHwa Motors, a North-South Korean joint-venture company. The country was moving. Colour was beginning to bleed back into North Korea's cities. The long march had begun.

PART II

Continuity and Change

5

Kim Jong Un

After the death of Kim Jong Il in December 2011, North Korea was called on to orchestrate the second leadership transition in its 65-year history. In 1994, the situation had been bleak. The 'Arduous March' was at its most gruelling, tens of thousands were dying every month from the effects of malnutrition, and the economy was melting down. Factories, farms, and workshops idled, then closed, as inputs dried up and the lights went out. The government had disappeared into limbo as Kim Jong Il spent three years mourning his father. The second time around, with barely a 100-day pause for mourning, Kim Jong Un took the helm. He seemed in control and on message. In his 15 years as leader, Kim Jong Il had uttered only a single sentence on the international stage; on 15 April 2012, Kim delivered a carefully crafted 20-minute speech that was Pyongyang's 'State of the Union'.

After his elevation, Kim systematically bolstered his personal authority by culling – literally, in some cases – those put in place to guide his early years. The execution of Jang Song Thaek, Kim's uncle, was the removal of a mentor who suffered the delusion that he was a regent, a kingmaker rather than confidant and mentor, and a power broker in league with and in hock to Beijing. Yet this was no purge in the manner of his grandfather Kim Il Sung, who condemned whole sections of the Party to the camps or the countryside, but a carefully orchestrated defenestration of a single potential threat.

Kim has become a cult figure – almost a 'rock star' – and has the charisma to carry it off. New statues and paintings clone the young Kim Il Sung's features as increasingly similar to those of his heir Kim Jong Un, while factories and institutions are adding a third set of 'history rooms' detailing the visits of the latest of the Trinity. At the opening of the Victorious Fatherland Liberation War Museum in

July 2013, I watched adulatory crowds of adolescents eddying around him as he walked the halls. In the soaring foyer of the Museum is a larger-than-life statue of a young Kim Il Sung that bears an uncanny resemblance to his grandson.

Politically, Kim Jong Un has made his mark by promoting his *byungjin* line of simultaneously developing the economy and the nuclear deterrent. This twin-track approach, endorsed by the Party in 2013, is designed to protect the North from outside interference, while also delivering the rising living standards that will ensure the regime's survival from both domestic and foreign threats. Where

Figure 15   The iconic, unfinished Ryugong Hotel from the courtyard of the Victorious Fatherland Liberation War Museum, 2013.

Kim Jong Il was a radical, his son is a revolutionary. Kim Jong Il was content with fitful progress towards nuclear deterrence and acquiescing to public/private markets; his son, by contrast, is going for broke. As Andrei Lankov argues, Kim Jong Un is 'the most pro-market leader North Korea has ever had', as 'he does not merely turn a blind eye to the activities of the increasingly influential North Korean private economic sector, but actually, if quietly, encourages such activities'.[1] It's full steam ahead: despite sanctions, the economy grew by 4 per cent in 2016.

Kim's base is the Party. His father had allowed it to decline and atrophy; its cadres were still at the wheel, but navigating on out-of-date maps to yesterday's destinations. In 2008, when Kim Jong Il started to prepare the succession, he revived and rebuilt it. After a decade and a half in the doldrums, the Party was back. The leadership structure that had withered since the last Party plenum under Kim Il Sung, in December 1993, was restored, with a new Central Committee and Politburo reflecting a generational change. The Party's symbol, the hammer, sickle, and calligraphy brush, suddenly sprang up everywhere. The 2010 Party conference declared its purpose to be 'the consolidation and foundation of the accomplishments of the revolutionary cause and to promote a new grand programme for building the socialist power through science and technology, playing a leading role in development, and the creation of an economic giant – a country that is strong and independent, self-reliant'.

Emerging Capitalism

Under the *byungjin* policy, the citizens – of Pyongyang, at least – have never had it so good. In the last decade, enormous resources have been funnelled into raising living standards in the capital. There are 100,000 new apartments in modern neighbourhoods that spring up year after year. Pristine sets of tower blocks march across the skyline. The zone around the Kim Il Sung University has been totally renovated. The new Science Street is finished. Traffic is jammed for the first time.

There are cash cards and ATMs and fleets of taxis. The Egyptian company Orascom has set up a public mobile-phone network that has around 3 million subscribers. There are pizzerias and hamburger joints, noodle bars and *okonomiyaki* grills. There are fashionable boutiques selling Italian dresses, handbags, stiletto heels, shirts, suits, and ties, and tailors ready to knock off 'made-to-measure' copies. Electronics stores have computers and DVD players, cameras, and watches. Blue jeans are still unacceptable, but black jeans pass unmarked by the fashion police. For women, skin-tight jeans with a flare at the bottom can be hidden under a coat in public. The North Korean 'iPad', the Samjiyon SA-70, is politically correct and comes pre-loaded with Kim Il Sung's *Collected Works* in the same way that Apple imposed *Stocks and Shares* on its early iPhones. A Deliveroo service hasn't arrived, but one can always dispatch a taxi for a pizza and pay with a cash card.

The entertainment industry is booming, with karaoke bars, restaurants and microbreweries opening across the city. Alongside are new state facilities with funfairs, waterparks and riding stables, a science complex – centred around a model of a Taepodong-2 rocket poised for blast-off – a natural history museum, a remodelled zoo, and even

Figure 16   Pyongyang fast food: burger, fries, and cola, 2014.

a dolphin aquarium whose denizens leap from seawater pumped from 60 kilometres away in time to stirring martial music. Tenpin bowling, ice-skating, and roller-skating serve the well balanced. The package holiday has arrived: sun or snow, beach or mountains. The trails of Mount Kumgang – which for a few years after the first North-South summit attracted South Korean tourists – is crowded in the summer with tour groups from Pyongyang. There have even been some attempts at promoting cultural exchange. In August 2015, the Slovenian avant-garde band Laibach played a mixture of martial and industrial music interspersed with Beatles numbers and tracks from *The Sound of Music*, to a bewildered audience.

Figure 17   Soldiers on a day out for military fun at the fair, Rungna Island, 2011.

The economy in Pyongyang is now market Leninism. Small-scale private enterprise operates under the close eye of the Party. In *North Korea Confidential*, James Pearson and Daniel Tudor term the system 'public-private capitalism',[2] with stallholders at the *jangmadang* (market grounds) paying the taxes of the tolerated. Ambitious parents scramble to place their children in trading companies rather than the Party. The *nouveaux riches* can buy a 'licence' to live abroad for $100,000 (€85,000) a year, while those lower down can 'ransom' themselves out of their state-allocated jobs in manufacturing – easier for women rather than men – freeing themselves to take their chances trading in the markets and kiosks. With the PDS increasingly limited to providing rice and other cereals intermittently, markets like Tong-il in Pyongyang are thriving and – almost – anything is available for a price. Given time – which is far from guaranteed – all the evidence is that change will come from within rather than from outside as the old makes way for the new and the North Korean economy increasingly resembles that of Vietnam. As Lankov says, 'It appears that the recent policies of Kim Jong Un have produced, at the very least, a limited but observable economic success, in spite of all the difficulties that have risen along the way'.[3]

After the agricultural and industrial reforms of 2002, the 'kiosk capitalists' grew in number and influence. Those who succeeded – though many fell into the clutches of loan sharks – were to be seen in bars and restaurants flaunting their wealth. The currency reform of November 2009 brought them to heel: overnight, the regime introduced new banknotes, with a low financial ceiling for exchanging old for new. With their bundles of 'old' currency turned into so much wastepaper, they learnt two lessons: curb conspicuous consumption, and ensure that the currency under the mattress is hard.

The main difficulty North Korea faces in introducing the market is that it lacks the mechanisms, institutions and laws necessary to regulate it. Even now, two decades on from its emergence, the market has no legislative footprint. This is one barrier to foreign investment. Nevertheless, consumerism is in North Korea to stay. As Tudor and Pearson write, the new system is 'so entrenched that the government itself must adapt to it'.[4] When the Party and government will take the next step and openly promote it remains to be seen.

Some Are More Equal than Others

Everyone is not equal. The very availability of expensive consumer goods and the emergence of a dual economy demonstrated a sharp rise in inequality. In the grim 1990s there was a surprising equality of misery, with a Gini coefficient trending close to zero. Now the gap in living standards between the best and the rest has become a chasm, with levels of inequality equivalent to those in Brazil.

In North Korea salaries are 5,000 to 10,000 won a day, which, at the 'grey'-market rate in late 2017, is €12.5 to €25 a month. Yet a suit is €180, stiletto heels €40, a pizza €2 to €6 and a burger and fries €3, while a game for four at the tenpin bowling alley is €10. Mobile phones cost €0.03 a minute to use for domestic calls, and the solid-gold Omega Speedmaster costs $40,000 (€34,000) – around 125 years' wages for a middle-ranking bureaucrat. In contrast, a month's season ticket on the metro is 200 won (€0.08). The middle class are the 'kiosk capitalists', while the seriously wealthy are those running the state, Party, and military companies and enterprises with international connections.

Just as 727 number plates – the date of the 'victory' in the Fatherland Liberation War – signal the travelling elite, 195 phone numbers distinguish those whose voices are heard from those who merely talk, with a separate server and higher levels of access. Influence and wealth are increasingly intertwined. The companies behind the new wave of consumerism are public-private partnerships: well-connected people in the military and Party use their contacts to import consumer goods for the market and split the profits between their institutions and themselves. The *nouveaux riches*, with their fashionably dressed daughters and pudgy sons, were making efforts in their own style at the first Pyongyang Taedonggang Beer Festival in 2016, as they worked their way stoically through the seven draught beers on offer. The 2017 event was cancelled.

Figure 18   First Pyongyang Taedonggang Beer Festival,
2016. Photo © Chiara Zannini.

Outside Pyongyang, urban life has marginally improved even in
the north-east, although admittedly from a very low starting point.
With the assistance of UK and EU aid, pipelines are bringing fresh
water from the mountains into Hamhung and Hungnam. This can
be 'purchased' from 'water shops' scattered across the cities for 20
to 30 won a litre (€0.002). This has reduced gastroenteritis by up
to 92 per cent. The hospitals are basic and suffer from high-tech
donor fads: Wonsan Hospital has barely used video intranet links –
intended to link them with doctors and consultants in Pyongyang

and the county hospitals – while, next door, new hospital buildings languish incomplete for lack of funds.

In the Hamhung-Hungnam conurbation – the heartland of heavy industry, rebuilt after 1953 largely with assistance from East Germany – the wheels are beginning to turn again after grinding to a halt in the mid-1990s. The Ryonsong Machine Complex, which sat gently rusting for a generation, is now up and running, with circumstantial evidence indicating that production restarted in 2010. Kim Jong Il visited three times in 2010 and four in 2011 the year he died. The manager's parking space held a car with one of the few 727 registrations seen outside of Pyongyang. The nearby Vinalon plant (Vinalon is the North's unique and scratchy clothing fibre, made from anthracite and limestone) shows the manifest pollution of production, with dark smoke leaking from rusty chimneys. Even the NGOs are getting in on the act. The orthopaedic unit in the city, run by Handicap International and staffed by amputees, has produced over 10,000 artificial limbs.

In the countryside there are high notes. On a visit three or four years ago to Yongkwang County, 20 kilometres outside Hamhung, we were shown an EU flood-control and irrigation project covering a population of 30,000 to 40,000 people with integrated pest management, new greenhouses and reforestation, plus a new bakery. This was, however, the exception rather than the rule. As we drove through the outskirts of Hamhung, we passed a water-park under construction.

Despite such striking changes, the country faces the danger of dismemberment. Peripheral areas are increasingly isolated and left to their own devices. Our 2013 drive up the east coast to Rason had to be abandoned because of dangerous roads – it had reportedly taken Rason's mayor seven days to drive the 800 kilometres to Pyongyang. Instead, we were rerouted from Hamhung back to Pyongyang, and then China – Dandong, Shenyang, Yanji, Hunchun – and Rason over three days. As of 2017, there is a train from Pyongyang to Rason seven times a month that is scheduled to take just under 30 hours – but it can run as much as 24 hours late, especially when hauled by

Figure 19   Steel works in Hungnam celebrating the end of the Fatherland Liberation War, 27 July 2011.

an electric locomotive. How often the carriages go on to Moscow is unclear.

Certainly the 'construction boom' in the capital is delivering 'Pyonghattan' at the expense of the rest of the country, beggaring and distorting other parts of the economy. In the north-eastern 'rustbelt', hunger and chronic malnutrition still stalk the streets, schools, and orphanages. In 2016, joint-venture mining operations returning high profits were forbidden from re-investing in improved facilities, instead forced to remit all the monies to the centre while their production facilities slowly degraded. Even in Pyongyang, monies set aside to purchase buses and trams ended up being swallowed by overruns in construction costs.

Investment and Special Economic Zones

Without a dramatic change in the political climate, the idea of North Korea as a destination for new foreign direct investment (FDI) is outlandish. The added sanctions after every nuclear test and long-range missile launch have moved prospects from improbable to virtually impossible. Nevertheless, Pyongyang recognises and acknowledges the importance of FDI. There has been some (predominately Chinese) investment in Rason, but the state has, at least until very recently, refused to acknowledge its contribution to shaping a noxious environment through arbitrary regulation, instead blaming structure or processes. The reality behind the underachievement is a combination of the external environment and the *post hoc* treatment of those who make money, with retrospective tithes on profits and capital equipment held hostage.

In theory, there are three possible options for FDI: equity joint ventures, contractual joint ventures, and exclusively foreign-owned businesses. The latter can only operate inside the SEZs. The North has tried a variety of iterations of SEZs as it hunted for what worked. The rapprochement with the South during the era of Kim Dae-jung's 'Sunshine Policy' of engaging with the North led to several joint ventures that married North Korean land and labour with South Korean energy and capital, management, and marketing. These were the Kaesong Industrial Complex (KIC) and the less significant Mount Kumgang Special Tourist Zone, both on the ROK border. The Party, particularly its United Front Department, was responsible for KIC and Kumgang and initiated the potentially colossal Wonsan-Kumgang International Tourist Zone.

Seoul closed the Mount Kumgang Special Tourist Zone in 2008, after a North Korean soldier surprised a woman tourist before dawn in an adjacent closed military zone and shot her dead. It has never

Figure 20   Frolicking on Wonsan Beach.

re-opened and now serves as a package-holiday destination for Pyongyang's middle class and Chinese tourists.

The KIC grew into a collection of more than 80 factories in a closed zone to which North Korean workers commuted in on a daily basis to work for South Korean SMEs. The work was predominantly in sub-assembly and fabrication, and the goods produced were shipped directly to the South. The original proposal for KIC had been that, after an initial phase involving around 50,000 workers, it would expand in two further phases: first to 250,000 workers, then ultimately to 450,000. At the start it thrived, employing 54,000 workers. It was politics that was the problem. The KIC was closed six times, for a few days or up to several months, serving as a convenient 'whipping boy' for both North and South when one wanted to make a point, whether it was Seoul's joint military exercises with Washington or the DPRK's nuclear tests and satellite launches. When tension grew with Seoul in early 2013, the KIC became an issue within the upper reaches of the WPK. The transformation of civic unrest in Syria into a full-scale civil war, aided and abetted by the West, exacerbated the situation. Was the KIC a 'cash cow' or a Trojan horse? For both the WPK's United Front Department and the Korea Asia-Pacific Peace Committee, it was the former, earning Pyongyang $50 million (€45 million) per year and a running total of at least $355 million (€300 million).

Elsewhere in the Party, the KIC was seen as a Trojan horse. The concern was that by the second or third phase – given that only one member of a family is allowed to work there at a time – between 1 and 2 million people could have been dependent on work in the complex, up to nearly 10 per cent of the North's population. At that point Washington and Seoul could wilfully close KIC, assuming that, after a couple of months, civil unrest and food riots would provide an excuse for outside intervention, patterned on Libya and Syria. After much argument the consensus in Pyongyang was to accept the *status quo ante* but curtail further growth for the foreseeable future.

Three years on, in February 2016, President Park Geun-hye announced the immediate closure of the KIC in retaliation for a satellite launch by the North. It was clear a few weeks later that – as far as she was concerned, at least – this was permanent when the government's contingency fund, secretly set up for such an eventuality, paid compensation to the 124 South Korean companies concerned for the loss of their facilities.

This was all to the chagrin of the United Front Department and the 'told you so' delight of much of the rest of the WPK. It also allowed Pyongyang's opponents to turn the screws on its cache of overseas workers. They contended that these were 'slave workers', the bulk of whose earnings were misappropriated by Pyongyang to fund its nuclear programme, even though in the North these were desperately sought-after posts. Yet persuading countries to give up this pool of cheap skilled labour when Seoul was profiting from over 50,000 such workers and a projected further 400,000 had always been a hard sell. This changed with Seoul's self-denial with the closure and the subsequent UN sanctions after the sixth nuclear test and the two ICBM launches over Japan, saw overseas workers first restricted and subsequently only allowed to serve out their contracts.

With Seoul's betrayal, attention turned, or rather returned, to the Raijin-Sonbong (Rason) SEZ. The Rason SEZ had been established way back in 1991 and, after the Inter-Korean Summit in 2000, became the 'ugly duckling' of the SEZs. Despite being wedged up on the China/Russian borders in the far north-east of the country, with good rail and road access to both, it initially failed to take off. Modelled on China's Shenzhen, it is an area the size of Singapore with a population of 200,000, fenced off from the rest of the country. As with Shenzhen, the fences are intended to stop people getting in rather than out. Away from Rason's border, the military and ideology are conspicuous in their absence. Instead, a pragmatic obsession with making a quick buck pervades. A visiting British ambassador returning from Rason in 2012 described it as a 'casino where they turn lights off at night'. Even then, she was behind the times.

It all started to change in the late 2000s, with substantial Chinese investment in manufacturing plants, port facilities, and a new 52-kilometre 'motorway'[5] from the Chinese border to the port, with a promised new bridge across the Tumen River to replace the one Japan built in 1938. Simultaneously, Moscow built a Russian-gauge railway into the port. Rason is ice-free in winter, unlike Vladivostok, thus making it the most northerly ice-free port in the region. In the future, it could allow for summer shipping through the Northern Passage if global warming continues to degrade Arctic ice. With China's railways at capacity, such a facility could serve as a valuable outlet for China's north-eastern provinces.

The problem the second time around was success, not failure. Despite the best efforts of the State Economic Development Administration and its predecessors to widen the FDI base, the Rason SEZ has become a virtual extension of China's Jilin Province. Investment has been all but exclusively Chinese, with token amounts from the Russians, Thais, and Mongolians. The four fish-processing plants load their production (mainly squid) directly onto refrigerated lorries bound for China, while seven clothing factories turn out Slazenger, Lands' End, Kappa, and NBA apparel with 'made in China' tags. The 2,000 workers in the processing plants and the 3,000 in the clothing industry receive $80 (€68) per month, the former for a 48-hour week and the latter for a 60-hour week. Thanks to 'unofficial taxes' in Rason, companies lacking ties to the administration or 'protection' either remain very small or merely trade and process on commission.

Figure 21   NBA shirts in Rason, complete with
'Made in China' labels, 2012.

In the large market in Rason, the default currency is the renminbi (RMB). Attempts to pay in won will have traders scrambling for a calculator. The exchange rate back around summer 2014 was 1,300 won for 1 RMB, 10,500 won for one euro, and 8,000 won for one US dollar – almost 50 per cent better than the 'grey' market in Pyongyang. Fruit and vegetables, fish and meat were available – although not rice – plus clothes, shoes, general household items, cigarettes, loose tobacco, stationery, and new and second-hand bicycles.

Chinese 'entrepreneurs' in Rason are building apartment blocks and selling and renting apartments, post June 2018 in a booming market. The Chinese feel is reinforced on the streets with the substantial presence of Chinese cars and lorries. The lack of a direct road to Russia does not help the mix. The only border crossing, a single-track railway, has seen annual trade shrink from 500 wagons a day in Soviet times to a handful, with total trade of less than 70,000 tonnes a year. Of this, 95 per cent is Russian imports, of which coal and timber make up more than half. There were rumours of a heliport and airport, although the latter would lie extremely close to the Chinese border. Rason is a geographic and economic outlier that is being pulled away from the rest of the country and toward China as the east coast road to Hamhung deteriorates.

Rason's internal bottleneck to development is, first and foremost, energy. The 200-megawatt *Sonbong (Unggi)* oil-fired power station is now closed and derelict. It had received HFO as part of the Agreed Framework, while North Korea waited on the completion of the Korean Peninsula Energy Development Organisation's (KEDO's) two light water reactors (see below). Washington walked away in 2001 abandoning the deal over allegations that Pyongyang was cheating on its nuclear programme. The HFO was so sulphur-rich that the corrosion from storing it destroyed the plant. The adjacent oil refinery isn't working either. Recently, much of the North's electricity has been supplied from power stations in Hunchun, just across the border in China, but whether and how long this arrangement can continue under the latest UN sanctions regime is far from clear. In 2013 the Chinese froze plans for further linkages into the Jilin electricity grid.

Pyongyang raises short-term money via one-off sales or long-term leases of Rason facilities to Chinese companies and organisations, making a continuous revenue stream impossible to maintain. The executed Jang Song Thaek's offences were many, but included selling off Rason's land, leases, and labour to China at 'friendship' prices.

Apart from KIC, Kumgang, and the promised Tourist Zone,[6] the other SEZs are run by the upgraded State Economic Development Administration (SEDA), under the Ministry of External Economic Relations. The former Joint Venture Investment Commission was absorbed into what is now the SEDA. There are now 25 SEZs – three under the Party (see above), 21 under SEDA, and Unjong, the high-tech SEZ, run by the State Academy of Sciences. Three, including Rason, follow the model of geographically based SEZs with 'captive' populations. The other two proposed SEZs – Hwanggumpyong-Wihwado (44 square kilometres), and Sinuiju (40 square kilometres), which both face Dandong, show at best patchy signs of development.

The remaining 19 SEZs – including Unjong – were announced in two tranches in November 2013 and June 2014.[7] These could be said to represent a 'Third Way'. They are small – varying from 1.37 to 8.1 square kilometres – and sectoral, split between high-tech, export processing, agriculture, and tourism. The first tranche included two export processing zones in or near Nampo and several industrial development zones: at Wiwon, on the Chinese border; in the Hyondong suburb of Wonsan; and in the Hamhung/Hungnam conurbation. Agricultural zones are in Pukchong and Orang. In addition, tourist zones are proposed in Onsung (to cater to Chinese trippers from Tumen) and Sinphyong (a scenic site not far from the Masik Pass Ski Complex, on the road between Pyongyang and Wonsan). There are economic development zones covering an area near the Chongjin Steel Works; in Hyesan, near Mount Paektu; and in Manpo. The second tranche had six zones: Unjong; an additional zone near Nampo; an environmental 'Green Zone' near Haeju; one near the Anju coalfield in Sukchon, in the centre of the North's rice-bowl area; and one in Chongsu, on the Yalu River, for Chinese day-trippers.

Energy and Mining

Outside of the SEZs, mining is far and away the most important industrial sector. Coal is the main energy source in North Korea, and this will not change in the near future. Though the quality of domestic coal is poor, it accounts for almost 90 per cent of the fuel for industry, 45 per cent for power generation and 80 per cent for household usage.

North Korea has massive coal reserves, enough for all its requirements and substantial exports, but most of the mines are run down and desperately need renovation. Another problem is the coal mix: there is not enough coking coal for steel production. There were well-publicised attempts to pioneer an innovative process substituting anthracite, with the upgraded Kangson Steel Works reportedly using domestic rather than imported coke. That has now gone quiet.

Other mined minerals include phosphate and the all-important rare-earth minerals used in the manufacture of mobile phones, electric cars, and other high-tech goods. China is keen to maintain its quasi-monopoly on the rare-earth supply and has invested over $500 million (€425 million) in all forms of mining since 2007.

Energy continues to be a serious problem. In rural areas, electricity is available for only three or four hours a day, at best; in Wonsan, the city's main streetlights are switched on for foreign visitors. The same is true for Pyongyang's metro stations. Yet the tower blocks in the capital's new streets are floodlit deep into the night, and there are few outages, though in February 2018 it was reported that in South Pyongyang, across the Taedong River, electricity was limited to one or two hours a day because of the sanctions.

The North has turned to renewables. Solar panels are now fitted as standard in new housing and are being widely purchased by private individuals for individual apartments in older buildings. (High-rise dwellers in Pyongyang should be concerned: while the traditional 10- to 12-storey blocks are just about functional with no electricity, the new 70-storey blocks will turn into vertical prisons during outages.) A 300,000-kilowatt hydroelectricity station came on stream in Huichon, and the Ministry of External Economic Relations boasts of solar, wind, geothermal, and hydropower schemes. Much of this new mix is 'soft', small-scale renewable energy – difficult to utilise to keep the wheels of the military-industrial complex turning. In the absence of major investment, this provides neither the quantity nor quality of energy required for economic modernisation and growth. The only realistic options are massively enhancing coal production from rehabilitated mines or returning to civil nuclear power, with all of the political and safety concerns that would pose.

Another outside possibility is a series of tidal barrage schemes that has enormous potential. Around 2010, a group of British engineers, who had worked on the aborted scheme for a tidal barrage across the UK's Severn Estuary, were invited to Pyongyang to discuss this possibility. These would be both conventional and renewable, addressing concerns about climate change as well as nuclear non-proliferation –

though that may not suit the machismo of Pyongyang. Some limited civil nuclear power may be a minimum demand from the North in a broader package: now that the DPRK has developed its own nuclear-weapons technology, the proliferation issue is moot. It's in a far better position to engage in proliferation now than it would be after any energy deal.

Pyongyang's potential indigenous resources of oil and gas are hard to estimate, although there is promising hydrocarbon geology offshore, particularly in the Yellow Sea. All attempts by the North to explore off the west coast have been physically blocked by China. The little-discussed maritime-boundary dispute between Beijing and Pyongyang is cryptically reported from time to time under the rubric of arresting Chinese 'pirates'.

Agriculture, Nutrition, and Industry

According to the FAO, the agricultural sector engages less than one in three of the working population, although substantially more when *corvées* from the KPA are helping with sowing and harvesting. Since the early 1990s agriculture has contributed 25 per cent of the GNP despite the challenge of geography, climate, and material; limited land; a propensity to flooding and drought; and chronic shortages of fertiliser, seeds, farm machinery, and equipment as well as fuel and energy. There have been efforts to expand arable lands by reclaiming tideways, but these areas were overwhelmed in the mid-1990s by storms that drove seawater far inland, rendering the fields sterile for many years to follow. The (re)construction of two fertiliser plants in Hamhung and Nampo has reportedly raised annual capacity to 1,300,000 tonnes. The country still needs to import fertiliser, but requests for it as aid have met with little response.

As late as 2012, the WFP estimated that around 16 million North Koreans (two-thirds of the population) continued to depend on the PDS for food. Delivered rations have, since the early nineties, been well below the official minimum of 573g of cereals per person per day, and in 2011 were closer to a harrowing 250g – even though the

sale of rice in the markets was banned in 2005. Anything over this
minimum is confined to a few high days and holidays: the Leader's
birthday, Victory in the Fatherland Liberation War–Armistice Day,
and so on. Even those who manage to obtain the official minimum
suffer: the relentless monotony of a cereal diet deprives the body
of micronutrients necessary for health. Using data from North
Korea's all-too-efficient family household-doctor system, UNICEF
estimates that one in four women aged 15 to 49 is malnourished and
that stunting affects 32 per cent of children under five, while 19 per
cent are underweight and 5 per cent wasting – and regional inequal-
ities make the picture distinctly worse in peripheral areas.

After 2002, productivity rose and harvests grew – albeit not to
self-sufficiency. That would require the best of all possible years. To
bridge the gap, the DPRK sought and received a drip-drip of food
aid, notably from the WFP and the EU. While such aid prevented
any prospect of sliding back into the horrors of the second half of the
1990s, starvation was replaced with hunger.

In July 2012, Kim Jong Un introduced the '6.28 instructions',
halving the size of the agricultural work teams to make them effectively family units, and allowing farmers to retain 70 per cent of
production. At a stroke he effectively de-collectivised agriculture,
leaving the PDS as supplier of last resort as the market took the
strain. These reforms brought a 10 to 15 per cent increase in grain
production, from 4.0 to 4.5 million tonnes between 2005 and 2010
to around 4.8 million tonnes after 2013.[8]

In the greater Pyongyang area, there have been attempts to diversify
production to satisfy the capital's more demanding consumers. The
Ministry of Public Security created an enormous apple orchard,
the Taedonggang Combined Fruit Farm, on former paddy fields to
provide the city with fresh and dried fruit, apple juice, and cider. The
same agricultural complex is also breeding bullfrogs and snapping
turtles for the tables of Pyongyang's gourmet restaurants, while
the Pongsu hydroponic farm, close to the capital, produces lettuce,
tomatoes, cucumbers, and strawberries. Meanwhile, the world's
third-largest ostrich farm delivers meat to the city.

Figure 22   Yosushi restaurant in Pyongyang.

Outside the capital, accessibility and logistics problems with food distribution are increasing. In the past the PDS distributed available cereals, meaning that – apart from at the very top – there was a shared equality of misery. Now, availability is not enough. Accessibility is increasingly determined by financial resources. Meanwhile, in the north-east 'rustbelt', hunger has reappeared as transport infrastructure deteriorates and the economic pull of these cities weakens.

In industry, unlike in agriculture, the reforms of 2003 failed. The means of production were outdated and poorly maintained, and managers untrained in the workings of modern economies. Serial attempts were made across the years to shift the emphasis towards light industry, but were thwarted by the inexorable marriage of the military with the coal, steel, and cement industries. In 2003, 95 per

Figure 23   Machinist in Pyongyang factory, 2012.

cent of industry was taken off the Plan and firms were allowed to hire and fire at will and choose process and product. But without energy and raw materials, this resulted in more firing than hiring. Financial reforms that monetarised the economy led to inflation and, in the absence of domestic production, imports. The goods in Tong-il Market, apart from basic commodities, are either made by or shipped through China.

The 30 May 2014 industrial reforms were more successful. Allowing managers to buy spare parts and raw materials on the market and to set workers' salaries gave significant autonomy to management, with sharp rises in earnings in successful companies, as well as for workers with skills in demand.

North Korea is hampered by labour shortages. Kick-starting the economy would require a pool of new workers. Unlike in China, there is no reserve army of labour on the land. A 150-day 'Speed

Battle' was launched in May 2009 and then extended for another 100 days, aimed at boosting productivity with 'voluntary' extra hours and harder work, especially in the coal, steel, and railway sectors – but any gains were incremental and temporary. There is little economic purpose behind hundreds of women sweeping roads or thousands of men, women, and children replacing railway ballast on lines that haven't had serious traffic in months, if not years. Toil can't replace technology. Rather than a developing economy making the rural-urban transition, the DPRK is a failed industrial state.

6
Daily Life in North Korea

Despite the transformation of the economy, North Korea remains as tightly controlled as ever. Andrei Lankov, a Russian commentator with extensive experience of Pyongyang, claims to have found a hidden third element to the dual-track *byungjin* policy: 'the maintenance of very strict surveillance and control systems domestically'. He argues that Kim Jong Un is in the process of transforming North Korea into a Vietnam-style 'developmental dictatorship'. Whether and how the economy develops is an open question, but the political system is here to stay, as far as Kim Jong Un is concerned. The vast majority of North Koreans have no 'outside' frame of reference. North and South have lived apart for almost 70 years, and the average North Korean has had no direct contact with anyone or anything outside the country. Access to the intranet (North Korea's closed internet, limited to domestic sources of information, with no international access), and domestic and foreign travel, and news – even football scores – remain tightly controlled. In March 2008, North Korea were scheduled to play South Korea in a World Cup qualifier. I travelled to Pyongyang with colleagues to see this historic encounter. Pyongyang refused to allow the South's flag to be flown or its anthem played. Consequently, the match was moved at the last minute to Shanghai. We were stuck in Pyongyang but expected to be able to watch it live on TV. It was not televised. Even the result, a 0–0 draw, was not announced for three days.

But cracks are appearing in the system. The North is an arbitrary society. What is not specifically allowed is forbidden. Thus *everyone* breaks the law, including the police. One Politburo member confided to me that the Party hierarchy shares the late London police commissioner Sir Robert Mark's ambition that the police should 'arrest more criminals than we employ'.[1]

There is a revolution under way behind closed doors, staffed by the *jangmadang* generation, the under-35s who became adults after the famine of the late nineties.[2] *Jangmadang* means 'market grounds', referring to the grey and black markets. The markets have sucked in a torrent of imports from China, including South Korean 'soaps' and K-pop, particularly as the price of DVD players tumbled. In Pyongyang the younger generation, of all classes, ride the *hallyu* (Korean wave) sweeping East Asia. Chinese and American films and box sets, such as the US spy series *Agents of S.H.I.E.L.D.*, are gobbled up. Private viewing shows itself in public fashion and lexicon. For Pyongyang's youth, to be out of touch with Seoul's latest fashions is to be marginalised.

Transportation

Just over 3 million people are permitted to live in Pyongyang, and checkpoints control movement into the city, though this is not a barrier for those with money and a car. Inside the city there are closed neighbourhoods, strictly off limits to ordinary people, where senior Party and military officials live and work. Multi-lane motorways stretch out from Pyongyang, but only a few cars make the trip. Those that do are at the disposal of the moneyed rich, who choose to live in the capital's satellite cities – like Pyongsong, site of the high-tech Unjong SEZ – where they can be 'out of sight, out of mind', but not so far out that they cannot come back for dinner parties and entertainment. The newest motorway, built in 1998, spans ten lanes and takes a handful of cars and lorries 46 kilometres to Nampo, Pyongyang's port city.

In Pyongyang, men commute on bicycles to and from work. Each bicycle has its own registration plate that requires annual renewal. Women are seen cycling less frequently after Kim Jong Il's guidance 20 years ago, apparently in the wake of a spate of accidents, that women cyclists were a traffic hazard (although they may drive buses and direct traffic). Any formal restriction has lapsed, but the taboo remains, at least in Pyongyang.

Figure 24   Cycling in the countryside.

Trams and trolleys function, electricity permitting; they are freezing in winter and boiling in summer. The public transport of choice is the metro, with the Hyokshin and Chollima lines traversing the capital, uncrowded former East German trains sedately trundling along its tunnels. The metro stations are extraordinary cathedrals to Communism, built deep underground; the people of Pyongyang will rush there with their gas masks to shelter behind enormous blast doors in the event of an air raid or nuclear attack. The platforms are clad in marble and the walls have stunning mosaics depicting the Great Leader leading the workers onward amid smoking factories, abundant crops, and doting women and children. Stirring tunes play and destination names are uplifting: Pulgunbyol (red star), Chonu (comrade-in-arms), Kwangbok (liberation), Kaeson (triumphant return). The terminus near the zoo is 'Paradise' (Raekwon). In contrast, the nationwide transport network is limited. Travel between towns and provinces requires a not-easily-obtained permit and, consequently, there is little demand. An extensive electrified rail network does exist, but apart from the international route to Beijing, service is unreliable.

Like in most capitals, living space in Pyongyang is hard to come by. To even enter the housing queue requires a political pedigree. The Party and military elite live in relatively spacious apartments in their gated communities. Since Kim Jong Un's elevation, construction has been booming. In 2015 Mirae Scientist Street was built near the river to serve the faculties and staff of the Kim Chaek University of Technology.[3] The academic staff of Kim Il Sung University had Ryomyong Street built for them the following year and occupied it in 2017. Its centrepiece is an 70-storey tower block. Successful athletes live in their own community. A South Pyongyang address is a disappointment.

Figure 25   Shopping for lipstick in Ryomyong Street, Pyongyang, 2017.

Nevertheless, Pyongyang standards are much higher than in the provinces and the countryside. In Pyongyang water comes out of the taps, even if only at a dribble; electricity is generally available. People used to pay a purely nominal rent for their apartments, but that changed with the 2002 wage and salary reforms and rents now consume a not-insignificant percentage of income. The general rule is that the taller, the newer, and the closer to the centre, the better and the more expensive. Hard cash can unlock availability. Everything from education to health, employment to living space, is based on class and position – and during the famine, these meant the difference between life and death.

Education: Shaping the Nation

The WPK was formally constituted in 1949 with the amalgamation of the North and South Korean parties (see chapter 2). The WPK is outlawed in the South. It rules the North as the dominant component of the Democratic Front for the Reunification of the Fatherland, the other two components being the Korean Social Democratic Party and the Chondoist Chongu Party. The WPK's most recent membership figures are from way back in 1988, when they were reported as 3 million, but there is no reason to suspect major change. Being *in* the Party – virtually every adult in the 'friendly' class is a member – is not the same as being *of* the Party. Like in all Communist states – including China and Vietnam today – it's the Party rather than the cabinet that takes the decisions, when it's not the leader himself. Kim Jong Il had let the Party leadership atrophy during his period of power, and a substantial section of the Central Committee were dead or in their dotage by 2008. Around then came the first signs that the Party was coming back into its own, with *Rodong Shinmun* reporting tens of thousands visiting the Party monument. The wave of visitors was entirely imaginary – I visited at the time – but that made the message much clearer to Pyongyang's residents. In 2010, as Kim Jong Un belatedly consolidated the succession, he announced a third Party conference for September. It was the first in 44 years:

the first was in 1958 and the second in 1966. The third conference renewed the Party, from the Central Committee up through the Politburo, and established Kim Jong Un as heir apparent. It provided him, young and inexperienced in a Confucian society that values age and experience, with a platform and a voice, speaking on behalf of a tried and tested institution to reassure the country it was in safe hands.

Education plays a central role in the North's society and culture. Its education system shares many features of those in China and Japan.

Figure 26 Pyongyang's new atom-shaped Science and Technology Centre, looking out towards the coal-fired power station.

The literacy rate is close to 100 per cent. Despite an over-emphasis in early years on rote learning, education standards in science and technology and languages are good or better, in Western terms, but in social sciences there are gaps because of the heavy emphasis on studying the Kim dynasty and Juche. The regime uses education to foster and promote collective ways of thinking.

Universal compulsory education (including educational facilities, textbooks, uniforms and, where necessary, room and board) is provided by the state for 11 years, from ages 4 to 15, including one year of compulsory pre-school education. But most children are placed in a nursery (*t'agaso*) from the age of three months to four years old, allowing their mothers to work. Orphans (and, during the famine, abandoned children) are raised in state-run children's centres. Standards there are low to adequate, but placement there does wipe clean the slate of family history.

The Party elite have their own schools. The Mangyongdae Revolutionary School, attended by Kim Jong Il, was founded in 1947 for the orphaned sons and daughters of revolutionary martyrs but is now the preserve of children of senior Party and army officials. This residential school fast-tracks its graduates into the Kim Il Sung Higher Party School, the equivalent of the USSR's Higher Party School and China's Central Party School, which delivers ideological training and retraining for Party cadres. After attending university (preferably Kim Il Sung University), the 'best' go on to run the country. After graduating from primary school, by contrast, ordinary students enter either a normal secondary school or a specialist school that concentrates on music, art, foreign languages, or computer skills.

The national curriculum is an amalgam of the academic and the political, with language, mathematics, physical education, drawing, and music – as well as the life and thought of the Kim family – constituting the bulk of education in the early years. From the beginning, the Kim dynasty is at centre stage. I visited a kindergarten classroom with a model in its centre of Kim Il Sung's birthplace; a primary school had a papier-mâché model of Mount Paektu that took up a whole classroom, with pupils arrayed around the perimeter learning the lessons of the Partisan War.

All classrooms, like all houses, have twin portraits of the Great Leader and the Dear Leader hanging together. On adjacent walls there are revolutionary posters and murals. For younger children, pictures of cartoon animals transform across the years into full-blooded battle scenes. Collective teaching is the norm, with the individual lost in identical school uniforms and expression channelled through group performances of folk songs, traditional music, and team displays of gymnastics or dance. What this translates to can be seen in Sonia Ryang's *North Koreans in Japan*.[4] Ryang, born in Japan to a Korean family who considered themselves 'overseas nationals of North Korea', attended a school run by Chosen Soren using a curriculum and textbooks set by Pyongyang.

History is taught through the lives of the Leaders. Moral and social study come under the 'childhood of Father Marshal Kim Il Sung' or 'revolutionary activities of the Great Leader Kim Il Sung'. There is no escape, even in maths classes. A textbook question is: 'Three soldiers from the Korean People's Army killed 30 American soldiers. How many American soldiers were killed by each of them, if they all killed an equal number of enemy soldiers?' Essays are littered with the Kims' sayings and aphorisms.

Language is controlled and its use disciplined. North and South show sharp differences in dialect, but not enough to hamper communication. What is noticeable for someone from the South is the North's strong political vocabulary, with words and phrases out of fashion or even forbidden in the South: *hyokmyong* (revolutionary); *sasang* (ideology); *tongji* (comrades); *ja-a bipan* (self-criticism); *wuidaehan* (Great Leader); *kyongaehanun ryondoja* (Dear Leader); *bandong* (anti-reactionary); and so on. A similar gap can be seen in China between many Mao-era political words and current language, with terms such as 'comrade' rarely used by ordinary people, except where appropriated by youngsters as a slang term for LGBTQ people.

To attend higher-education institutes in the North requires approval by the local, county, and provincial college-recommendation committees. Students are from the 'friendly' class, salted with bright orphans and abandoned children. From the 'neutral' class it is the exception that proves the rule. Higher-education institutions include universities; teachers' training colleges; colleges of advanced technology; medical schools; special colleges for science and engineering, art, music, and foreign languages; and military colleges and academies. In total there are about 280 universities and colleges and over 570 advanced technical and specialist institutions. The 'Oxbridge' of North Korea is Kim Il Sung University, with 12,000 students, including a very small foreign contingent from China, Mongolia, and Vietnam. For the Chinese, it's the cheap way to learn Korean if you can't afford a university in the South, with tuition plus board and lodging totalling around $5,000 (€4,250) a year.

Outside of formal school hours, 'social education' takes place through extracurricular activities. In Pyongyang and elsewhere, 'children's palaces' with gymnasiums and theatres have been built. These offer a wide variety of computer courses, calligraphy, circus, music, science, sport – especially the North's variant of Taekwondo. The Mangyongdae Schoolchildren's Palace and the Pyongyang Students'

Figure 27   Mass Games with the North Korean People's Marines, 2011.

and Children's Palace are two institutions where the fiercely competitive classes are on show to foreign tourists. Children are visible practising at weekends in Kim Il Sung Square or on the banks of the Taedong for their role in the next commemoration, celebration, or Mass Games. It's not all song and dance. The Pioneer Corps and the Socialist Working Youth League provide work experience to teenagers, drafting them to help with the harvest and construction projects.

Controlling the Nation

In Western terms, North Korea is closed, isolated, and tightly controlled. Only Turkmenistan, Saudi Arabia, and Eritrea come close. Apart from at the highest levels of the Party and the military – where a daily news digest is distributed – there is no official access to information other than that propagated by the regime. The state controls the media and the intranet. Only authorised books are available. Travel at home and abroad requires a permit. Uniquely, there is no sign of a domestic dissident movement.

The pre-eminent paper is *Rodong Shinmun*, the organ of the Central Committee of the WPK. It is Pyongyang's *Pravda* or *Renmin RiBao*. *Rodong Shinmun*'s editorials reflect the thinking at the highest levels of the Party and introduce and reinforce the leader's messages. Until 2012, its New Year's editorial set Party policy for the coming year, published jointly with *Kulloja* – the Party theoretical journal – and others. In 2013, this was replaced with a New Year's address by Kim Jong Un that serves the same purpose. Newspapers and TV are dominated by the Leader's visits and 'on-the-spot' guidance and by the North's economic achievements and successes in sport and elsewhere. There are human-interest stories, informing and heart-warming, with tales of individual heroism. International news denounces US and Japanese foreign policy, while the treatment of the South is more nuanced depending on who is president. There are stories of the horrors of capitalism, some references to China's economic success, and plenty of news of foreign visitors arriving, staying, and departing. *Rodong Shinmun* is not for sale. Copies are displayed in every park, metro station, public square, and workplace in glass-fronted cabinets, which passers-by and commuters group around to read.

The DPRK's only newswire is the Korean Central News Agency (KCNA), which publishes daily press releases in English, Russian, French, and Spanish, while the monthly magazines *Korea Today* and *Korea* are published in English, Spanish, French, Russian, and Chinese. These are complemented by the weekly *Pyongyang Times* and a glossy pictorial magazine called *Democratic People's Republic of Korea*. The only foreign press agency with a bureau in Pyongyang is the Associated Press Television News, staffed by North Korean 'journalists' who provide footage of Pyongyang's calendar of events. There is little danger of any cutting-edge reporting.

There are three TV stations. Korean Central Television broadcasts daily while Kaesong and Mansudae only broadcast at the weekend. The Koryo Hotel, where visiting political delegations stay, once offered a range of foreign TV networks, but BBC World and CNN have fallen into disrepute; Al Jazeera English, Russia Today, TV5 Monde and Chinese Central Television are available.

There are 11 radio stations on AM and FM; the two main ones are Radio Pyongyang (also known as Voice of Korea) and Korea Central Radio. News is broadcast overseas in Chinese, Russian, Japanese, English, French, German, Spanish, and Arabic. The overseas content follows predictable storylines: the greatness of North Korea as compared to the evil US and unrepentant Japan; the wisdom and prescience of the Kims. One suspects the number of listeners (apart from the broadcasts in Japanese) can be counted on the hands of Britain's Juche Study Group. There are also a score of radio stations with more or less hostile intent broadcasting from South Korea and elsewhere, such as the Voice of America and BBC Korean Service.[5]

In urban areas most households have radios and televisions that receive only domestic broadcasts. However, when combined with DVD players and USB sticks, they make the South's 'soaps' illicitly available. The day's TV consists of news, films, documentaries, soaps, 'pop' music (performed by the now-famous Moranbong

Band), and stand-up comics – no laughing matter in North Korea. Their shows owe much to Chinese crosstalk (*xiangsheng*), an old stand-up art form, now cleaned up and politically correct but still widely appreciated. The Moranbong Band, sometimes rather glibly, billed as Pyongyang's answer to the Spice Girls, is a group of young women, mini-skirted and high-heeled but clearly classically trained musicians, whose repertoire includes songs like 'Let's Study', 'He's Our Comrade Kim Jong Un', and 'Without a Break'.

For Western 'pop' you either have to go to the Grand People's Study House, where you can listen to Western music as modern as the Beatles, or catch one of the Slovenian avant-garde industrial group Laibach's rare concerts. Jazz seems to be forbidden. In 1964, Kim ordered musicians to compose only certain types of music and did not approve of jazz, saying, 'We should never allow the penetration of jazz in the future as in the past' – a sentiment the Nazis would have approved of. 'It depraves and emasculates the youth and dulls their revolutionary consciousness. Jazz is an ideological weapon of the imperialists to degenerate revolutionary people'.[6]

Radios are in every household, factory, workplace, and public space, with a steady diet of speeches and news interspersed with military music, propaganda songs, and traditional melodies. Each radio has a registration number and can be checked to deter tampering. Nevertheless, many refugees and migrants claim to have listened to broadcasts from the South, and the depth of knowledge of South Korean pop music amongst younger members of the Party suggests they do too, if for very different reasons. Controls are fast eroding as more and more radios and cheap DVD players are smuggled in from China. Around 2010 Pyongyang bowed to the inevitable and started its own production line for DVD players, though not DVDs. A domestic intranet has been up and running since 2001. All those with access are 'friendly', but they are exactly the class from which the winds of change will blow.

The computer revolution hit the North at the turn of the century, with *Rodong Shinmun* reporting new computers in factories, offices, and schools and announcing the establishment of a series of specialised IT training centres. The Korean Computer Centre supervises and controls the examination, registration, and dissemination of software. The North has joined the cyber-warfare race, both offensively and defensively. The US's successful hacking of computers for Iran's uranium-enrichment programme did not go unnoticed; there were grave suspicions that a series of missile test failures in the DPRK had the same cause. That risk seems to be resolved, at least for the moment. Outside of Pyongyang and a small number of other cities and R&D centres, the population is lucky to have electricity for more than two or three hours a day, let alone a computer and modem.

North Korea's e-mail service is confined to government, Party, and state operated enterprises. Its Internet domain name, .kp, was only obtained from the Internet Corporation for Assigned Names and Number (ICANN) after a three-year delay, supposedly for failing to provide sufficient information. One suspects this was politically driven, as ICANN authorised .io for the British Indian Ocean Territory decades after the UK expelled the whole population. Quite who provided the sufficient information on this occasion is unclear. Email addresses appear only rarely on the business cards of even senior officials and are normally generic to the organisation or department concerned. Business cards are kept simple, with name, position, telephone, and fax number and, more rarely, office address. Embassy staff and regular travellers outside the country often resort to Gmail.

National Health

The country boasted an extensive public health system before its economic collapse. The institutional architecture of hospitals, clinics, and dispensaries remains in place, but these lack basic necessities, including medicine, functioning medical equipment, heating, clean water, and sanitation. Most drugs are no longer available, except from hard-currency shops or foreign NGOs. The 'showcase' Pyongyang Maternity Hospital was built to impress, with 1,500 beds, but now its X-ray machines lack film and its anaesthetists gas. There are few working ambulances and no epidurals.

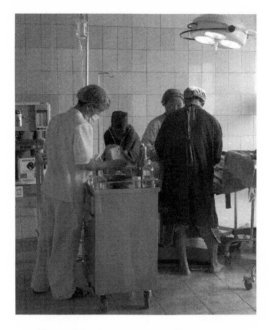

Figure 28   An operation in Pyongyang.

Disproportionate resources are devoted to the care of triplets, which have a special place in Korean folklore. There are special facilities for the elite and the wealthy. The ophthalmic hospital that opened in 2017 has a VIP floor and a shop selling designer glasses frames. Medical care is available abroad for the most important, but even then, it's normally Moscow rather than Zurich or Paris.

With these exceptions, medical care is rudimentary. I have both observation and personal experience in this matter. In 1998 I visited Huichon Children's Hospital during the famine (described in chapter 3). Fifteen years later, my 16-year-old son was a patient at Hamhung Provincial Hospital. He was on a visit with me and contracted severe food poisoning. We were hurriedly taken there, where he was put into a stark room on a metal bed with a bare mattress and was attached to a drip that used an upturned bottle with the base removed. When he started spasming, three nurses and two doctors sat on him until the spasms died away. After we decided to take him back to Pyongyang by car – a five- to seven-hour journey – I was given a solitary white pill wrapped in a fold of newspaper. I was, and still am, immensely grateful for the care and attention of the hospital staff. I have, as yet unsuccessfully, tried to go back and thank them. But the cupboard was bare. The strain they must be under on a daily basis is impossible to appreciate.

As a result of such shortages, traditional medicines and medical procedures such as acupuncture, cupping, and moxibustion are making a comeback – though they never entirely went away.[7] Supporting the argument that shortages of medical supplies are one driver of this renewed interest, the diagnoses are Western and the therapies Korean. Some traditional remedies cure better than others. Ginseng is reportedly good for metabolism, mental and physical well-being, detoxification, and strengthening the immune system; bear bile treats liver and intestinal diseases; bear-bone powder treats rheumatism; and Pyongyang medicinal water cures everything from chronic gastritis to dermatitis. Lake Sijung, about 50 kilometres south of Wonsan, has a guesthouse specialising in hot mud treatments to cure skin complaints, bronchitis, and heart trouble. I sampled it once. It was enjoyable, with no noticeable impact for good or ill.

Malaria, thought to be eliminated in the 1970s, is back, along with tuberculosis. Climatic conditions in 1998 led to limited outbreaks of malaria in China and both Koreas. Those in China and South Korea were rapidly brought under control, but in the North there were no insecticide, no drugs, no equipment – one Chinese expert reported that the only laboratory equipment available was a single Russian microscope from the 1940s. The outbreak spiralled out of control. Within five years, up to 300,000 farm labourers had been infected with relapsing malaria, which lays its victims low repeatedly for months on end. As of 2016 there were just over 5,000 cases; the number is falling each year, but it is far from eradicated.[8]

At school, recreational exercise is mandatory and hygiene, sanitation, and healthy living are part of the curriculum. Kim Jong Un is a heavy smoker, however, and is pictured smoking on visits to children's hospitals. A campaign to reduce smoking – which is close to universal amongst men, though virtually unknown amongst women – started in 2010 with exhortations in *Kulloja*. There are now smoke-free zones in hotels and public buildings, and some long-term smokers have given up. In the foreign media, even the anti-smoking campaign was used as a stick to beat Pyongyang: the *Taipei Times* reported it under the headline 'No College for North Korean Smokers'.[9] Yet the original report in *Rodong Shinmun* revealed a campaign little different from those run in Europe.

Crime and Punishment

North Korea has a dire human-rights record. There are no published figures, but indications are that executions could run into hundreds a year. Those held for political offences are detained – with their families – in camps. Yet, like in 1930s Japan and 1960s and 1970s China,[10] one of the main obstacles is not so much the camps as the cult nature of the regime. Millions are locked inside their own minds, in prisons of their own construction. Most people are true believers. Social conformity is based less on threats than on indoctrination and belief.

North Korea has its common criminals, whose crimes range from petty theft through drunkenness and hooliganism to assault and murder.[11] Though Pyongyang is reluctant to admit that criminality is on the rise, circumstantial evidence suggests so. With the emergence of a market economy, there are more things to steal. The market has brought with it gangs and prostitution, drugs and loan sharks. If their presence is a sign of progress, then the North is doing far better than most political commentators report. Tong-il Market has an increasing number of shady characters lurking in its shadows, willing to exchange foreign currency at rates marginally better than those in the market. In older apartment blocks, the bars and wire mesh protecting windows and balconies climbs ever higher.

The Ministry of People's Security (MPS) and the State Security Department (SSD) are in charge of internal security, the former for general policing and social control and the latter for surveillance and intelligence.[12] The MPS, with 144,000 personnel, is one of the country's most powerful organisations. It has 27 departments, 12 provincial offices, and branches down to village level. It maintains law and order, investigates common criminal cases, administers the detention camps and prisons, and manages traffic control, transport, and fire-fighting. It guards Party and government buildings, state facilities, and senior officials' houses; keeps census records and civil registration data; classifies citizens by social background; controls individual travel for business or family reasons; handles the government's classified documents; carries out construction of roads and major state facilities; and directs propaganda activities.

The SSD conducts intelligence work, investigates political suspects, and manages the camps for political prisoners. Unlike the MPS, which is under Party control, the SSD reports directly to Kim Jong Un. It manages collective supervision and collective punishment. It has agents everywhere: in workplaces, organisations, and neighbourhoods. Groups of 20 to 50 families are brought together and then subdivided into groups of five. The head of each sub-group monitors the group's activities and attitudes and passes the information up. A typical offence would be 'making and listening to anti-revolutionary remarks'. This monitoring mechanism mirrors that of the Japanese Koban system from the 1930s, although Kim Il Sung claimed to have invented it in 1967. The SDD is also responsible for monitoring senior officials and staff seconded to government organisations, embassies, factories, and co-operative farms.

Those who engage in 'everyday, non-political' crime are tried and sent to prison. There are prisons for minor offenders and petty thieves as well as for recidivists and those convicted of more serious offences. Until 1987, prisoners could be condemned to hard labour. While this form of punishment was officially abolished, several labour camps have been identified.[13] The political camps are far worse. These are normally in remote mountainous areas, though satellite evidence points to some consolidation and shrinkage in recent years. What constitutes a political offence is largely arbitrary and trials are perfunctory. To come to trial is to be guilty. Who you are determines your fate more than what your crime was. Political re-education camps and prisons are not for ordinary Koreans but former Party members and their families, relatives of defectors, and high-level officials accused of corruption.[14] Those who make a quick buck or mistake take their families down with them – although it is reported that incidents of family punishment are on the decline under Kim Jong Un. The first published account of the political camps came from Venezuelan poet and Communist Ali Lameda, recruited to the North in 1966 to translate Kim Il Sung's *Collected Works* into Spanish. Within a year of arriving, Lameda had been arrested, convicted of spying for the US, and sentenced to 20 years in a camp near Sariwon. International pressure from sources as diverse as Amnesty International and Romanian dictator Nikolae Ceauşescu finally led to his release in 1974. In 1979 he published his experiences in an Amnesty International report.[15]

PART III

The Diplomatic Stage

7

The Nuclear Factor

North Korea has the world's fifth-largest army, and it is the backbone of the state, consuming around 25 per cent of GDP, with 1.2 million troops in uniform, 7 million in reserve, and 100,000 Special Forces designed to operate behind enemy lines during wartime. The DPRK is still technically at war with the world's largest military superpower, which means that the ability to ensure regime survival is a constant pre-occupation. Without the shelter of the twin nuclear umbrellas of Moscow and Beijing, North Korea was labelled by George W. Bush as a 'rogue state', 'outpost of tyranny', and founding member of the 'axis of evil' and incurred Donald Trump's threats of 'fire and fury' early in his presidency.

The North's determination to complement its conventional military forces with a nuclear deterrent is a direct consequence of the US and UK's ferocious interventionism. Despite its enormous comparative expenditure, the military budget is a minnow: just under 2 per cent of the combined military spending of the US, Japan, and South Korea, and falling further behind every year. Seoul spends more on its military than Pyongyang's total GDP and is one of the world's top arms purchasers. Pyongyang's paranoia doesn't mean someone's not out to get them. As one senior Party figure in Pyongyang said, 'The lesson of Iraq, Libya, and Syria shows that the real problem was not that they had weapons of mass destruction but that they did not have them'. This has been burnt deep into Pyongyang's psyche. After Gaddafi gave up his primitive nuclear programme in December 2003, North Korea was urged to follow Libya's example. But the North saw the upshot all too graphically, live on global TV, with Gaddafi's brutal rape and murder barely a month before Kim Jong Un took over. Pyongyang's leadership is in no mood to commit suicide. Completing their nuclear deterrent provided a guarantee against future US-inspired attempts at regime change.

On top of this, the protection offered by a nuclear deterrent was seen as the key to unlocking economic growth. As long as North Korea remained vulnerable to outside intervention, it saw no alternative to maintaining its million-man army and spending a quarter of its GDP on defence. Once it has its own nuclear deterrent, Pyongyang could relax its desperate efforts to stop being lapped by Seoul, Washington, and Tokyo in a conventional arms race it is all too aware it can never win. Resources and labour can then be shifted out of the military and into the civilian economy. Weapons of mass destruction are a necessary, if not sufficient, condition for kick-starting the North's economy.

Washington's response was and is deploying, in conjunction with Tokyo and Seoul, theatre missile defence (TMD) and, more specifically, theatre high-altitude area defence (THAAD) arrays. The very names come close to a contradiction in terms: 'missile defence' is as much offensive as defensive. It enhances Washington's ability to launch a preventive or pre-emptive strike against the North and to defend South Korea, Japan, and itself against any odd missile the attack might have missed.

In a first strike from Pyongyang, the South's missile defence and THAAD, with its limited deployment, would be hard pressed not to be overwhelmed, even by a North with only limited numbers of nuclear weapons. The North could 'haystack' a light mix of nuclear and conventional warheads and challenge THAAD's algorithms to distinguish between them. Furthermore, the real figures for the effectiveness of some US missile-defence systems are criminally lower than advertised. The Patriot missile system misses an order of magnitude more than the incoming missiles it hits.[1]

Particularly after Trump's inauguration in January 2017, Washington orchestrated maximum pressure on the North via the UN and the sanctions regime to try to force it to abandon both its nuclear and missile programmes. Pyongyang's response was that, despite its sustained efforts to the contrary between 1994 and 2002, the continued 'US hostile policy towards the DPRK' left it no option but to continue development.[2] So who is a threat to whom?

Military Perception

That North Korea is a military regime on a semi-permanent war footing should hardly be a surprise. After all, it is still technically at war with the US and the rest of the UN Command countries. The military, now under the command of Kim Jong Un, has been at the core of North Korean society since the start of the civil war in 1950. In a country with a population of 22.3 million, it comprises the entire male population between the ages of 17 and 50 (including reserves).

But turn the telescope round. North Korea is no match for the military might of the US, with 2.25 million personnel (including reserves) and a budget in 2015 of $598.5 billion (€476 billion) – 3.8 per cent of its GDP and 54 per cent of the federal discretionary budget. The US military budget accounts for 37 per cent of world spending – in a country with 4.4 per cent of world population – and it's the world's biggest arms exporter, with 31 per cent of its arms sales going to 94 countries or entities. The US military is also the most technically advanced, with multibillion-dollar research programmes maintaining a technological cutting-edge. North Korea's military budget may be close to a quarter of its GNP, but it is barely 2 per cent of that of the US, Japan, and South Korea combined. South Korea alone has a military budget close to five times larger than that of the North, with 625,000 highly trained military personnel, reinforced by 58,000 US troops based in the South and in Japan. Japan's image, engendered by its imposed Peace Constitution, also belies the reality: Tokyo will spend $48 billion (€40 billion) in 2018 on its military, making it the world's fifth-biggest spender. The analysts at Global-Firepower, in their 2017 assessment of military power, put the US at number one, Japan at number seven, and the ROK at number twelve. North Korea comes in at number 23, behind Australia. North Korea's military would be a serious obstacle to any invasion from the South, but its offensive threat as an invasion force is close to zero.

Pyongyang has long had the capacity to launch intermediate-range ballistic missiles capable of hitting mainland South Korea and much of Japan. It massively extended this footprint in 2017 as it tested a further series of intermediate-range missiles and ICBMs; as of the beginning of 2018, Pyongyang has the ability to hit the island of Guam and its US bases with intermediate-range missiles as well as the potential to strike anywhere in the mainland US with an ICBM. However, serious problems and deficiencies remain. As yet there is no proven marriage between vehicle and package. They have a bomb and they have an ICBM. Whether the missile even has the payload capacity to carry the warhead is still far from clear: they have not proved they can shrink to fit bomb to missile. What is certainly untested is the ability to put them together as a functioning unit.

There are four further qualitative and quantitative obstacles to be overcome before North Korea can be an existential threat to the United States: re-entry, defensive measures, targeting, and numbers. Taking the first of these, when a warhead re-enters the atmosphere, the air friction generates enormous heat. Unless the warhead is protected, it will be destroyed during this phase of its trajectory. South Korea's Deputy Defence Minister announced in August 2017 that it would take the North another year or two of continued testing before mastering the technology.[3]

Regarding defensive measures, to enhance the effectiveness and survivability of the missiles, Pyongyang needs to deploy multiple independently targetable re-entry vehicles (MIRVs) containing several warheads with different targets. These massively advantage the attacker over the defender and are made more effective by the addition of cheap decoys or diversionary warheads that threaten to overwhelm missile-defence shields. This consideration requires the North not only to miniaturise its nuclear weapons (which is an order of magnitude more difficult than producing a simple nuclear bomb) but also to enhance its missile payloads.

As for targeting, Pyongyang's most pressing need is for enhanced guidance systems for its missiles. As noted, currently the US estimates that there is only a 50 per cent chance that a missile would land within 80 kilometres of its intended target.[4] On this basis there is currently no strategic targeting, just hopeful lobs in the direction of major conurbations.

All of this means that numbers are crucial. The North will need to produce a lot more missiles and warheads for quantity to overcome the lack of precision, and it will need to increase the yield of its weapons by further developing thermonuclear capacity. China, it should be said, was able to do this in the absence of testing, so a simple nuclear test freeze doesn't solve this problem.

The North's announcement after its third ICBM test in late November that it had completed its programme – reiterated in Kim Jong Un's New Year's address – left the world to guess whether it was a bluff or a genuine indication that they have successfully concluded a viable weapon design that can be put into production to churn out 30 to 85 warheads from the available plutonium. This put Washington in a quandary: global support for a preventive strike has evaporated, leaving the US the options of either malign neglect (or, as Trump prefers to call it, 'maximum pressure') or conceding an arms control dialogue with a 'fellow' nuclear state.

Nuclear weapons may not be the only weapon of mass destruction in Pyongyang's armoury. The assassination of Kim Jong Nam, Kim Jong Un's older half-brother, in Kuala Lumpur in February 2017, using VX (a third-generation nerve agent), gave a hint of the North's level of sophistication as regards chemical weapons. The US claims the North has a stockpile of 5,000-tonne chemical weapons pre-loaded into munitions and dispersed throughout the country. It claims to know of two chemical weapons factories, in Kanggye and Sakchu, respectively. Alongside Israel, Egypt, and South Sudan, North Korea is one of only four UN member states not to have ratified the Chemical Weapons Convention, which outlaws their use.

By contrast, Pyongyang acceded to the Biological Weapons Convention in 1987. A CIA assessment from 2002 states that

Pyongyang's resources include a rudimentary (by Western standards) bio-technical infrastructure that could support the production of infectious biological warfare agents and toxins such as anthrax, cholera, and plague. North Korea is believed to possess a munitions-production infrastructure that would allow it to weaponize biological warfare agents and may have biological weapons available for use.[5]

There is concern over the proliferation of weapons of mass destruction by Pyongyang. In the past, certainly, it exchanged expertise with Pakistan, but that was more of a case of Islamabad doing the proliferating, with the notorious A.Q. Khan supplying Pyongyang with second-generation P-2 gas centrifuges in return for missile expertise. The North has sold missiles and missile technology in the past, to the tune of $3.5 billion (€2.9 billion) – to Iran, Pakistan, Syria, and Libya, amongst others.

As for future proliferation, Pyongyang has said it won't happen. Few nation-states are willing to buy in the current circumstances; Pyongyang is well aware that while non-state actors would purchase for immediate use, the source would inevitably be traced by chemical signature, and retaliation would follow.

The final area of concern is cyber-warfare. The US and South Korea claim Pyongyang has 5,000 hackers, run as congregations, with denominations such as Hidden Cobra, Cyber Command, and the Lazarus Group. These are associated with, among other things, the attack on the Sony corporation over the film *The Interview* – a 'comedy' about the assassination of Kim Jong Un – in 2014; and with the release of the WannaCry malware in May 2017 that infected almost a quarter of a million computers worldwide and badly hit the UK's National Health Service computers.[6] The perpetrators demanded payment in Bitcoin. Fortunately, a British security expert discovered found a 'kill switch' and stopped the attack. Security services in the US blamed Pyongyang. A leaked memo from the NSA claiming with 'moderate confidence' that it was linked to North Korea's spy agency, the Reconnaissance General Bureau. Michael

Chertoff, the head of the Department of Homeland Security under George W. Bush, also claimed that the culprits were agents or allies of Pyongyang.

This US view was shared by London, with the UK's National Cyber Security Centre concluding that a government-led North Korean hacking group known as Lazarus was behind the attacks. In a diplomatic demarche, the British Foreign and Commonwealth Office raised the issue with the North Korean ambassador to the UK, who vehemently denied any involvement in the attacks by the North. He reiterated what Pyongyang's deputy ambassador to the UN, Kim In Ryong, had stated at a press conference: 'Relating to the cyber-attack, linking to the DPRK, it is ridiculous.... Whenever something strange happens, it is the stereotype way of the United States and the hostile forces that kick off a noisy anti-DPRK campaign deliberately linking with DPRK'.[7]

Is it a case of 'give a dog a bad name'? Certainly there is no proof of who was behind the attacks, and the accusations are cut to fit political agendas. Why Pyongyang would want to attack the British National Health Service is unclear. The most probable scenario indicates a Chinese-speaking group recycling material from the 2014 attack on Sony Pictures. Even here, there is only circumstantial evidence of North Korean involvement. The uses of the hacked emails showed an awareness of US mores and sensitivities that most would have put well beyond Pyongyang. The linguistic analysis indicated the authors were fluent in Chinese and proficient in English, leading to the counterintuitive conclusion that it therefore must be North Korea. In the North itself, they avoid using Windows and its built-in 'backdoors' in favour of their own operating system, Red Star Linux.[8]

It continues. The front-page headline of the 7 February 2018 *Japan Times* was 'N. Korea Tied to Coincheck Heist; Seoul Spy Agency'. The story started, 'It's a possibility that North Korea could be behind the theft,' but then concluded that 'there is no hard evidence North Koreans were behind the theft', leaving the headline to damn Pyongyang for those who skim rather than read.

In fact, the North Koreans are almost certainly more victims than perpetrators. After the US and Israeli governments' Stuxnet malware operation – to compromise Iran's nuclear programme by causing the gas centrifuges to malfunction and shatter – it is hardly surprising that Pyongyang was deeply suspicious when a series of its medium-range Musudan missiles exploded during testing or spun out of control immediately after launch. Up to 88 per cent failed, when the normal failure rate should be closer to 10 per cent.[9] The North saw it as a combination of cyber-sabotage and 'faulty parts' being deliberately fed into the illicit supply chain by Washington. Total rewiring and new software solved the problem.

How Did We Get Here?

The origins of the North's nuclear programme go back to July 1955, when a delegation from the North Korean Academy of Sciences was invited to Moscow for a conference on nuclear energy. The following year, Pyongyang and Moscow signed an agreement for a team of North Korean scientists to be trained at Dubna Nuclear Research Institute. In 1959 a further agreement was signed with Moscow, bookended by a first agreement with Beijing. After China's nuclear test in 1964, Kim asked Mao for the bomb. Presumably Moscow had already said no. Mao made the decision unanimous. Kim's ill-advised civil war had burnt deep.

Moscow made concessions. In the early 1960s Pyongyang established a Nuclear Scientific Research Centre at Yongbyon, 100 kilometres north-east of the capital, and in 1965 Moscow sold Pyongyang an IRT 2-megawatt pool-type research reactor, with Soviet scientists providing on-the-job training.

Kim received a second refusal from Mao in the early 1970s, just when Seoul started its own initial programme, although there is no evidence Pyongyang was aware of the South's initiative. It was not until the late 1970s that the North was able to do the same. By 1980, with Soviet help, it had a 5-megawatt experimental graphite-moderated reactor under construction in Yongbyon. It went critical in 1986. Not only was the reactor capable of producing weapons-grade plutonium, it also had the enormous advantage of a fuel cycle that required neither heavy water nor enriched uranium, using indigenously mined natural uranium. This made Pyongyang independent of outside resources once on stream. Alongside it they constructed a fuel-fabrication plant, a short-term spent-fuel storage facility, and a reprocessing facility to extract plutonium. It was the right choice. After the collapse of the Soviet Union, the IRT reactor was moribund as fresh fuel supplies went undelivered.

By the early 1990s a 50-megawatt graphite-moderated reactor was close to completion in Yongbyon, while construction had just begun on a second 200-megawatt reactor nearby. Neither ever became operational; construction was frozen as part of the 1994 Agreed Framework. Both are derelict.

Both Russian intelligence and CIA believe that the world came closer to a nuclear war in 1994 than at any time since the 1962 Cuban Missile Crisis. This began in 1992 when both – erroneously – informed their governments that the North had up to five nuclear weapons, made from diverting plutonium from its Yongbyon reactor. Because the reactor was built with Soviet assistance, Moscow pressed Pyongyang to adhere to the Non-Proliferation Treaty (NPT) and to submit to IAEA inspections. Pyongyang finally signed the NPT in 1992 and allowed the IAEA to conduct four rounds of ad hoc inspections between May and November. This confirmed the existence of a plutonium-extraction facility, although the North denied access to two sites where the inspectors believed plutonium reprocessing might be taking place. Any such inspections would have revealed whether plutonium had been diverted to a nuclear-weapons programme.

International pressure to open the sites for inspection grew. Under NPT rules, access could not be refused. In March 1993, Pyongyang announced it was withdrawing from the NPT. Not unreasonably, it used as its get-out clause Article 10(1) of the Treaty, which allows a state to withdraw after three months' notice should 'extraordinary events' jeopardise its supreme national interests. Although the North was within its rights, it was the first and only time that any of the

191 state parties had ever invoked the article. This triggered a major crisis in Washington and Seoul, with claims that the withdrawal proved Pyongyang either already had or was about to obtain nuclear weapons. Yet this was massively overstated: as we have seen, it's a long and winding road from weapons-grade material to weapons. Pyongyang wanted neither to be caught out diverting plutonium nor to allow IAEA inspectors to act as surrogate partners for US intelligence.

Three months later, and the day before its withdrawal from NPT became definitive, North Korea stopped the clock in exchange for direct negotiation with the US. Resumed inspections in March 1994, however, ran into immediate problems. Pyongyang wanted to be allowed unsupervised unloading of spent fuel rods, which would destroy evidence of earlier plutonium reprocessing. When the IAEA confirmed that spent fuel was being removed in May 1994, the crisis threatened to spiral out of control, with the Clinton administration threatening military action. Plans for preventive strikes on the North's nuclear facilities were prepared and approved by President Clinton.[10] F-111 fighter-bombers based at Kadena Air Base in Okinawa were fuelled and ready to fly.

All par for the course, as *Foreign Affairs* notes:

In 1950, the Truman administration contemplated a preventive strike to keep the Soviet Union from acquiring nuclear weapons but decided that the resulting conflict would resemble World War II in scope and that containment and deterrence were better options. In the 1960s, the Kennedy administration feared that Chinese leader Mao Zedong was mentally unstable and proposed a joint strike against the nascent Chinese nuclear program to the Soviets. (Moscow rejected the idea.)[11]

Pyongyang responded to Clinton's threats by threatening to turn Seoul into 'a sea of fire'. In January 2005 I interviewed one of the key US players, Bill Perry, Clinton's secretary of defence from 1994 to 1997, who confirmed the air strikes were prepared and ready to go.

He then said, rather incredulously, that he 'now' believes Pyongyang felt genuinely threatened by the US. Apparently this had not crossed his mind a decade earlier, when the planes were warming up on the runways.

The cavalry arrived at the last minute. The situation was rescued by the maverick intervention of former president Jimmy Carter, who invited himself to Pyongyang at the height of the crisis.[12] He spent hours with Kim Il Sung – Kim Jong Il refused to meet him – and negotiated an unauthorised deal involving direct US-DPRK talks and a compensation package. Announcing the deal on CNN, he forced Clinton's hand, despite serious reservations in parts of the White House. (Carter tried to repeat his trick in October 2017. Both Trump and Pyongyang said no.)

The resulting negotiations in Geneva, from 23 September to 21 October 1994, produced an Agreed Framework signed by both parties. This promised Pyongyang two proliferation-resistant 1,000-megawatt light water reactors (LWRs) by 2003 in exchange for freezing its Yongbyon reactor and halting construction of its two new reactors. In the interim, before the LWRs were completed, the North would get 500,000 tonnes per annum of HFO to compensate for the shortfall in energy supplies. In reality, if they had ever gone online, the North's rudimentary and aging electricity grid would have been unable to cope. Washington promised to lift the 40-year economic embargo and normalise relations. When the reactors were ready to come online, and not before, the North Koreans would permit the requested inspections to establish whether, and how much, plutonium had been diverted and allow the spent fuel rods, held in safe storage in the interim, to be shipped out of the country. It was a technological fix designed to resolve a political crisis.

Whether the US ever seriously contemplated delivering on its promised LWRs seems unlikely. Washington signed the Agreed Framework in bad faith as a way to buy time until North Korea collapsed. It was the next domino after the foundering of the Soviet empire in Central and Eastern Europe. If Pyongyang's fall was running unfashionably late, the brakes could always be put on the reactors' construction. Ambassador Robert Gallucci, Clinton's chief negotiator, certainly worked on the assumption that the US would never have to deliver. When asked privately at the time about the difficulties of delivering the LWRs, Gallucci assured questioners not to worry, since the North was disintegrating. He was far from alone. Similarly, declassified documents from the National Security Archives show a CIA panel of experts in 1997 predicting collapse within five years.[13] They also noted that South Korea, which would step in and take over the North, would have conveniently at hand two concrete sheaths where nuclear reactors could be slotted in later.

Unfortunately for the US, the wish was father to the thought. North Korea weathered the crises of the 1990s. The North's national 'Communism' was not of the same brittle variety imposed by Moscow on Central and Eastern Europe, a Communism that crumbled the instant Gorbachev's reforms in the Soviet Union kicked away the crutches that supported it. North Korea's ideological superstructure, by contrast, was deeply rooted in Korean history, experience, and culture. Marxism-Leninism had mutated into a version of the Japanese emperor cult, with Kim Il Sung as philosopher-king. Unlike in Eastern Europe, there has been no internal surrender by the North Korean people. Washington failed to recognise the difference between the imposed regimes of the Soviet Empire in Europe and the indigenous character and historical continuities of Kim's deeply heterodox Communism.

Whatever the intention, the US never delivered. Economic sanctions against North Korea were never lifted, nor did the promised normalisation of relations take place. In a neat sleight of hand, Washington, having chosen the menu, left others to pick up the bill. It contributed nothing save the cost of the HFO. Despite this, the operational arm of the Agreed Framework, tasked with building the two LWRs by 2003, was to be the KEDO, based in New York and run by Washington. Seoul was to be responsible for 70 per cent of the cost, estimated to be $4.6 billion (€4.3 billion), with Japan strong-armed to put up the rest. Tomiichi Murayama from the Japanese Socialist Party, the first left-wing prime minister in almost half a century, balked at going it alone with Seoul. He agreed to put up $1 billion (€950 million) if the EU would chip in to provide political cover. It did – under the auspices of the European Atomic Energy Community (EURATOM) – but only with a paltry $75 million (€71 million) over five years, while a rag, tag, and bobtail coalition of nine other states, including New Zealand, Uzbekistan, and Argentina, were meant to plug the $300 million (€283 million) funding gap. From the beginning, costs crept up, and while Seoul's contribution went up in parallel with them, the other contributors' payments were fixed. A funding gap yawned.

The North Koreans complained at the slow progress. As early as 1996, KEDO was warning that the 2003 deadline for the completion of the LWRs might not be met because of financial difficulties. From the start there was a fraught relationship with Russia, which wanted to join on the same basis as Japan, but without paying. They argued that their earlier assistance on nuclear power to Pyongyang should be taken into account – the repentant thief seeking a reward for returning the swag. It wasn't until 1999 that the turnkey contract for the reactors was signed with the Korean Electric Power Corporation (KEPCO) Consortium in the South. Concrete was finally poured in August 2001. Pyongyang, constantly frustrated at the stop-go pace of work, demanded compensation as early as April 2001.[14] Washington did not so much move the goalposts as the whole pitch when it demanded, first, a halt to the North's missile programme and missile exports and, second, inspection rights to suspected underground facilities. At the same time, the Republican Congress was proposing to substitute 'clean-coal' power stations for the LWRs in March 2001. The US finally threatened to disallow the delivery of key nuclear components until after the IAEA 'completed' its inspections, in contradiction to the initial agreement. KEDO was a dead project walking long before it's final 'murder'.

The US was a serial discoverer of secret nuclear programmes in the North. In the late 1990s, satellite reconnaissance identified an underground chamber near the village of Kumchangri, and swiftly 'identified' it as an underground nuclear-weapons facility. Washington demanded inspection rights. Pyongyang finally agreed, granting a visit in return for 100,000 tonnes of potatoes.[15] It was a political debacle. The supposed nuclear site turned out to be secure storage for holy artefacts, namely Kim Il Sung statues and other icons, during wartime.

Bush's people were determined to find a secret North Korean nuclear-weapons programme. During the October 2002 meeting between James Kelly, US assistant secretary of state for East Asian–Pacific affairs, and Kang Suk Ju, first vice foreign minister, Pyongyang was confronted with evidence that it had a uranium-enrichment programme and enough plutonium for at least two nuclear weapons. A furious Kang reportedly retorted, 'Your President called us a member of the Axis of Evil. . . . Your troops are deployed on the Korean peninsula. . . . Of course we have a nuclear programme'.[16] This was taken as a confirmation of a secret highly enriched uranium (HEU) programme.

The reality was more ambiguous. Kang's 'confession' was not on record, with neither tape nor transcript. The North Koreans angrily countered that the vice foreign minister had been misinterpreted, that what he said was that North Korea had the *right* to a programme – not that it had one.[17] It was an interpreter's nightmare, given that in the Korean language there is a subtle but crucial distinction – even for native Korean speakers – between 'is entitled to have' (*kajige tui-o-itta*) and 'has come to have' (*kajige tui-otta*). The US turned a deaf ear and suspended deliveries of HFO.[18]

This did not come as a surprise to Pyongyang, whose faith in the US's commitment to the Agreed Framework had been sharply eroded when promised shipments failed to materialise on time in the coldest months of the year. This suspension was the final nail in the coffin. The promises had all come to nothing. North Korea had no alternative. While it is not clear whether it actually had the components of a nuclear weapon before the end of 2002, it now made a dash for the bomb.

The North's nuclear programme had been frozen for eight years at a total cost of $1.56 billion (€1.4 billion), a bargain even if Washington had paid – and it hadn't. A combination of cock-up and conspiracy by the George W. Bush administration turned the heat back on. The North put the Yongbyon plant back online and completed its withdrawal from the NPT in January 2003. Citing once again that its 'supreme national interests [were] jeopardised', Pyongyang again had a point, given Bush's new strategic doctrine of pre-emptive deterrence and the 1994 plans for a preventive strike.[19] Reopening the plant enabled them to reprocess 8,000 spent fuel rods and extract 45 kilograms of weapons-grade plutonium, enough for five or six nuclear weapons, and produce a further 5 kilograms of plutonium a year. On 10 February 2005, North Korea declared it had now become a nuclear-weapons state. Head of state Kim Young Nam insisted that the 'nuclear deterrent force' was purely for self-defence and there would be 'no first use' of nuclear weapons.

The US's action and response showed all the tactical skill of General Custer at Little Big Horn. It turned North Korea into a nuclear power in barely two years. While North Korea denied it had a parallel HEU weapons programme, even if it did, it would have taken six to ten years to produce enough to make a bomb. Worse, uranium weapons are heavier and more difficult to mount on missiles than plutonium weapons. Thus Pyongyang was able to develop nuclear weapons that serve its purposes better and more quickly than if HFO deliveries had continued. The cost was not a factor either. At 2002 oil prices, 500,000 tonnes of HFO cost less than $200 million (€184 million), six months' running costs for an aircraft carrier.

North Korea acquired the blueprints for an HEU programme from the entrepreneurial efforts of Pakistan's nuclear scientist A.Q. Khan, who sold his secrets to Libya, Syria, and Saudi Arabia as well as North Korea. Khan visited the North a total of 13 times. The only two states where Khan didn't hawk his nuclear secrets seem to have been India and Israel. Pakistan almost certainly gave Pyongyang some – possibly up to 20 – of its P-2 high-speed centrifuges, as well as warhead design and weapons-testing data from Pakistan's own nuclear tests, in return for missiles and missile technology.[20]

An HEU programme requires highly specialised materials and components, plus a quantity and quality of electricity – 100 to 200 megawatts – which requires a plant large enough to run a medium-sized city, and with a constant current. This is not a feature of the North's normal electricity output, where lights constantly flicker even if they don't actually go out. Any HEU facility would also require access roads; a large plant capable of holding a thousand centrifuges, arranged as a cascade, to produce enough fissile material for one to one and a half bombs a year; and to be near a railway siding. All would be difficult to hide or disguise from America's eyes in the sky. In 2010, Siegfried Hecker, the former director of Los Alamos National Laboratory, was taken to Yongbyon and shown what he estimated was a 2,000-centrifuge array modelled on Pakistan's P-2 centrifuge.

The North certainly attempted earlier to obtain quantities of the special aluminium alloy necessary to construct the minimum of a thousand gas centrifuges. A shipment of 214 aluminium tubes destined for North Korea was intercepted in Hamburg, Germany, in April 2003.[21]

Yet the North's experience of US backsliding provided good reasons in the late 1990s for them to seek uranium enrichment capability. LWRs, unlike Yongbyong's reactor, are fuelled by enriched uranium, which would make the North dependent on Washington for future supplies of nuclear fuel. A capacity for low-level enrichment – to 10 or 15 per cent rather than the 93 per cent needed for weapons-grade HEU – would have insulated the North's LWRs from any future US embargo on fuel imports. It turned out Pyongyang was too trusting: while they thought that the US would be an unreliable long-term partner, they had believed it would at least deliver the LWRs. The HEU programme may well have been the driver for the later construction of the experimental light water reactor at Yongbyon; its construction was first observed in 2010, but it was still not online in summer 2018.

North Korea's Nuclear Tests

North Korea carried out a first underground nuclear test on 9 October 2006 in the mountains near Kimchaek in the north-east. The blast registered a 4.2 on the Richter scale, and radioactive xenon was subsequently detected in the atmosphere. It was a whimper rather than a bang, yielding a blast equivalent to only 1,000 tonnes of TNT, an eighth of that anticipated when the North gave Beijing a couple of hours' early warning of the test. While it showed that the North had the material and the technology to build a nuclear device, it was a failure. Technically it was a 'fizzle', where poorly engineered components lead to an early core breakup and sharply reduced yield. If the two pieces of subcritical material are not fused fast enough, nuclear pre-detonation (fizzle) can occur, with a small explosion blowing the bulk of the nuclear material apart. This test holds the record as the smallest yield from any initial test ever.

It briefly looked as though that might be it when, in February 2007, Pyongyang agreed to close its main nuclear reactor in exchange for $400 million (€310 million) in aid. In June 2008 it destroyed a water-cooling tower at Yongbyon, and Washington removed North Korea from its 'terror-state' list. The reconciliation was short-lived. By December, talks had broken down again after Pyongyang refused international inspectors access to nuclear facilities. North Korea's second nuclear test in May 2009, with a yield of 5.4 kilo-tonnes, showed slow progress.

February 2012 saw the outlandish 'Leap Day' agreement, in which Pyongyang (on the face of it) renounced its whole missile programme for a paltry 240,000 tonnes of food aid. (More than a decade earlier, the US had delivered 100,000 tonnes of aid to inspect a hole in the ground.) After a bilateral US-DPRK round of meetings, both sides put out incongruent press statements as to what had been agreed. Neither appeared to have read what the other had said. Washington assumed that 'no missile testing' covered the North's space programme, while Pyongyang believed satellite launches were not covered. Sure enough, the agreement collapsed into mutual name-calling within less than three weeks, when Pyongyang announced a launch to celebrate Kim Il Sung's centenary. During the launch, on 6 April 2012, the Kwangmyŏngsŏng-3 exploded less than 90 seconds after lift-off, in front of hundreds of international observers. The US abrogated the deal.

A year later, Kim Jong Un oversaw his first, and the nation's third, test, with a yield of 14 kilo-tonnes (the same order of magnitude as the US 'Trinity' test of July 1945). North Korea seemed to have finally arrived at the starting gate. The following year it claimed, but failed to demonstrate, the capacity to miniaturise nuclear weapons.

January 2016 saw a 10 kilo-tonne test, followed nine months later by another test with double the yield. All this was topped by a sixth test in September 2017, where the yield leapt a magnitude and more, to between 70 and 280 kilo-tonnes. It apparently exceeded even the North's high expectations, damaging if not destroying the test site. Pyongyang claimed it as its first hydrogen-bomb test. More likely it was a boosted fission weapon, a kind of halfway bomb that allows high yields and small weapons.[22] As of early 2018, it probably does have the capacity to launch intermediate-range missiles with nuclear warheads and the range to hit Guam's Andersen Air Base, but not the targeting. Intermediate-range weapons don't have the same problems with atmospheric re-entry as ICBMs.

A combination of ill will, bad faith, poor crisis-management, and incompetence by past US administrations has helped to produce a situation where Pyongyang has, to all intents and purposes, become the world's ninth nuclear state: after the US, the UK, France, China, Russia, Israel, India, and Pakistan. Blackballed from the nuclear club for the moment, it is castigated as the source of nuclear proliferation. That point has power if you substitute *cause* for *source*, although the blame must be shared with Washington. If Seoul takes its own path to an independent nuclear deterrent, it will be closely shadowed by Tokyo – and both will be driven by the ramifications of Pyongyang possessing nuclear weapons.

Nevertheless, most global nuclear proliferation has been driven by one country and one man: A.Q. Khan and Pakistan, which, like India and Israel, refuses to sign the NPT and which has actively engaged in proliferation, conducted by a nuclear establishment riddled with Islamic fundamentalist fellow travellers. Pakistan had a flourishing nuclear programme in the 1980s, when it was working hand in glove with Washington to undermine Afghanistan's Communist regime and its Soviet support troops. But by the mid-1990s, the US's love affair with Pakistan had cooled and Islamabad was in deep financial trouble. To keep up in the arms race with India, it traded Pyongyang nuclear know-how for missiles.

A connection should be made between the West's collusion – in particular France – with Israel's nuclear-weapons programme and the consequent imperative for Iran, a competing regional power, to follow suit. Apparently it is only a nuclear North Korea that threatens world peace, not a nuclear Israel (it went nuclear in 1966), India (1974) or Pakistan (1998). For Washington, some proliferators are more equal than others. Back in the 1960s the US even pondered encouraging India to develop nuclear weapons as a counter-weight to China's bomb.

Yet, in a sense, this is no longer relevant. The United States is in denial, with its semantic, logic-chopping arguments about whether or not North Korea is a nuclear-weapons state. The fact is that it has failed to prevent Pyongyang acquiring nuclear weapons and missiles that can certainly reach Guam and the US mainland. The North no longer poses a non-proliferation problem; it poses a nuclear deterrence problem.

Missile Trade

North Korea's ballistic missile technology owes debts to the former Soviet Union and China. In the early 1960s Moscow provided surface-to-air missiles and artillery rockets, along with engine and guidance designs. In the 1970s it was Soviet Scud-B missiles, further updated between 1985 and 1988. From this Pyongyang reverse-engineered the Hwasong-5 and Hwasong-6. China's contribution was surface-to-air missiles and anti-ship cruise missiles.

A joint Chinese-North Korean programme, East Wind 61, was initiated in 1975 to develop a 600-kilometre-range mobile ballistic missile. The programme was cancelled three years later. Despite its brevity, it provided North Korean engineers with training in missile development, engine design, and production processes.

The North subsequently refined these Soviet and Chinese designs with Soviet missile technology bought – illicitly in some cases – from Egypt, Iran, Libya, Pakistan, and Syria. The Nuclear Threat Initiative, a US think tank, claims that a number of Soviet Scud-B missiles were re-exported to the North from Egypt between 1976 and 1981, while Pyongyang was pursuing a joint ballistic missile programme with Egypt.[23] After the collapse of the Soviet Union, redundant and poorly paid Russian missile experts enticed to the North proved invaluable..

A quarter of a century later, the North has an impressive armoury. It includes hundreds of short-range missiles capable of hitting anywhere in mainland South Korea; Rodong medium-range missiles (up to 1,500 kilometres) carrying a payload of 700 kilograms and capable of striking most of Japan; and Hwasong-15 missiles, with a range enabling them to hit anywhere in the US, but possibly without the payload capacity to carry a nuclear weapon.

Pyongyang has been happy to share. Iran's Shahab missiles and Pakistan's Ghauri are both virtual clones of the Rodong, while Libya's Al-Fatah missiles contained elements of Rodong technology. Pakistan's Ghaznavi was a close copy of the Taepodong-1. Syria settled for the earlier Hwasong-6, which, with a range of 500 kilometres, contains all the range it needs in its standoff with Israel. Yet there were teething problems. Early reliability and range were less than impressive. Iran and the United Arab Emirates, which purchased the missiles, were disappointed by the unreliability of the Hwasong-5. In the second phase of the Iran–Iraq War, during the 'War of the Cities' in 1988, Iran fired 77 of these missiles, and at least 10 to 15 per cent exploded on launch. North Korea's early missiles were definitely second-rate, but beggars couldn't be choosers. North Korea has been successfully exporting missile technology to the world's less fashionable regimes for decades. In all, $3.5 billion (€3.0 billion) worth of Hwasong and Rodong missiles were delivered to Iran, Pakistan, Syria, Libya, the United Arab Emirates, and Yemen – though none to Iraq.

The North's arms exports began in the 1960s, as assistance in the form of military equipment, training, and local advisors to national liberation movements throughout the Third World. The full extent of North Korea's involvement is very hard to establish, but scarce resources limited it to comparatively low-cost training and advice programmes. According to the US Library of Congress's Country Reports, prior to 1990 Pyongyang provided military assistance and training to groups in 62 countries: 25 in Africa, 19 in Central and South America, 9 in Asia, 7 in the Middle East, and 2 in Europe. It also trained more than 5,000 foreign personnel in the North and dispatched more than 7,000 military advisers, primarily from the Reconnaissance Bureau, to 47 countries.[24]

In Asia, the main beneficiary, as we've seen, was Cambodia's Norodom Sihanouk, for whom Kim Il Sung's support had few limits. Strong political support was matched with material. At one point Kim offered troops to fight in Cambodia, which Sihanouk rejected, but he did take up the offer of a palace in Pyongyang – where he indulged his passion for film-making – and Korean bodyguards for life. He called Kim 'my surest and most sincere friend and the most steadfast in my support'.[25]

In Africa during the 1970s, Kim provided support and some modest quantities of military equipment to Polisario in the Western Sahara, fighting for independence against Morocco, as well as to governments or revolutionary groups in Angola, Benin, Burkina Faso, Congo, Ethiopia, Ghana, Madagascar, Mozambique, the Seychelles, Tanzania, Uganda, Zambia, and Zimbabwe. In the 1980s, North Korea equipped and trained the Zimbabwean Army's Fifth Brigade for counterinsurgency and internal security duties. Pyongyang provided almost all of its equipment and about $18 million (€15.3 million) worth of small arms and ammunition. The result was less than entirely successful. By 1986 the Zimbabwean government had

had the unit re-trained by British military instructors. North Korea provided Malta with an unspecified amount of arms, plus military training, for its forces in 1982. Officially a generous gesture to strengthen DPRK–Malta friendship and solidarity in the 'common struggle against imperialism', it was a backhand payment to a country whose GDP per capita was higher than its own, as a quid pro quo for Kim Jong Il's yearlong residence there. John Sweeney's dreadful *North Korea Undercover* claims that the Official Irish Republican Army (IRA) sent its armed wing for weapons training in the late 1980s (more than 15 years after abandoning the armed struggle) and also makes claims about the Official IRA's role, possibly alongside the Provisional IRA, in laundering the North's counterfeit $100 'superbills'.[26]

In South and Central America during the 1970s, North Korea provided similar assistance to anti-government groups operating in Argentina, Bolivia, Brazil, Chile, Guatemala, Mexico, Nicaragua, Paraguay, Peru, and Venezuela. Documents seized during the US invasion of Grenada in 1983 revealed plans for Pyongyang to provide arms, ammunition, and two patrol boats. The North did provide Nicaragua's Sandinista government with patrol boats and other unconfirmed assistance. Yet money talked louder than politics, and by April 1986 North Korea was selling small arms to the Peruvian government to help put down the previous recipients of its bounty – the Maoist guerrilla movement Sendero Luminoso (Shining Path).

Pyongyang is also suspected of being involved in military operations in the Middle East. There are reports that North Korean pilots flew Egyptian aircraft during the Yom Kippur War of October 1973, and from 1979 as many as 100 North Korean pilots and air crew were in Libya training local pilots to fly Soviet aircraft. Pyongyang's support for the Palestine Liberation Organisation started in the late 1970s and continued until the early 1990s.

By the early 1990s, North Korea was capable of supplying a much wider range of weapons. Although supporting leftist revolutionary movements remained a component of its military assistance, the political dimension was superseded – as in the earlier case of

Peru – by a demand for hard currency in the aftermath of the Soviet Union's collapse. Military sales expanded to include missiles, tanks, and armoured vehicles; self-propelled and towed heavy field artillery; and naval vessels. North Korean weapons technology was – and is – far from state of the art, but its two advantages are cheapness and availability to those with no alternative source of supply.

The Nuclear Threat Initiative claimed in 2011 that that some Libyan material handed over by Gaddafi had Korean markings.[27] Technicians from Pyongyang were certainly helping with the Syrian nuclear programme before the Israeli Air Force destroyed its partially completed nuclear reactor in September 2007. More interesting is the case of Myanmar. As mentioned previously, Pyongyang attempted to assassinate South Korea's president, Chun Doo-hwan, in Rangoon in 1983, and relations between North Korean and Myanmar (then Burma) were consequently severed. Just over two decades later, relations were restored as the military dictator Than Shwe explored the prospect of going nuclear with help from Pyongyang. Opposition within the military and the slow pace of progress killed the programme.

The first Taepodong launch was as a platform to put the Kwangmyŏngsŏng satellite into orbit on 31 August 1998, at the tail end of Clinton's second term. The rocket's trajectory passed over Japan, but the third stage failed to ignite, scattering debris across the Pacific. (Tokyo stubbornly maintained, against all evidence to the contrary, that it had been a missile test rather than an abortive satellite launch.) This nevertheless demonstrated to the world, all too graphically, the DPRK's rapid advance in missile technology, which had progressed at a rate no-one had anticipated. This successful development of a satellite launch vehicle put them well down the road to having the capacity to construct and launch an ICBM. As a consequence, Bill Perry headed a delegation to Pyongyang in May 1999 that came very close to a deal to buy out Pyongyang's missile programme.[28] Pyongyang was told that, if on top of freezing its nuclear ambitions, it abandoned the development of long-range missile technology, Washington would offer diplomatic ties and trade. It was clear that there was precious little on offer that had not already been covered by the Agreed Framework, yet Pyongyang did not dismiss it out of hand.

Distracted by the run-up and preparations for the Kim Jong Il–Kim Dae-jung summit in June 2000, the North didn't respond to Washington until September 2000, when Marshal Jo Myong Rok delivered a letter to Clinton in the White House saying that the North was willing to negotiate away the 'production, sale, and use of long-range ballistic missiles'. Secretary of State Madeleine Albright was sent hotfoot to Pyongyang to seal the deal, but events conspired against them. The deal's death sentence came with Florida's hanging chads, as George W. Bush lost the vote to John Kerry but gained the presidency. It was too late for Clinton to fly to Pyongyang, and the North knew there was no point dealing with a Republican adminis-tration in waiting.

Two years later, John Bolton, then undersecretary of state for arms control, was able to record in his memoir that 'September 11 pushed North Korea to the side, but by the year's end I was able to move on to the offensive toward dismantling the failed Agreed Framework and its various manifestations'.[29] The US military-industrial complex, seeking profits from Star Wars technologies, and robust neo-cons, who wanted to see an American empire enforce regime change, were delighted. Snatching defeat from the jaws of victory, the Bush administration deliberately destroyed the last best chance of stopping Pyongyang's drive to develop a nuclear deterrent capable of hitting the US mainland. In the absence of a deal, Pyongyang continued to develop, deploy, and export its missiles and restarted its nuclear programme.

North Korea's development and sales of missiles were all perfectly legal, even after the 1994 Agreed Framework, which included no provisions regarding missile testing, deployment, or sales. Pyongyang never signed any agreement restricting missile exports. Nor was it against international law. In December 2002, the US was forced to allow a North Korean–registered ship, the *So San* – intercepted in a joint US-Spanish operation in the Indian Ocean while it was heading to Yemen carrying Rodong missiles – to continue into port when the Yemenis demanded delivery of the weapons they had bought and paid for. At that time, there was no provision of international law prohibiting the ship or the cargo.

This changed after Pyongyang's July 2006 satellite launch and missile tests. UN Security Council Resolution 1695 of 15 July 2006 interdicted all future missile sales from the North and authorised stop-and-search operations to intercept missile deliveries. The resolution prohibited UN member states from trading with North Korea in missile-related goods and technology.

It was the launch of the Taepodong series that created the 2006 crisis, with Washington claiming the two-stage variant would have a range of 6,200 kilometres, sufficient to strike Hawaii and Alaska, together with a putative three-stage variant that could extend to the whole of the US mainland.

The second satellite launch was provocatively timed for 4 July 2006, Independence Day in the US (though it was already 5 July in Korea's time zone). The North fired a phalanx of seven missiles, including the Taepodong-2, which crashed into the Sea of Japan after only 43 seconds. But the six simultaneous successful Rodong and Hwasong launches showed that Pyongyang's technological capacity and reliability were continuing to grow rapidly. In financial and technological terms, these were the more important tests. August 1998 had potential buyers observing Taepodong's launch. The same was likely true on 4 July 2006. Yet the failed satellite launch was the excuse to widen the sanctions regime to indict the North's missile programme.

However, the notion that Pyongyang makes any substantial contribution to the world's arms market is exaggerated. Its arms sales are a minute fraction of the global arms market, less than 0.4 per cent of annual US arms sales, and bring in less money than those renowned military powers Australia, Canada, and Sweden. The only rationale for declaring it a security threat is its claimed readiness to export to any willing buyer. North Korea's customers are, by definition, those who are *persona non grata* at the US and Europe's arms fairs. Its arms sales certainly do contribute to exacerbating civil and regional conflicts, as well as assisting authoritarian governments to maintain their control. Yet the same could be said of the US and UK supplying Saudi Arabia's surging demand for weapons – it spent $9.3 billion (€7.4 billion) in 2015 – in its promotion of the civil war in Yemen, threats to Qatar, and increasing regional tensions with Iran. In the context of the international arms market, Pyongyang is more an itch to scratch than a global threat.

Star Wars

The threat of the North's missiles and nuclear weapons made for the perfect sales pitch for the US to sell TMD and THAAD to Japan and South Korea as part of its wider national missile defence (NMD) system.[30] Ever since the 1998 satellite launch, Japan's conservative politicians, particularly in the ruling Liberal Democratic Party, have painted Pyongyang as a threat to Japan's security.

Article 9 of the Japanese constitution states:

Aspiring sincerely to an international peace based on justice and order, the Japanese people forever renounce war as a sovereign right of the nation and the threat or use of force as means of settling international disputes.

In order to accomplish the aim of the preceding paragraph, land, sea, and air forces, as well as other war potential, will never be maintained. The right of belligerency of the state will not be recognised.[31]

Despite this, Tokyo has rapidly expanded its military capabilities, with Aegis cruisers at sea, airborne warning and control systems in the air, Patriot surface-to-air missiles, and THAAD on the ground. Patriot supposedly had a proven track record in the first Gulf War (even if recent research tells a different story[32]) and Japan already has 24 operational missile-launch pads near urban centres and airbases. Yet the North's real threat to Japan lies with its medium-range missiles rather than its ICBMs. These were first deployed back in

1993. There is absolutely no reason for the North to waste ICBMs on targets in Japan.

However, Pyongyang's advancing long-range missile capacity and capability serve the purposes of both Japanese neo-cons and the US military-industrial complex. The former were seeking a credible threat to justify calling – and winning – the referendum required to remove Article 9 from the 1947 US-imposed constitution, which they rightly regard as a political obstacle to Japan becoming a 'normal' country. For the latter, Pyongyang's capability has resolved the dilemma that missile defence, on the grand scale, had become a solution in desperate search of a problem. The 1998 North Korean launch, which cost a few hundred million dollars, was the answer to its martial and material prayers. It provided the justification for a US missile-defence programme with a budget two hundred times larger than the North's – and amounting to ten times North Korea's annual GNP.

The Bush administration took office determined to push ahead with NMD, driven by military contractors and ideology. The idea, born during the Reagan presidency with the neo-con Heritage Foundation as midwife, was to erect over the United States an impenetrable shield of anti-ballistic missiles for immunity from the threat of the Soviet Union's 1,500 ICBMs. The original motive vanished with the USSR. Few believe that a surrogate China – let alone Britain or France – will threaten the US with ICBMs. For Star Wars, NMD, and THAAD to have any rationale, the US needs an enemy that is a malignant state entity. It is just too difficult to justify deploying it against the Islamic State (ISIS), the Taliban, or Al Qaeda and their fellow travellers, whose weapons of choice are the terrorist bomb and the suicide attack.

Thus NMD was reborn to defend against the threat from North Korea – albeit a threat two orders of magnitude smaller. As a bonus, once deployed, TMD and THAAD would enable a preventive or pre-emptive strike against a nuclear North Korea with a limited number of nuclear-tipped missiles. Those not destroyed in the initial strike would be severely winnowed by missile-defence interceptions

– if not eliminated entirely – before they could hit Japan and its US bases.

The simple idea behind missile defence is rather more complex in practice, with success rates barely above 50 per cent – the US tests fail time and again. Nevertheless, the ultimate efficacy of the technology is an act of faith in Washington. Those sounding warnings about the technological absurdity of Star Wars were silenced. In 1995, the Republican Party, led by House speaker Newt Gingrich, abolished the highly respected Office of Technology Assessment (OTA), which had been responsible for the production of independent evaluations of complex scientific and technological issues for Congress. The OTA had offended neo-con Republicans by publishing some of the most damning and authoritative indictments of the technology behind Star Wars.[33]

Initial planning – which emphasised hitting speeding missiles in flight – switched in favour of boost-phase technologies, which strike immediately after launch, as the missiles are accelerating up out of the atmosphere, before they can deploy MIRVs. These enable multiple targets from single launches and virtually neutralise all but these launch-stage NMD technologies. Using multiple warheads, mixed with decoys that deploy separately once the missile is outside the atmosphere, complicates re-entry defence by an order of magnitude or more, way beyond any defence currently available or projected.

Early-stage missile defence is technologically simpler but countered by the risk of fatal mistakes, since there are only minutes – or seconds – in which to make the right call and act accordingly. The Pentagon, on a hair-trigger, will have three or four minutes at most to decide whether any future ICBM launch is a pre-emptive strike or a further test of developing technology, with a trajectory dictated as much by geophysics as politics and an indistinguishable electronic signature. Any error of judgement could well precipitate the very conflict NMD was intended to prevent.

Deploying TMD and, especially, THAAD in and around Japan and the Korean peninsula threatens to neutralise Beijing's ICBMs and trigger a regional arms race. China, in its 2011 Defence White

Paper, reiterated its policy of 'maintaining a minimum deterrent with a no-first-use pledge'.[34] Whatever that 'minimum' represents will need to be sharply factored up to counter enhanced offensive and defensive deployments, and will force China to increase military spending to develop and deploy new additional ICBMs to restore the *status quo ante*. Beijing believes that Washington and Tokyo – not so much Seoul – view the TMD deployments as serving simultaneously as an offensive deployment against North Korea and a deterrent for China.

NMD defends neither against a 'rogue state' like North Korea nor against Russia or – if it adds new banks of ICBMs – China. If that is Washington's intention, then it is the 21st-century tactical equivalent of the Maginot Line. The only purpose it serves well is to enable offensive action.

As noted above, as of early 2018, Pyongyang had short-range missiles capable of carrying plutonium-based nuclear weapons and almost certainly intermediate-range ballistic missiles that could carry the same weapons to anywhere on the Japanese archipelago. As for launch capability, the move in 2017 from liquid to solid fuel removed the umbilical link to a static launch site and sharply reduced prepa-ration time with transporter erector launchers (TEL) that can launch rapidly in remote locations at night. The TELs were purchased from the Chinese Wanshan factory, ostensibly for lumber transport, and were converted into TELs with the addition of hydraulic gear and controls. To avoid destruction during launch, the TELs separate from an independent launch pad. The move to solid fuel also benefits Pyongyang's early submarine-launch missile programme. At the same time, the possibility of Pyongyang using decoy aircraft or unconventional means, such as a cargo ship flying a false flag, to evade NMD should not be discounted.

Impact and Solutions

The North's nuclear and missile programme is an entirely rational response to the situation in which it finds itself.[35] Since Kim Jong

Un came to power, any remaining ambiguity about the seriousness of its intentions has been put to rest. Its nuclear deterrent is central to national defence and can only be eventually bargained away as part of a grand deal with Washington that guarantees the regime's survival and is backed and buttressed by the global community. Until early 2018, the last time Pyongyang had mentioned even the prospect of denuclearisation was 2010, when Kim Jong Il was still leader.

Pyongyang's nuclear doctrine reflects weakness and an asymmetric balance of power. Mutually assured destruction was never a possibility. The best Pyongyang can hope to achieve is to deliver a handful of nuclear strikes against US cities in exchange for being wiped off the face of the earth. With little probability of much, if any, of its arsenal surviving a US first strike, it pursues a 'Scorpion Policy' of a punishment pre-emptive first strike. Use them or lose them. Pyongyang can make no distinction between military and civilian targets or between 'counter-force' (military) targets and 'counter-value' (civilian, non-military) targets. This reflects its rudimentary intermediate and long-range guidance technology, which makes precision strikes impossible. It also reflects the reality that many of the US bases on South Korea and Japan are embedded within civilian population centres, such as Yongsan Garrison in Seoul and Futenma Air Station in Okinawa.

Several factors make it impossible for Pyongyang to plan for a step-by-step escalation. These include the US's refusal to rule out a nuclear first strike; the 2015 US-ROK Operations Plan 5015, which proposes pre-emption in response to a perceived threat of military action from the North; and November 2016's joint military exercises between the US, ROK, and United Kingdom, Operation Invincible, training for the regime's 'decapitation'. Iraq, and the dropping of the 'Mother of All Bombs' in Afghanistan in April 2017, made it clear that pre-emptive retaliation is the last throw. There is no possible victory. It's hara-kiri by proxy.

Why is nuclear development in some countries, notably Iran and North Korea, perceived a threat to world peace, but not the equal dangers posed by Israel and Pakistan? The priority for North Korea is regime survival. Nuclear deterrence certainly suits the millions who would die in a new war on the Peninsula or the hundreds of thousands who would probably perish after any forced economic collapse. The North wants a negotiated solution. US neo-cons want regime change.

To take the step of compensating Pyongyang in the short term for abandoning its export trade in missile technology and their nuclear programme would be no different, in principle, from the US paying the Taliban $40 million (€34 million) in June 2001 for limiting its opium production. It's just a mite more expensive, but then, as we saw with the Agreed Framework, it will be someone else's money. To provide, at the same time, assistance to establish new export industries based on the North's mineral wealth as a substitute for weapons exports would make good sense. The EU and China should supply the political impetus to overcome US opposition, while South Korea, in its own best interests, and Japan (if it can resolve the abductees' issue to public satisfaction) as a part of the settlement of the legacy of World War II, could provide the bulk of the financial resources required.

In terms of solutions to the nuclear crisis, the first point to stress is that the Six-Party Talks are dead. As Pyongyang says, 'The talks are about stopping us from becoming a nuclear power, but we are already one – what's to talk about?' They are looking for new institutional structures that could serve as a framework for a renewed dialogue, and that would not include surrendering their nuclear deterrent as a pre-condition for negotiations. Pyongyang's priority has been a bilateral dialogue with Washington alongside a concurrent dialogue with Seoul, all eventually topped off with a multilateral dialogue of donors and guarantors to allow a comprehensive plan to solve all the elements of the crisis.

Thus a window of opportunity came with Donald Trump's initial acceptance of Kim Jong Un's offer in March 2018 of an early summit. Yet the summit barely started the process. It merely laid a foundation on which to build. If the process fails, Washington will return to 'kinetic solutions' – preventive military strikes to try to take out the

North's nuclear facilities and decapitate the leadership. While Beijing (and France) are most concerned with further nuclear testing, logically the red line for Washington is evidence of Pyongyang getting close to developing a platform capable of marrying with a nuclear weapon that could hit US territory and has re-entry capabilities.

In Washington, some have argued the US should demonstrate intent early on by giving Pyongyang a 'bloody nose': for example, taking out a TEL vehicle after using THAAD or, more likely, Aegis systems, or 'disappearing' one of the North's submarines. Its recent successful testing of solid-fuel rockets gives the North a quick and mobile capability not previously demonstrated. US concern has been amplified by claims that Pyongyang is making significant strides in advancing its missile-guidance technologies. The US will continue to attempt to disrupt the North's programmes through the surreptitious supply of defective components and through cyber-warfare.

There is evidence that a 'coalition of the willing', some of which is a hangover from the Obama administration, may assemble. This is evidenced by the joint exercises in Japan and South Korea, together with a squadron of British Typhoon aircraft, in Operation Invincible in November 2016. There was also Operation Vambrace Warrior, where British, American and Japanese Special Forces launched a seaborne assault to 'capture' the moribund Trawsfynydd nuclear power station in Wales (interestingly, it has the same design as Yongbyon). December 2017 saw a Vancouver conference of UN Command member states, plus South Korea and Japan. In January 2018 the UK sent a military delegation to South Korea to co-ordinate evacuation plans with US commanders for the country's 8,000 British residents if the Peninsula should edge towards war. Beijing has its own plans for a military intervention to 'save the revolution'. Perhaps unsurprisingly, given the US's recent history of military interventions with no clear endgame or exit strategy, the civilians in the Trump administration are considerably more enthusiastic than the military at turning from dialogue to destruction.

EU involvement could ameliorate the situation as a global economic power, given Europe's marginal involvement in the

Korean War. Nevertheless, Brussels – like Washington – fails to appreciate that the commitment to economic reform is becoming the primary obstacle to short-term de-nuclearisation of North Korea. For Pyongyang, a nuclear deterrent has been the necessary, if not sufficient, condition for economic renewal.

Relations with South Korea

In the 65 years after the end of the Korean War, the citizens of North and South Korea had little contact. There was effectively no contact at all until the late nineties. South Koreans are not allowed to travel to the North without explicit permission from the government. The South's National Security Act made it illegal to praise or support the North. Sanctions ranged from imprisonment to death. This was not just rhetorical. In 1975, in the 'People's Revolutionary Party incident', eight South Koreans were tried and executed. A subsequent tribunal in 2002 retrospectively concluded that they were almost certainly innocent and that their confessions had been tortured out of them.

There had been earlier attempts to talk, but the first real window of opportunity came after Kim Dae-jung, running for the fourth time, won the presidential election in 1997.[36] With its Sunshine Policy, based on a pro-engagement, non-threatening approach, the incoming administration abandoned previous hard-line positions that tried to drive the North to collapse. The genesis of this new approach was his defeat in the 1992 election. Kim Dae-jung took a sabbatical from South Korean politics and went to Cambridge University to study the lessons of German reunification. His research gave him pause. West Germany had found East Germany difficult to absorb, to the extent that it threatened German economic and political stability. It had failed to fully appreciate exactly how dire was the state of the East German economy: the standard of living in the East, estimated to be 40 per cent of that of West Germany, turned out to be substantially lower.

Yet the situation on the Peninsula was far worse. Comparatively, the North was significantly bigger than the East. The standard of living in North Korea was less than a tenth of that in the South – it's closer to a fortieth in 2018 – with scarcely any industry or infrastructure worth rescuing. And while the East Germans had some appreciation – and envy – of Western lifestyles and standards, North Koreans lived in a solipsist society and most knew of no alternative. The North's economy shrivelled, the South's boomed, and the estimated costs of a possible unification to South Korea clicked rapidly upwards, to a point where it would threaten to bankrupt Seoul. On the eve of the 21st century, with the South's fragile democratic transition far from fully concluded, economic hazard was thus paralleled by political peril. Would the North's convinced Communists want to play the democratic game, and would the South's generals let them? Kim Dae-jung was forced to challenge the assumptions of the South's political class, which had always favoured early unification. Pyongyang, Kim argued, needed to be buttressed, not demolished. Early unification was replaced by 'one nation, two countries, two systems'.

Korean unification was part of the catechism on both sides of the 38th parallel, and Pyongyang was initially deeply suspicious and resentful. The two had been fighting to beat each other to the same goal for half a century – and now Seoul was walking away, saying it had lost interest? Surely it was a subtle subterfuge designed to make the North economically dependent, to facilitate later absorption. Yet, when Kim Dae-jung successfully lobbied Washington to ease sanctions, Pyongyang began to warm to the Sunshine Policy despite itself.[37]

On 15 June 2000, Kim Jong Il greeted Kim Dae-jung on the tarmac of Pyongyang's Sunan International Airport. Images of the two leaders hugging were beamed around the globe, transforming perceptions of the North in Seoul. The summit appeared to be a resounding success, with a five-point Joint Declaration in which the two leaders acknowledged common grounds in their approach to unification, with pledges to work 'independently', to 'promptly resolve humanitarian issues', and to 'consolidate mutual trust by promoting balanced development of the national economy'. All would be delivered through 'dialogue between relevant authorities' and Kim Jong Il would pay a return visit to Seoul 'at an appropriate time'.[38]

The Declaration produced results. By March 2004, there had been 13 rounds of inter-Korean ministerial talks, a meeting of defence ministers, numerous economic talks, six rounds of talks on reuniting separated families, and an agreement that saw athletes from North and South entering Sydney's Olympic Stadium during the opening ceremony as a single team under a single flag. Despite its domestic critics, the Sunshine Policy gave momentum to reconciliation, cooperation, and exchanges between South and North.[39]

Kim was succeeded as president by Roh Moo-hyun (in office from 2003 to 2008), who shared his thinking. The South has a one-term limit for its presidency. Roh's support base saw a sharp shift to the '386 generation': in their thirties, born in the sixties, and active in the democracy movement in the eighties. They gave him political space to be even more radical and he pushed rapprochement with the North harder, straining the South's relationships with Washington and Tokyo. Despite the nuclear crisis, inter-Korean exchange and cooperation accelerated. Inter-Korean travel and trade soared. Regular governmental working-level meetings progressed projects such as the Kaesong Industrial Complex, reconnecting rail and roads, promoting Mount Kumgang tourism, and constructing a Centre for Separated Family Reunions.

But it was not to last. Bush's deliberate demolition of the Agreed Framework and the ensuing fate of Iraq made Pyongyang increasingly nervous, to the point that security concerns trumped reconciliation. Roh Moo-hyun's trip to Pyongyang and the Joint Peace Declaration were the last hurrah of the Sunshine Policy. National Security Advisor Condoleezza Rice and Defense Secretary Robert Gates labelled Roh 'anti-American'.[40] (From their perspective, he was: one of the Wikileaks cables from Seoul reports him questioning how the 'US mistreated North Korea'.)

Roh gave way to the conservative Lee Myung-bak as president (2008 to 2013) and was hounded to breaking point; he committed suicide in May 2009.[41] After that, North-South relations went downhill all the way until 2017. In March 2010, the South Korean navy corvette *Cheonan* was torpedoed, killing 46 sailors. Lee responded by cutting all trade with the North, which responded by cutting contact with the South. In November 2010, when the South's navy was engaged in live-firing exercises across the disputed NLL, the North used the 'hotline' to ask them to desist. When the South refused, the North shelled Yeonpyeong Island, one of the South's fortress outliers deep inside North Korean maritime waters, killing two marines and two civilians. The South returned artillery fire.

The North's subsequent nuclear tests prompted more and new US–ROK joint military exercises. Lee's conservative successor was President Park Geun-hye (2013 to 2017), the daughter of former South Korean dictator Park Chung-hee (1963 to 1979). She responded to the Kwangmyŏngsŏng-4 satellite launch in February 2016 by closing the Kaesong Industrial Complex, the last functioning manifestation of North-South cooperation and a source of revenue for Pyongyang.

North Korea's ICBM launches in July and November 2017 were not just 'game-changing' for Seoul, but rule-changing. Seoul is now in a much more dangerous world, threatened with a loss of control over its destiny as the US threatens to look first to its own interests. The contradictory and incoherent responses from Washington exacerbated the situation. The progressives around and supporting President Moon Jae-in were deeply worried as to what might happen in the absence of any settlement on the Peninsula.

Until now, the bedrock of the ROK's security has been the solid axis of the Seoul-Washington military alliance. This effective partnership locked the two allies' military resources together and gave Seoul a role, albeit subordinate, in decision-making. No US president since Carter has done other than provide unquestioning support to Seoul, serving as it does the US's interests in East Asia. Since Trump's election, the basis of this arrangement has been crumbling. There is a real danger that the ROK's interests will be seen as increasingly peripheral in Washington, as Pyongyang is seen as primarily a challenge to US domestic security rather than in the context of the US's interests in north-east Asia. There is no part of 'making America great again' that has the US threatened by a small Asian rogue state.

Moon Jae-in won a special election in May 2017, consequent upon the Constitutional Court ruling in March that ratified Park Geun-hye's impeachment by the National Assembly. In the first months of his administration, he travelled to Washington to meet Trump and to Hamburg to meet the G20. He subsequently reported to his cabinet, 'We are helpless'. Clearly this was not completely true, but he had a point. Trapped between the inexorable logics of Pyongyang and Washington, Moon wanted a third way. Special envoys toured the globe – save Pyongyang, much to the North's ire – Tokyo, Beijing, Moscow, the Vatican. They went to Brussels in an attempt to understand and learn the lessons of the Iran nuclear deal and the Joint Comprehensive Plan of Action (JCPOA).

Every contact with the North had been cut, including back channels and secret links, after Lee Myung-bak's election almost a decade before. When the South, shortly after Moon's victory, returned a group of North Korean fishermen and their boat that had strayed into South Korean waters, they were forced to rely on megaphones to communicate with the North. None of the three telephone 'hotlines' were operating. The one on the east coast had been destroyed in a scrub fire, and the two on the west coast just rang unanswered.

Pyongyang argued that the South Korean government was talking but not listening. For the North, the priorities are security and economic engagement, not family reunions and participation in the Winter Olympics. In theory, Seoul is opposed to recognising the North as a nuclear-weapons state. Nevertheless, the basis of Moon's position is more nuanced: 'four nos' (no hostile policies against the North, no intention to attack the North, no wish for regime change or collapse, no plan for artificial reunification). Yet the South's military establishment was not necessarily on board, at best frustrating progress, at worst threatening to sabotage it.

Seoul's early proposal for a joint team for the PyeongChang Winter Olympics February/March 2018 had a problem: in the absence of winter-sports facilities, barely any North Korean athletes met Olympic standards. The North had not had a single athlete at the Games in Sochi, Russia, four years earlier. When Chang Ung, the North Korean member of the International Olympic Committee (IOC), visited Seoul in early summer 2017 with the North's tae kwon do demonstration team, his initial response was to comment politely that the South was 'naive', 'hopeless', or both. Yet, in the end, political will and a complicit IOC solved the problem.

The breakthrough was the twin declaration and offer in Kim Jong Un's New Year's address. He announced that, with the North's nuclear and missile programme complete, he was putting nuclear tests and ICBM launches in abeyance. He also offered to send a delegation of high-level officials and athletes, accompanied by a large contingent of pretty cheerleaders, to the Games. The IOC offered North Korea 'wildcard' spots for its athletes, and the South offered a joint North-South team for women's ice hockey. Pyongyang offered joint training for the South's skiers at its Masikryong resort.[42]

During the Cold War the US protected Berlin at the risk of a nuclear threat to New York, Los Angeles, and Washington. Until now the US's nuclear umbrella over Seoul and Tokyo – threatening to obliterate Pyongyang in reparation for any attack on either or both – has not been at the expense of the US homeland. It is far from clear whether extended deterrence would be applied to north-east Asia were the fate of Washington or Chicago in the balance. Consequently, in the short term, many in the US administration prefer to fight a war today 'over there' rather than tomorrow 'over here'. A less trustworthy Washington needs to be hugged tighter. The result is that, while presidents Kim Dae-jung and Roh Moo-hyun had the space to challenge Washington's hegemonic thinking, this luxury is no longer available to Moon Jae-in. If he's to retain any residual influence with the Trump administration, it is as loyal servant, not dissident. This poses a series of dilemmas for his administration.

Pyongyang will seek real security or economic benefits, preferably while creating tensions within the Seoul-Washington alliance.

The argument was that joint military exercises are legal, while the North's nuclear and missile tests are in breach of international law. These exercises have been normalised since the sinking of the *Cheonan* and are now tied up by bureaucracy in Washington. Yet, in his press conference after the Singapore summit, Trump unilaterally announced a suspension of the joint military exercises, which he termed 'war games'.

As for THAAD, the problems lie not with the first Array, but the rest to come. The initial THAAD deployment was designed by then-president Park to punish Beijing for failing to rein in Pyongyang. From a military perspective, it makes little sense. The prevailing military opinion is that to provide any realistic defence against 'haystacking' (when one or two nuclear-tipped missiles are included in a bouquet of others, to be found like a needle in a haystack), five or six further arrays will be necessary. Seoul keeping a balance between Washington and Beijing will be extremely tricky, with the US taking pole position by default. In the current climate, with the military urging him on and further economic threat hanging over Moon's head as the US gets tough on trade, coupled with Trump's threat to renegotiate the Korea–US Free Trade Agreement, few believe Moon will be willing or able to say no. Worse, Seoul will be required to pay for its own subordination.

In the longer term, Seoul wants to recover its autonomy. Moon will attempt to veto any military action against the North, although it's impossible to imagine the South's military standing aside when action starts. They face the same prospect on the basis of interventions by other regional actors. Tokyo's new defence minister, Tomomi Inada, has threatened to shoot down any future North Korean missile that flies over Japan, even though such an action could trigger war.

Thus, there is growing recognition by politicians and the public in the South of the need for Seoul to develop its own independent nuclear deterrent. There will likely be a very strong negative reaction from Beijing – but if China is already 'sanctioning' the South for

THAAD decisions, there may be not much more it can do. Japan will go through the motions – although Abe may be secretly not too unhappy with a further nail in the coffin of Article 9 and an excuse down the line to follow suit.

For many in Seoul, the tightened sanctions regime moved sharply away from the former 'carrot and stick' approach, replacing 'carrots' with a virtual economic blockade of the North. If fully implemented – and here China is the key – these sanctions will over time not only have a major impact on the living standards of the North's 'middle class' – the people who matter – but will trigger misery, hunger, and possibly famine in the north-eastern 'rustbelt' and other peripheral regions. There were reliable reports in November 2017 that around Chongjin the population was already living on little other than potatoes. In Pyongyang's markets, sales of consumer goods have slumped, and those who can afford to are stockpiling non-perishable food at home.[43]

The success of the North's Olympic excursion and the follow-up summit should not be taken as a prelude to Pyongyang allowing Seoul – and later Washington – to 'cherry pick' the easy options. Pyongyang wants two things from Seoul. First, it wants Moon to force Washington to engage meaningfully with the objective of finding a negotiated road map for peace. This mapping only began with the Trump–Kim Jong Un summit. Second, hard on this, it wants economic engagement over soft symbols of reconciliation, such as family reunions. It wants to reopen the Kaesong Industrial Complex (KIC) and the Mount Kumgang Tourist Zone. During the special election campaign Moon Jae-in, in light of ongoing protests from the small and medium enterprises adversely hit by the closure, promised to look at reopening the complex. North Korea needs the money and, whatever the formal position, any 'breach' of the strictest embargo on Pyongyang would not encourage officials and traders who are suffering collateral economic damage from the sanctions in China's Jilin Province and in Russia's border region Primorsky Krai to continue their sacrifices.

8
Foreign Affairs: Between Rapprochement and Standoff

North Korea is not a Hermit Kingdom, and never really was. It might have preferred it that way, but there was just too much traffic, with near neighbours jostling for power and influence. There were times during the Cold War when Pyongyang could probably count its real friends on the fingers of two hands. Even now, after three ICBM launches and six nuclear tests, the North retains substantial links to the outside world, despite pressure in 2017 from Washington for states to degrade – if not entirely sever – diplomatic relations.

Their only major success was with Madrid. Pyongyang opened an embassy there in January 2014, mainly intended to look after dozens of young Korean footballers to be brought in for training with Spanish La Liga clubs. (In addition, two players have signed professional contracts in Italy: Choe Song Hyok for Serie A's Fiorentina and Han Jwang Song for Serie B Perugia.) In September 2017 the Spanish government declared Ambassador Kim Hyok Chol *persona non grata*. It has been joined in this position by Kuwait, Peru, and Mexico. Malaysia, after the assassination of Kim Jong Nam, expelled the North Korean ambassador. Since Singapore – and a new government – it has reversed its decision. None of the other countries involved have broken off diplomatic relations. More than two dozen embassies remain in Pyongyang, but North Korea's relations with the outside world took a sharp turn for the worse.

When Kim Jong Un first took power, there were new leaders in the ROK, Japan, and China, and the US had a second-term president, released from the electoral cycle. North Korea had wanted to open up economically and politically, at least in terms of foreign relations.

Yet the twin needs for internal consolidation and external security – accompanied by the loss of faith in the country's Chinese 'friends' – prejudiced it against concessions and for confrontation. If it had to be done, 'twas best done quickly. To deter Washington, Kim Jong Un concluded it would be necessary to have a nuclear deterrent capable of threatening the mainland United States. Once the technology was proven, the regime would be safe, but there would be a dangerous interregnum between commission and conclusion, overshadowed by the prospect of a preventive strike by the US.

The goal was economic development, but the means were rocketry and nuclear technology. For long-term economic gain, Pyongyang was willing to take short-term pain, with more and tougher sanctions. While UN Security Council resolutions might just have some wriggle room for the 'peaceful use of space' – although far less after 2005 and 2006, when the US's neo-con ambassador to the UN, John Bolton, got his hands on the sanctions resolutions – the same was never true for nuclear weapons. The consequence was an endless ratcheting up of sanctions, all punctuated by the UN Commission of Inquiry in March 2013, with its inevitable attempt to refer Pyongyang to the International Criminal Court for crimes against humanity (ultimately vetoed by China in late 2014).

The sanctions imposed in August and December 2017 further tightened the garrotte around Pyongyang's economy. Pyongyang drove ahead with its missile and nuclear development throughout 2017. In a series of missile tests it demonstrated a good beginning in submarine-launch capacity and successively the ability to hit Guam, then the mainland US, and finally all of the country with its November 2017 Hwasong-15 test firing. Then it paused for breath – or for good – and announced its programme was complete. Kim Jong Un's New Year's address reiterated that the development of the nuclear deterrent was complete, with the less helpful addendum that now was the time for mass production.

In September 2016 Pyongyang demonstrated what it described as a miniaturised weapon, with a yield somewhere between the 15 kilo-tonnes of Hiroshima and the 20 kilo-tonnes of Nagasaki. In September 2017 it tested what it identified as a hydrogen bomb but was more likely a tritium-boosted fusion weapon. This was supported by Pyongyang's claim of a variable yield. The yield was estimated at up to 250 kilo-tonnes.

Donald Trump has made the passage more unpredictable, colourful, and erratic, but the journey would essentially have been the same had Hillary Clinton, a hawk on North Korea, won the electoral-college vote as well as the popular vote in November 2016.

Washington's Cold War victory in the late 1980s and early 1990s saw Pyongyang's crop of friends and associates wither. As red banners were furled and statues tumbled across the former Soviet Empire, Kim Il Sung had the opportunity in the run-up to New Year 1989 to watch the televised executions of Elena and Nikolae Ceauşescu by firing squad. Post-Communist leaders looked to the booming South rather than the destitute North. The 1988 Seoul Olympic Games showcased the South's economic success. South Korea's bilateral trade doubled with China and tripled with the Soviet Union between 1987 and 1989. The Soviet Union set up a trade office in Seoul in 1988, and its successor state, the Russian Federation, established diplomatic relations in 1991. Beijing followed, to Pyongyang's fury, a year later. It was the recognition of a new reality.

By the early 1990s, the first Russian president, Boris Yeltsin, had totally written off the North in favour of the South. The economic consequences for Pyongyang were dire. As we have seen, China and the Soviet Union had historically competed for influence with the North by providing oil and other imports at 'friendship' prices, in exchange for increasingly shoddy and barely functional manufactured items from the North. With the fall of the Soviet Union, it became a seller's market. Trade between Russia and the North vanished, going from $3 billion (€2.6 billion) in 1989 to $40 million (€30 million) in 1999, barely 1 per cent of the earlier figure, as hard currency replaced delinquent goods as the means of exchange. Losing heavily subsidised food and energy imports as well as captive markets for its poor-quality countertraded manufactured goods left the North economically marooned. China followed Russia's lead: for the first time since Mao's victory, it began demanding payment in hard cash.

There are 24 foreign embassies in Pyongyang, including those of Cambodia, Vietnam, Laos, India, Germany, the UK, and Sweden, which also acts as the protecting power for Australia, Canada, and the US.[1] Sweden established diplomatic relations in April 1973 more than 21 years before it joined the EU. Currently, seven EU member states have embassies in Pyongyang: Bulgaria, Czech Republic, Germany, Poland, Romania, Sweden and the United Kingdom. The UK will leave the group on 29 March 2019, when it exits the EU. In turn, North Korea has almost 50 embassies overseas, including in Syria, Senegal, Indonesia, and Venezuela. It also has missions to the UN in Geneva, Paris, and New York. Pyongyang has long wanted to open an embassy to the EU in Brussels, but due to a combination of French objections and Belgium intransigence, the request has been denied, despite the establishment of diplomatic relations in 2001.[2]

Key to understanding and dealing with the North's foreign relations is to note that it is not the Foreign Ministry that makes policy but the Party, as in China and Vietnam. Alongside the Foreign Ministry's departments for Europe, Asia, Africa, and America, the WPK's International Department has its own organigram, with separate departments for China, former Soviet Union and Eastern Europe, Europe, Asia, and the Americas. Alongside these geographical divisions within the Party, there are horizontal departments dealing with organisation and guidance, research, etc. Relations with South Korea are considered domestic, not international, and so are dealt with by the Korean Asia-Pacific Peace Committee (which acts as a ministry in its own right) and, within the Party, by the United Front Department.

Japan

After the collapse of the Soviet Union, North Korea had a very pragmatic motive for attempting rapprochement with Tokyo: money. Japan had effectively paid 'reparations' for its occupation and colonisation when it normalised relations with the South in 1965, giving $300 million (€255 million) outright and a further $500 million (€425 million) in soft loans. A similar normalisation with the North, it is estimated, is worth, in contemporary prices, as much as $12.5 to $25 billion (€11.7 to €23.4 billion), equivalent to between $475 and $950 (€430 and €860) for every man, women, and child in the North.

In March 1989, Japanese prime minister Noboru Takeshita, speaking in the Diet, expressed 'deep remorse' for the excesses of Japan's colonial rule on the Korean peninsula and called for the North to open talks. This signal was followed in September 1990 by a delegation of Diet members visiting Pyongyang, and was succeeded by eight rounds of negotiations on normalising relations between January 1991 and November 1992. Pyongyang – as with its claims against the US – wanted additional compensation for the post-colonial period. Talks finally collapsed after the CIA briefed Tokyo on Pyongyang's nuclear ambitions.

Despite the failed 1998 satellite launch over Japan, dialogue did finally resume in April 2000. It was suspended in December 2001 after Japanese coast guards chased a North Korean spy ship out of its territorial waters, sank the boat, and captured the crew. A year later, in September 2002, Prime Minister Junichiro Koizumi travelled to Pyongyang for a summit meeting with Kim Jong Il. They signed the Japan–DPRK Pyongyang Declaration, in which North Korea agreed to maintain its ongoing moratorium on missile tests while Kim and Koizumi traded apologies, with the former apologising for the North's abductions of Japanese citizens and the latter for the Japanese occupation of Korea. Pyongyang disclosed that a 'rogue unit' had kidnapped 13 Japanese between 1977 and 1983, of whom 8 had subsequently died. The five survivors were allowed to travel to Japan for a 'temporary' visit. Tokyo never allowed them to return. They landed in Japan less than 48 hours before the US announced that Pyongyang had 'confessed' to a secret HEU programme. In May 2004, Koizumi returned to Pyongyang for a day trip, bringing family members of the five abductees, who denied rather unconvincingly that this was a swap for the food and humanitarian assistance Tokyo had just approved.

Kim Jong Il made a strategic mistake in assuming that his apology for the abductions and releasing the five survivors would improve relations with Tokyo. This was not to be the case. Partly fanned by the media, the Japanese public was outraged both by the North – and, to a lesser extent, their government for too long ignoring the issue. It continues to fester.

In October 2006, after the North's first nuclear test, Tokyo banned all imports from the DPRK. Progress on both bilateral relations and the Six-Party Talks were stalled during 2007 and 2008 by Japan's continued pre-occupation with the abduction issue. Tokyo proved unwilling to contribute to the provision of HFO to the North while the issue remained unresolved. Relations became even worse in 2009, when Pyongyang launched a number of ballistic missiles and conducted another nuclear test. Japan responded with a total export ban to match the earlier import ban.

Kim Jong Il's death and Kim Jong Un's accession did nothing to improve relations. Pyongyang's two satellite launches in April and December 2012 and its third nuclear test in February 2013 saw further unilateral sanctions from Tokyo. The Japanese government exacted further retribution in 2013 by co-sponsoring, with the EU, the UN Human Rights Council resolution establishing the Commission of Inquiry.

In an attempt to break the deadlock on the abductee issue, in 2014, further talks took place in Stockholm, Beijing, and Berlin. Pyongyang announced a fresh round of investigations into the fate of the eight 'dead' abductees and promised a full report within a year. In exchange, Tokyo allowed representatives of the North Korean residents of Japan to visit Pyongyang for the first time in six or seven years. The report never materialised. In July 2015, Kang Suk Ju stated that, subsequent to May 2014's Stockholm agreement, the North's promised investigation had been concluded without locating any of the 'missing' abductees. As far as Pyongyang was concerned, the matter was now closed. Japan continued to protest loud and long, with organised lobbying in the US and Europe, accompanied by film documentaries and relatives. North Korea's continued nuclear and ballistic missile tests – particularly its August 2017 test, which passed high above Japan – have reinforced the antipathy. Now all Japanese mobile phones are enabled with a feature that allows the government to issue an alert when North Korea launches missiles over Japan.

The DPRK sees no role for Japan in future negotiations arguing that their obsession with the fate of the abductees will obstruct progress. Part of the problem is the central role played over the years by Abe, now prime minister. He was Koizumi's chief of staff in 2002 and was responsible for flouting the promise to Pyongyang – overriding opposition within the LDP – to return the five abductees to the North and their families after their visit to Japan. The issue has taken on a life of its own in Japan, with new 'abductees' constantly being discovered. In the following years, civil society groups have logged over 900 names. Abe played to that constituency after he replaced Koizumi as prime minister in 2006, establishing a high-profile stand-alone Ministry for Abduction Issues. Then he allowed the press and public to force him to take the position that 'all [presumably 17] abductees as yet unreturned are still alive and Japan will not rest until their final return'. This is wishful thinking at best. The oldest would be 93 and two more would be in their 80s, in a country where male life expectancy is 66.

The North returning the ashes and remains of other abductees proved just as controversial. The Japanese government performed DNA analysis on remains purported to be of abductee Yokota Megumi and concluded they were not hers but rather those of two unrelated people. Pyongyang was lying. The response was an article in *Nature* – one of the world's most prestigious science journals – divulging that the analysis at Teikyo University had been carried out by a junior faculty member with no previous experience in the analysis of cremated specimens, utilising a technique no longer accepted by forensic laboratories in the US because of the risk of contamination.[3] Even the researcher, Yoshi Tomio, had claimed his tests were 'inconclusive'.

Chief cabinet secretary Hosoda Hiroyuki attacked *Nature*'s article as 'inadequate and a misrepresentation'.[4] *Nature* responded in a highly unusual editorial, arguing that Japan's 'interpretation of the DNA tests has crossed the boundary of science's freedom from political interference' and that 'dealing with North Korea is no fun, but it doesn't justify breaking rules of separation between science and politics'.[5] Pyongyang's demand for the remains to be returned for independent testing was rejected and new unilateral sanctions were imposed by Tokyo even as it sat in the Six-Party Talks.

An additional stumbling block is the fate of the 'Yodo Group' of Japanese hijackers from 1970. Four are still in Pyongyang, having been granted political asylum.[6] Despite their offer to return to Japan – with Pyongyang's approbation – to face close to a decade in prison in exchange for Japan dropping allegations that members of the group were involved in abductions, the Japanese Ministry of Foreign Affairs has consistently refused to take them back. For many years

Figure 29   The remaining Japanese Red Army Faction hijackers, 2016. Photo © David Yarrow.

their presence in Pyongyang served as the proximate excuse to keep the North on the US's 'terror state' list.

Japan is thus likely to be side-lined in any multilateral group trying to resolve the crisis on the Peninsula. Japan is in denial, both that the Six-Party Talks are dead – here they are not alone – and that they are largely responsible. While the next stage is likely two parallel and interlocking sets of bilateral negotiations, North–South and North–US, any solution is likely to require a multilateral group of 'donors' and 'guarantors'. In Beijing, Pyongyang, and Seoul, Tokyo are seen as wreckers rather than builders, spoilers rather than sceptics.

China

China was Pyongyang's greatest ally, and many still perceive it as such. With the collapse of the Soviet Union, it became the only major power the North could rely on. For many years, around 90 per cent of North Korea's foreign trade was conducted with and through China, with minerals, seafood, and textiles traded principally for oil. Prior to the latest rounds of sanctions in the second half of 2017, trade was booming. Chinese official reports showed that their trade grew by 37.4 per cent in the first quarter of 2017, compared to the same period in 2016.[7]

Nevertheless, Beijing's trade with Seoul dwarfs that with Pyongyang. The DPRK is more political problem than economic opportunity. Hu Jintao urged 'socialist modernisation' to Kim Jong Il after the two declared 2009 a 'Year of Friendship'.[8] A year later, however, China refused to condemn Pyongyang for the sinking of the *Cheonan* – motivated as much by the cynicism of Washington as the North's innocence – and labelled the Commission of Inquiry report 'unreasonable'.

Nevertheless, 'as close as lips and teeth' has not described the relationship between the two countries for a more than decade. The key turning point was Kim Jong Un's succession. Under his father there were frequent visits between the two, even if more arrived in Beijing than departed to Pyongyang. This all changed in 2011 with Beijing unenamoured with the new leader backing the wrong horse twice. Jang Song Thaek was executed and Kim Jong Nam assassinated. More recently, Beijing's estrangement with Guo Wengui – a billionaire exile in New York who was close to Jang and the leadership – has deprived them of their eyes and ears.

Beijing has 'resolutely opposed' the North's nuclear programme as an indirect threat to its own security. A nuclear North Korea justifies close containment of the Peninsula by Washington, the deployment of missile-defence technologies in both South Korea and Japan, and Tokyo's abrogation of Article 9 of Japan's US-imposed constitution – all of which copy across as threats not only to Pyongyang but Beijing. While Kim Jong Il saw the nuclear programme as an option to be explored, for Kim Jong Un it was a core objective.

Beijing routinely condemned all the North's tests, but became serious after the SPA amended the constitution in 2012 to make the North a 'nuclear-armed state'. In the Security Council, Beijing – and to a lesser extent Moscow – did a political shuffle from blocking sanctions to abstaining, from abstention to support, and finally back home – from going through the motions to making them real.

As of early 2016, China was still not serious about sanctions. This changed when Pyongyang publicly snubbed its envoy, sent to urge North Korea to suspend February's satellite launch. This was a slight Beijing did not forget, after Beijing had just softened its stance. Complicating matters was that, the previous December, Chinese authorities had sent the North's Moranbong Band packing after they refused to drop their 'mushroom cloud' backdrop. China suspended coal imports. Pyongyang went from feeling disillusioned to feeling betrayed.

China is no longer the North's best friend. Until recently the relationship has been a toxic one; it would be difficult to underestimate the degree of mistrust on both sides. China has precious little influence on Pyongyang, save that over trade. China would like to keep the status quo. China does have the economic leverage to bring Pyongyang to its knees, but is all too aware of the North's willingness to fight it and the prospect of millions of refugees flooding Jilin

Figure 30 Rason Port, waiting for business.

Province – they were constructing refugee camps there in early 2018 – and US troops on the southern banks of the Yalu River. Washington wants to 'save the armistice'; Beijing wants to 'save the revolution'. My enemy's enemy is my friend. The question is who's who.

The sudden rapprochement with China, with Kim Jong Un travelling to Beijing, Dandong, and back to Beijing after the Singapore summit to meet with Xi Jinping in March, May, and June, reflects the feeling in Pyongyang that Washington is trying to treat it as a 'surrendered state' that has lost the war. North Korea is looking for Xi's – and Moon's – support for a 'phased and synchronous' denuclearisation, over the Libyan model that John Bolton is trying to foist on Trump.

United States

In May 2009, four months after Barack Obama's inauguration, Pyongyang conducted its second nuclear test. The president, on the surface, did nothing, neither negotiation nor threat. Obama was waiting for the other shoe to drop. 'Strategic patience' was intended to let the pressure of sanctions change hearts and minds in Pyongyang. There were to be no incentives to come to the negotiating table. In the meantime, technology would hold the line. THAAD and other missile-defence weapon systems would be deployed, and if it helped the bottom lines of US defence contractors, that was all to the good. Obama also stepped up the pressure on the North's surrogate partner, China, to make them see sense. Needless to say, strategic patience (or, more accurately, malign neglect), didn't work. Pyongyang went on to conduct another three nuclear tests, two satellite launches, and close to 70 missile tests during Obama's watch.

Despite all claims to the contrary, the first year of the Trump presidency brought more continuity than change. It had a darker hue and was peppered with promises of 'fire and fury', yet Washington was loitering with intent. Publicly, each long-range missile launch and nuclear test saw the US and UN ratcheting sanctions up further. In Washington, even after Kim Jong Un's New Year's address, this continued, as Trump extolled the efficacy of 'maximum pressure'.

Behind closed doors in the US, the talk was of covert action, with attempts to find, create, and exploit cleavages within the ruling family and friends of the regime and incite civil unrest, using the Iraq playbook. Pyongyang's responses were unsurprising, with statements cut and pasted from past ultimatums – with the addition of a very specific threat to bracket the US military outpost on Guam with missiles around the island and hints at firing a conventionally tipped missile into the deep South Pacific.

In many senses, Washington and Pyongyang collude and collaborate. Pyongyang's exaggerated claims about the range and accuracy of its missiles, the success of its nuclear tests, and its miniaturisation of its warheads are all supported by some in Washington, to serve their own paranoia and economic interests or both.

On 2 January 2016, Otto Warmbier, an American student on a tourist trip, was arrested for trying to steal a framed poster from an off-limits floor of the Yanggakdo Hotel in Pyongyang during a tour. Otto's father, Fred, was part of Vice-President Pence's entourage at the Winter Olympics. Pyongyang claims Warmbier was taken ill with food poisoning immediately after his trial and sentencing and received medication and a sleeping pill. Overnight, he choked on his own vomit, cutting off oxygen to the brain. (Others in the North privately claimed it was a failed suicide attempt using the curtains from his room.) In the morning Warmbier was discovered unconscious. Those immediately responsible panicked and failed to inform those higher up the chain of command, hoping he would eventually regain consciousness. He never did. When he was returned to the States, he was in a persistent vegetative state. He had been well looked after in the Pyongyang Friendship Hospital. On his return he had no bedsores, no weight loss, and no injuries, despite claims to the contrary.[9]

Exactly when the leadership and Kim Jong Un were made aware of Warmbier's state is unclear. There are suspicions that it may have been several months before his repatriation, when there were some unexplained and sudden personnel changes at the top of the Ministry of State Security (MSS). Certainly the MFA was unaware of his condition until very late on. When the American team arrived to take him home, both the MFA and the hospital authorities refused to move without the authority of the MSS, although his release was formally the province of the courts. Warmbier's fate precipitated Trump's travel ban: individual US citizens can apply for a special passport to visit the North on humanitarian or national-interest grounds. Those with a dual nationality can travel on their non-US passport. The ban has remained, despite the summit.

The tightening of US sanctions is having a detrimental impact on all forms of engagement. Any meeting involving US citizens has to be authorised by the State Department; even paying for transport, hotels, and meals is seen as financial support for the regime. The impact is not limited to the US: organisations like the International Committee of the Red Cross having to deal with the UNSC Sanctions Committee. Even though the Committee is more tractable than the State Department, obtaining the necessary permission can take four to six weeks.

From Pyongyang's standpoint, the US is not to be trusted. If negotiations didn't work in the past for Washington, they didn't work for Pyongyang either. They had a letter from President Clinton promising to deliver the Agreed Framework, but that failed to stop President Bush from reneging on the deal. Some senior figures in the Trump administration are sceptical that the summit and dialogue can ultimately lead anywhere. One or two would be delighted if that were the case. As far as they are concerned the US have tried to negotiate three times and failed. Three strikes and you're out.

The March 2018 double bombshell of Kim Jong Un inviting Trump to a summit and, even more surprisingly, Trump accepting threw everything up into the air. Trump's intentions, however, were initially called into question by the virtually simultaneous dismissal of his tough but pragmatic national security advisor, J.R. McMaster, and his replacement by Bolton. Yet, in the end, Bolton was side-lined by Pompeo.

Pyongyang demands an early confirmation that the war is over followed by a peace treaty/settlement. In Washington, some argue that any such settlement would be a de facto recognition of North Korea as a nuclear-weapons state. Quite how a diplomatic agreement confers technological competence escapes others. The freeze in ICBM and nuclear testing after November 2017 has the North poised on the red line that in all likelihood would have triggered a preventive US military strike. Pyongyang claims that Trump committed in Singapore to announcing the end of the war on 27 July.

What would be required for Pyongyang to denuclearise? Would they want to return to the terms of the Agreed Framework and demand LWRs to compensate for the potential electricity production foregone by closing Yongbyong and its new experimental LWR?

This would be highly problematic politically, but using conventional power stations to break the energy blockage in the North's economy would suffer from an unacceptable dependence on imported fuel. Reviving the LWR plans would have the advantage of shortening the timeline, with the foundations already in place and an institutional architecture that could be rapidly tweaked to match current realities. Renewables might partially fill the gap, but for Pyongyang, virile power politics may well favour form over substance. Yet nothing works without a new national electricity grid.

Washington is neither willing nor able to pay the tens of billions of dollars any settlement will require. Trump is looking for a cheap solution, in US terms, and even if he wanted to pay, Congress would never approve the budget. Squaring the circle brings in more players.

United Nations

Given that the US intervened in the Korean civil war under the flag of the United Nations, which still flies alongside the Stars and Stripes in Panmunjom, it is hardly surprising that North Korea's relations with the UN have been problematic. For decades neither North nor South were members, but in 1991 General Assembly Resolution 46/1 admitted both simultaneously.

From the famine in the mid-nineties until today, the UN has juggled a constantly tightening sanctions regime and the provision of humanitarian aid (see chapter 4). Not dropping either ball has required increasingly frantic manoeuvring. For example, in April 2018 the UN launched a campaign to raise $111 million (€94 million) to combat the North's food insecurity, and as recently as August 2017 it committed $6 million (€5.1 million) in aid to help cope with the consequences of a severe drought. Yet the new sanctions have seen millions of dollars of emergency medical kits held hostage on the Chinese border because they contained scissors. Meanwhile, the financial sanctions have made it increasingly costly and convoluted for the UN to transfer legitimate funds into Pyongyang to cover the costs of its agencies on the ground.

Figures 31 and 32   Panmunjom, as entered from
the North (*left*) and from the South (*right*).

In response to Pyongyang's first nuclear test in 2006, the UN
banned the import of luxury goods and the export of technologies
that might assist its nuclear programme. A wider arms embargo
followed in 2009, after a satellite launch. In January 2013, after
another satellite launch, the UN agreed on the ability to seize and
destroy cargo intended for military R&D, with 2013's third nuclear
test leading in March to a ban on money transfers and an asset freeze.
January 2016's test brought a March embargo on the export of gold,
vanadium, titanium, and rare-earth minerals – the last sop to Beijing
to help it protect its semi-monopoly in the world market – while coal
and iron exports were limited to 'livelihood purposes'. November
2016's test added a further cocktail of metals and minerals to the
mix and a cap on total coal exports. In February 2017, under pressure
from Washington, Beijing unilaterally announced a moratorium on
coal imports for the rest of the year.

In 2017 there were two further rounds of sanctions. The first tranche targeted coal, iron ore, lead, and mineral exports generally, alongside seafood and textiles, and were expected to cut the North's annual exports by at least $1 billion (€850 million). It also capped the numbers of North Korean workers in all third countries and imposed draconian restrictions on the foreign trade bank. The second focused on cutting oil imports and closing the last loopholes, ending the continued employment of North Korean contract labourers in Russia and elsewhere. Since 2006's first sanctions, the UNSC has tightened the screws seven times.

As for the North's 'foreign workers' working abroad – principally in China and Russia, as well as the Middle East and to a lesser degree Europe – they are estimated to generate between $750 million (€637 million) and $1 billion (€850 million) with a substantial proportion going to the state each year. A global campaign against 'North Korean slave labour' helped to push the ban. The reality is these were eagerly sought-after positions in the North, with people calling in favours to secure what are seen as lucrative opportunities.

One issue with the sanctions is sanctions implementation. In February 2017, a UN panel reported that 116 of the UN's 193 member states had failed to submit the required report on implementation.[10] The result has been a massive drive to push the indolent and recalcitrant into action, with US envoys touring places like Myanmar and Somalia to force them to toe the line, while hunting out and pointing out to governments where the North is making money from using its embassies to host weddings in Bangladesh or as hostels in Germany.

The US started to get organised. In December 2017 it called a conference of the foreign ministers of the UN Command states – plus, as hosts, the South Koreans and the Japanese. The aim was to assemble a 'coalition of the willing' to, if necessary, continue the war after a 65-year hiatus. The UN was pointedly not invited. Neither were the EU, Russia, or China (to the fury of Xi Jinping). In March the US called an 'experts meeting' in Washington with the same format, adding countries like Liberia to discuss 'enforcement of sanctions and control of smuggling'.

A second area of contention is human rights. No one argues there are not grave concerns about the situation in the North, but the issue is being used by elements in the US and elsewhere as a hammer, not an anvil. The Commission of Inquiry was primarily the responsibility of member states. Damning as the material was, it was decades out of date, with some reporting experiences in the camps long before Kim Il Sung's death in 1996. Some of those giving evidence were false witnesses (see chapter 4). Even accepting the contents and thrust of the report does not axiomatically mean that the most obvious outcome was to refer Kim Jong Un to the International Criminal Court; he had scarcely been in power a year when the report was commissioned. If the UN wants to improve human rights, the effective mechanism is the Universal Periodic Review, where Pyongyang has seriously engaged and adopted a majority of recommendations.

There have been discussions on the fringes of the Security Council about invoking either Article 5 or Article 6 of the UN Charter: the former allowing for the suspension of a member state 'against which preventive or enforcement action has been taken by the Security Council' and the latter allowing expulsion for 'persistently' violating the Charter. Pyongyang is as likely to jump as to be pushed. The UN continues to support 1.6 million malnourished children in the North, but this is virtually entirely dependent on its own emergency fund, as funding from member states has totally dried up.

The US, South Korea, Japan, and the EU have all imposed additional sanctions measures over and above those mandated by the UN. In the case of the US, these relate to financial transactions and suspicions of money laundering. There is also a 180-day ban on any aircraft or ship that lands in North Korea or meets with North Korean vessels from visiting the US. After the death of Otto Warmbier, American citizens are prohibited to visit North Korea and North Koreans to travel to the US. After the *Cheonan* sinking in 2010, Seoul severely restricted trade and banned North Korean vessels from landing. Tokyo, around the abductee issue, imposed unilateral sanctions forbidding all trade and money transfers and allowed asset seizures from suspicious entities or individuals. Brussels has a list of trade restrictions, mainly against goods the North has never exported to the EU, and a ban on luxury exports. All five, with the UN, have semi-coherent lists of sanctioned individuals, with some on one, two, or three of the lists but not the others. In Iraq, the allies produced packs of cards featuring the 52 'most wanted'. Here they are playing with different decks.

European Union

In Pyongyang they know everything, but don't always understand. This is especially true of the EU. They see a continent struggling to cope with austerity, the refugee crisis, Islamic terrorism, and populism. Yet, for all that, it was the EU that negotiated the JCPOA and signed with Iran to freeze and reverse its nuclear ambitions. There are two sides to the subsequent chapters of the story. The negative face is Trump's abrogation of the Iran deal over issues outside the deal's remit: Iran's political and logistical support for the 'wrong' sides in the Middle East nexus of conflicts and its missile programme not being covered by the deal. All this leads Pyongyang to wonder whether a sustainable deal is possible with Washington. The positive face is the continued support for the Iran deal of the EU, France, Germany, and the UK, despite threats and pressure from the Trump administration, encouraging the North to see a wider eventual deal on the Peninsula sustainable with the right set of guarantors.

Though Pyongyang perceives the EU as a potentially 'neutral' force, untainted by intervention in the Korean War – despite 6 of the current 28 member states dispatching troops – the increasing tendency of EU policy-makers to follow Washington has seen it leaning heavily to one side. For Pyongyang, EU member states fail to appreciate the extent of US provocations. The German contract to sell over 250 Taurus KEPD 350 air-to-surface missiles to Seoul in 2014 was a surprise and a disappointment. It denounced the sale of these missiles, which have a range of 500 kilometres and can penetrate 6 metres of concrete, as 'an anti-peace action that makes one wonder whether Germany really wants peace on the Korean peninsula'.[11]

The EU had no diplomatic relations with Pyongyang until the visit by the Troika of Göran Persson, Chris Patten, and Javier Solana in May 2001, but a political dialogue had been established in December 1998. By 2000 the EU had already provided food and humanitarian assistance both directly ($95 million, or €106 million) and via the World Food Programme ($44 million, or €50 million) and EU NGOs ($9.9 million, or €11 million). By the beginning of the 21st century the EU seemed ripe to become an independent political unit within the global economy. After industrial and economic union, the next stage was political union, manifested as self-interest rather than subordination. Some saw this in the EU's engagement with Pyongyang. The EU, in a strategy paper, set out a sharply different approach from that of the US, partly spurred by Kim Dae-jung in Seoul.[12] The May Troika visit had garnered a moratorium on missile launches until 2003 and an EU-DPRK human rights dialogue modelled on that of the EU-China dialogue. Now the EU was offering continued humanitarian aid: food and medicine, capacity building, technical assistance and pilot projects in agriculture, help with sustainable natural-resource exploitation and transport infrastructure, and improved market access for textile exports to the EU. This was the heyday of relations with Brussels. *Rodong Shinmun* was peppered with editorials arguing that the EU was the only hegemonic power capable of challenging the United States.

It turned out to be premature. The independent Common Foreign and Security Policy was stillborn. Brussels had got too far ahead of the game and Washington slowly reeled it in again. The EU continued to provide humanitarian aid and participate in political dialogues. When Pyongyang announced in September 2004 that it wanted to phase out short-term food aid in favour of long-term development assistance, it gave special permission for European NGOs to continue their activities, with the NGOs rebranded as units of the European Commission.

The EU's human rights dialogue was sabotaged early on by the Heritage Foundation and the French government. In 2003, after three or four rounds of the dialogue that European Commission officials said was just beginning to yield results, the EU was persuaded to co-sponsor a resolution with Japan at the Human Rights Council in Geneva condemning North Korea (see chapter 4). They never warned Pyongyang. Unsurprisingly, the dialogue was frozen.

The last grudging contact was a visit by the director-general of the DPRK Ministry of Foreign Affairs in April 2018 for what Pyongyang considered the 15th political dialogue. Paris, London, Washington, and Tokyo all expressed their displeasure. The 14th Dialogue had been back in June 2015 in Pyongyang and the 13th back in 2010. Increasingly EU positions and statements have echoed – sometimes anticipated – Washington and New York, with the European Parliament not far behind. In January 2017 it condemned 'breaches of human rights, democracy, and the rule of law' with 65 in favour, 2 against, and 10 abstentions.

The internal divisions within the EU are stark. On the one side, as we've seen, there is Paris, aided and abetted by London, both taking an extremely hard line hostile to any engagement and frustrating EU high representative Federica Mogherini. As permanent members of the UNSC, they have a disproportionate influence. The hostility seems rooted deep in the French Ministry of Foreign Affairs, transcending the changing political kaleidoscope that is the presidency. France is the only member state with no diplomatic relations with the DPRK, and is always at the tip of the spear demanding additional sanctions above and beyond those of the UNSC. It was also Paris which was most reluctant to sign off on the Iran deal in 2015 and which, in spring 2018, tried to get Tehran to give something for nothing on missile control. Were President Emmanuel Macron to shift France's position decisively under pressure from Germany decisively, any remaining objections by London – already leaving the EU and keen to curry favour with Washington – would get short shrift.

The second outlier is the Scandinavians, in particular Sweden, who favour engagement, dialogue, and negotiation. It was no accident that the 2001 Troika visit to Pyongyang was led by Göran Persson, then president of the Security Council and Swedish prime minister. Japanese diplomats were particularly critical of Sweden's role in the Security Council during 2017, saying the Swedes were acting as if they were North Koreans themselves.

The EU and its member states will continue to follow the US line at the UN, despite Mogherini shaking hands with DPRK foreign minister Ri Yong Ho in August 2017. In the past, the EU has been more payer than player in north-east Asia. Under pressure from Seoul, Tokyo, and Washington, Brussels was persuaded to chip in to KEDO to allow the Japanese to join. A purely South Korean and Japanese operation was politically unthinkable in Tokyo. The EU was also invited to join the Six-Party Talks, but Patten turned it down.

In the last decade, the situation has changed enormously. The rise of China, the 2011 FTA with the Republic of Korea, and the latest 2018 FTA with Japan – the world's biggest trade deal to date – mean a new balance of interests in Brussels. The advent of the Trump administration has reinforced the point. The Republic of Korea's increasing misgivings about the US administration are strengthening Seoul-Brussels relations, with the South's interest in an Iran-style deal leading to an interest in some involvement in the EU.

9
Conclusion – After Singapore

The Trump-Kim summit in Singapore in June 2018 was more spectacle than substance; indeed, the summit itself was conceded on a Trump whim. On 8 March, a senior South Korean official just back from Pyongyang reported that Kim had requested an early meeting with President Trump. Trump agreed without consulting his staff and ordered its immediate announcement. Three months later, with some bumps on the road, it happened. Kim glad-handed and charmed the Singaporeans in a series of bilateral meetings and a late-night walkabout, while Trump tried to bring the summit forward to get it out of the way. In the end he didn't ad lib and stuck to his part of the script.

After a symbolic handshake in front of a tableau of the two countries' alternating flags, Trump and Kim met privately – with only interpreters – for 40 minutes, then brought in their respective teams of three for wider talks before a working lunch. The result was a statement less than 400 words long that promised US security guarantees in exchange for progress towards complete denuclearisation of the Peninsula, a new era of US–DPRK relations with a lasting and stable peace regime, a renewed search programme for the remains of Korea War missing-in-action soldiers in the DPRK, and the immediate repatriation of the remains already stored there.

At Trump's press conference, he used Kim's language to announce the suspension of the US–ROK joint military exercises – or, as he called them, 'war games' and 'provocations'. It was subsequently hinted that this was the first of a series of moves agreed upon by the two leaders in their private meeting, with more to come: the North demonstrating progress through action and Washington looking to 'amend' the armistice.

As friends from the North of England might say, it was 'summat and nothing'. Nevertheless, it was progress, in that it was at least a base on which to build, leaving the world in a far less critical and safer place than in the early months of the year. Yet, getting there turned out to be as exacting as expected, making clear that any step off the narrow diplomatic path Washington and Pyongyang are walking could land them, the Peninsula, and the rest of us back on the road to war. If this is to be avoided, Washington must curb its ambition.

The US overreached on the way to Singapore, with John Bolton, as Trump's newly appointed national security advisor, demanding on Fox News that Pyongyang give up both its nuclear weapons and its civil nuclear-power programme, chemical and biological weapons, and long- and intermediate-range missiles and return the unaccounted-for abductees to Tokyo before the US would ease its 'maximum pressure' at all. This set of 'transitional demands' went way beyond what Pyongyang was willing to offer or Kim was capable of delivering. It was a security shopping list for a conquered country – Bolton was treating the North as if it was Japan in August 1945. The final straw was his subsequent reference to 'following the Libyan model'. It was so over the top that it looked more like an act of sabotage than a search for settlement. No surprise, then, that Pyongyang reacted with fury, having Kim Gye Gwan, the first vice foreign minister and former Six-Party Talks chief negotiator, respond angrily. He was subsequently echoed by high-flying vice foreign minister Choe Son Hui, who will play a central role in future negotiations.

The global community's concerns about the North are embodied in the UNSC's set of nine sanctions resolutions over the past twelve years.[1] These focus on nuclear weapons and proliferation as well as human rights, with sideswipes at the North's space programme and long-range missiles. Thus there is no justification for endangering a successful outcome by overextending the agenda. A sense of realism and proportion is required. In response to Kim, Trump switched the Singapore summit off, then back on again after a rhetorical retreat from Pyongyang. At this the US backed down on its demands, and Trump acknowledged that it would be a process and not a one-night stand.

Washington's key objectives are to halt and reverse the North's nuclear weapons programme and its potential, to the point of complete, verifiable, and irreversible denuclearisation. If this process extends over years, Pyongyang may need to surrender or destroy its ICBMs and ICBM testing and manufacturing capacity early on – or at least place them under international lock and key in the interim. The counter-argument that the US needs to give precedence to nuclear weapons over missiles misses the crucial political point that the North will not go naked into the negotiating process. The counter that the North could then launch an attack without ICBMs (e.g., on ships) has long been true. The obvious question is: Why should it launch such an attack?

The reason for the extended period is not technical but political. Washington argues that North Korea could denuclearise within twelve months to two years if it is prepared to ship out the weapons' nuclear engineers to disassemble them. Even if (and it's a big if) Kim was prepared to consider such an accelerated timetable, the menace for Pyongyang is that the US strips it of all its qualified scientists and engineers by offering them enhanced asylum at the end of the process. The obvious counter is to have the process carried out in the North, under international supervision. On the issue of verification inspections, the parties will likely to need to come to terms with the disparity between the politically acceptable level of intrusion and what is technically required. Pyongyang has signed up for a denuclearized Peninsula – but if it remains unlikely that we will see North Korean inspection teams checking the Yongsan Garrison in Seoul for nuclear materials, there is a limit on what can be done in the North. The North resists verification inspections by the IAEA, giving Washington preference over the world and thus avoiding the necessity of re-joining the NPT. It is unclear how sanguine the international community would be about another US venture into unilateralism, if this proves to be the final position.

The US – and Pyongyang – both need to be clear on the content of the agenda. Addressing the UNSC concerns should be the minimum and maximum. Denuclearization and non-proliferation, long-range missiles, and human rights will just be a heavy load. It might be that the EU could take the lead on the last, as since 2014 Pyongyang has been offering to reopen the EU-DPRK human rights dialogue, which could be done in parallel with reviving the moribund political dialogue. The North's focus, like China's, would be on social and economic rights.

In the past, to the detriment of earlier agreements, the North has considered its space programme to be separate from long-range missile development. Is it included here, as Washington wants, or can the US ultimately live with it, since putting satellites into orbit does not require re-entry technology? Should someone offer launch facilities for the North's satellites? Past experience of negotiating with Pyongyang has shown that you only get what's on the box.

Washington is also concerned that the North doesn't become the proliferators' Walmart. As we have seen, in the mid-2000s Pyongyang provided help to the nuclear programmes of Iran, Syria, and Burma. But if Pyongyang provides a full and complete inventory of its nuclear holdings relatively serious counter-proliferation oversight can bring the material aspects under control. This will not be simple. The Yongbyon complex alone has more than 200 buildings. Yet an early, even partial, declaration and inspections would be an important signal of Kim's commitment. More problematic are the North's nuclear scientists, whom Pompeo suggested handling through mass extradition. A better answer could be retraining them to maintain a civil nuclear-power programme, as with many 'orphaned' nuclear scientists after the collapse and breakup of the Soviet Union.

Between Washington and Beijing

Pyongyang initially had two alternate gambits. The first was a bold, radical switch: to relinquishing its last lingering ties with Beijing and pivot to Washington. The Cold War play-off between China and the Soviet Union served Pyongyang well. Kim Jong Un's aim was to replicate it with Washington. The idea was that the North becomes an adjunct, a ward of the United States for a generation or maybe more. There were even hints of US bases. Rason is, after all, the most northerly ice-free port on the east coast of Asia. The lock on American good behaviour was Beijing: if Washington's commitment slackened there was another suitor waiting in the wings.

Yet early exchanges between Pyongyang and Washington showed a lack of awareness of Kim's embrace of the Palmerston doctrine: 'There are no eternal allies and no perpetual enemies'. Nor did Trump's administration show any understanding of the North's singular efforts to escape from China's tutelage and entanglement. The more perceptive among them hinted that Kim could demonstrate seriousness by abandoning Tehran, making commitments on human rights, or offering the complete inventory of nuclear materials mentioned above. It was just beyond imagination. When it became clear to Pyongyang that Trump was passing on the offer, Kim looked to Plan B: reluctant reconciliation with China. The Xi-Kim meetings, in Beijing in March and June, sandwiching Dalian in May, said it all. The North was now looking for an external partner to underpin its negotiations and police the process. The Singapore summit was a shocking success for Xi and Beijing. Though they had been concerned weeks earlier that North Korea was about to desert them, China went in the political revolving door after Trump and came out ahead. The optics of Kim arriving in an Air China plane were priceless.

The US radicals, in contrast, were looking to finesse the deal by working behind the scenes with Beijing to plot reunification of the Peninsula. There they had an even harder sell, flying hard in the face of north-east Asian realities. Beijing greatly prefers the status quo over any prospect of a united Korea allied to the US on its borders; Pyongyang, as has been said, sees early unification as nothing more or less than assimilation. As for South Korea, even if President Moon could be persuaded to renege on his promise of no forced unification, there is little enthusiasm amongst the population for bearing the costs that would inevitably follow. It would mean 'only a 20% drop in living standards', as one conference in Brussels was told – a prospect that generates more horror than enthusiasm in Seoul, especially amongst the young.

Figure 33 Cards and cigarettes on Pyongyang's pavements.

Part of the problem is that those at the top in the US are just not listening. They are misreading Pyongyang. Trump offered the prospect of McDonald's, condos on the beach, and US-based multinationals taking over and running the economy, but what the North wants is normalization of relations, security guarantees, and release from Washington's economic fetters to allow Kim to pursue *his* vision of an economy with 'North Korean' characteristics. They want to be strong, secure, and prosperous – closer to the economies of Vietnam and China, or even South Korea or Japan, with their state-owned enterprises, Chaebol, and Zaibatsu rather than US free-market capitalism. This is the industrial architecture of choice for economically vibrant, effective one-party states in Asia. Any serious US investment in the North will be more a concession from

Pyongyang than a reward from Washington. It's more likely that the dysfunctional political system in Washington will self-harm and block investment by US companies by failing to lift domestic sanctions against the North until long after South Korea, China, and Germany are fully engaged.

Before Singapore, Washington talked about maintaining 'maximum pressure' on Pyongyang until final denuclearization. Afterward, the sentiment remained, even if the two magic words didn't readily trip off the tongue. Never believe your own propaganda. Washington did. It's true that the final rounds of sanctions were beginning to have an impact in the North by the end of 2017. There were food shortages in the north-east and electricity was in shorter supply than normal. But this was not what triggered the announcement that the nuclear deterrent was complete. It was the technological success of the 28 November ICBM launch, which proved the North had the range to hit the whole of the mainland US, prompted Kim's New Year's address, and set in motion the diplomatic avalanche that followed.

Whether the cause was science or suffering, 'maximum pressure' was doomed after the announcement of the Singapore summit in March and Kim's serial trips to see Xi. After the summit, it was well and truly buried. Beijing was the last in and first out, the final country to sign, implement, and enforce sanctions. It is aware of the dangers of Pyongyang slipping out of its orbit, and that some of those worst affected by the sanctions regime live and work on the Chinese side of the border. Strict enforcement went, while implementation became increasingly generous. Gone are the days when tens of thousands of emergency medical kits were held up because they contained a small pair of scissors. As of July 2018, there was a property boom in Jilin Province. Real estate prices on the border with the North boomed and, for the more adventurous, houses and apartments were available on the North Korean market. For Washington to attempt to retain its 'maximum pressure' policy is to be in denial, and to surrender to Beijing goodwill with Pyongyang for political correctness back home.

The UN sanctions were imposed notch by notch, with each screwing more tightly than the one before. Logically, that process

Figure 34   Rason fish-processing workers loading refrigerated
lorries bound for China.

should be reverse-engineered as the North runs the tape of history
backwards. For Pyongyang to get nothing until the tape finally
unreels makes no sense, nor is it good politics by Washington. Kim
is taking a bold risk, with tolerance rather than enthusiastic endorse-
ment from the military leadership. Failing to reward his efforts would
threaten to undermine and weaken him. That's clear from his spring
appeal to the public to pay close attention to the guidance coming
from the Party, and from his back-channel messages to Washington
when Trump threatened to cancel the summit. Deferred gratification
works least well for the cold and hungry. Beijing will be followed by
Seoul in wanting to reward progress, and in doing so will serve their
own interests. Washington should lead, not follow.

Where Can It All Go Wrong?

There are three principal dangers of this process. The first is ill will.
Certainly, in Washington, there are those who – almost as an act

of faith – believe no good can come of engagement. They refuse to recognise that Kim is a different man from his father. They believe it will not be possible to reach a deal and that if by some chance one is reached, Kim and Pyongyang will cheat. Others believe in principle that it is an obscenity to do a deal with a ruler like Kim Jong Un. There is no reason to believe that the other face of the same scepticism is not to be found in the North, if less public.

The second is gullibility. The classic example here is Muammar Gaddafi, who was in the end impaled by his credulity in trusting Washington and the West. No matter what's been signed, sealed, and ratified, Pyongyang cannot be assured that the current or future US president will be capable of forbearance in the face of food riots, revolt, or rebellion in the streets of Kaesong. On the other side is Kim playing Trump for a fool, with no intention of delivering on his promise to denuclearise. If so, the US returns to the *status quo ante*. These are both real dangers, but they can be countered with commitment, investment, and belief. That requires ownership of the project and process by a mesh of individuals and institutions that tightly bind those involved, with mechanisms in place to prod progress forward and manage and settle disputes.

The third is the most perilous: ignorance of the intrinsically possible. This infects Washington and Pyongyang. Neither understands the other. Unknowing and unaware of the art of the attainable, they will ask the impossible, demand the undeliverable, and seek the unfindable. Both need the self-awareness to appreciate that they are surrogate players in a game where getting it wrong means millions of people, on both sides of an arbitrary line drawn on the ground three-quarters of a century ago, lose and lose badly.

Where does the Peninsula go from here? The situation is still singularly dangerous. There is a long, complex, and arduous journey ahead. Heaven may be easier to attain than peace. All the options facing Washington take the world to hell in a handcart, save for diplomacy. The only difference is the pace of the march. The roads to war include a military strike, 'regime change' through covert action and subversion, and the imposition of an increasingly brutal sanctions regime barely short of an economic blockade and trade embargo. In practice, this deadly trinity is a three-lane highway to armed combat.

Another War Is Possible

If the Peninsula goes back to the future of early 2018, there is also the prospect of another war, unforeseen in the West. Formally, the Sino-North Korean Mutual Aid and Cooperation Friendship Treaty commits China to come to the North's aid if attacked. It was signed in 1961 and remains in force, with automatic twenty-year renewals, until 2021. However, Beijing made it clear in 2017 that this would not apply if Pyongyang was doing the attacking, nor if, in its opinion, Pyongyang had provoked the war. Conversely, Beijing doesn't believe the US's pledges that they will not deploy troops or establish bases north of the DMZ after any conflict; Washington reneged on such promises to Moscow regarding Central and Eastern Europe. Frankly, the US might have little option if insurrectionary and civil violence continued after such a conflict.

How can China resolve the contradiction? It doesn't want to fight the US with North Korea and doesn't want the US to attack Pyongyang. The answer: China could resolve the problem of the North itself. On the eve of destruction, China could jump the gun and intervene, all carefully stage-managed, with a senior North Korean general or party official beseeching Beijing to intervene to 'save the revolution' (resonating with the language of the Chinese People's Volunteers in the Korean War). The intention would be a quick and reasonably bloodless *coup d'état*, securing the country and the North's stockpile of nuclear weapons, replacing Kim Jong Un with a befitting figurehead, putting in place a Beijing-compliant regime, and then rapidly withdrawing. This is possibly easier said than done. As early as autumn 2014, Kang Suk Ju, then international secretary of the WPK, said that Pyongyang would fight China if necessary. The question is: If China intervenes, how will Washington – and Seoul – react?

In the North, as we have seen, the US and Japan are totally demonised. China, however grudgingly, is acknowledged as providing assistance in the Korean War – even if its contributions are woefully pared down from reality. When the Victorious Fatherland Liberation War Museum re-opened in 2014, there were hundreds of Chinese veterans in attendance. While the Chinese leadership is criticised for its 'betrayal' of the North in recent years, the Chinese people, in particular the ethnic Koreans in the border provinces, go unremarked.

Beijing is sufficiently concerned about prospects for the Peninsula that it has conducted military-to-military coordination with Washington. Of the four bilateral dialogues Donald Trump kicked off in 2017 at Mar-a-Lago with President Xi – economics, law enforcement, people-to-people, and military-to-military – only the last is functioning, and it remains largely restricted to North Korea. There were press reports that a hotline has been established between China's Northern Theatre Command in Shenyang and US forces in Seoul, though Beijing denies this. It could not deny the August 2016 visit by the Marine Corps general Joe Dunford, chair of the Joint Chiefs of Staff, to General Song Puxuan, head of the Northern Theatre Command, to observe troop manoeuvres adjacent to the North's border. The same is true of then–secretary of state Rex Tillerson's response to questions about the prospect of regime collapse in the North, as it was announced that China was preparing camps for the anticipated flood of refugees that would follow the outbreak of war. Tillerson referred to

> conversations about . . . in the event that something happened – it could happen internal to North Korea; it might be nothing that we on the outside initiate – that if that unleashed some kind of instability, the most important thing to us would be securing those nuclear weapons they've already developed and ensuring that they – that nothing falls into the hands of people we would not want to have it. We've had conversations with the Chinese about how might that be done.[2]

The locations of the North's nuclear sites favour China winning any race for arms – but it is less clear that Washington wouldn't see the North falling to Beijing as putting it in 'the hands of people we would not want to have it'. The cure might just be seen as worse than the disease. After all, if successful, it would enormously enhance China's status at the expense of the US – and make Trump look impotent in the bargain. Seoul would also be furious that the North was in limbo between suzerainty and colony, with even distant unification an illusion.

Therefore, it is difficult to imagine the White House standing aside. But how then could a US intervention keep from transforming the nature of the war from conventional to nuclear? How could the two 'liberators' be kept apart in what would then be a race to seize political and military control over Pyongyang and its nuclear weapons sites, missile sites, and production facilities? Beijing would face fewer hurdles, politically and militarily, than Washington. The North's demonisation of America and Americans would likely keep the KPA fighting to the death against the US, while the North's massive forward deployment of forces just above the DMZ would slow the US advance, compared to that of the Chinese from the north, just through sheer weight of numbers.

Yet the success of any 'smash and grab' strike depends upon knowing where the weapons, missiles, and nuclear material are stored. After the fiasco of Iraq's 'weapons of mass destruction', few believe the CIA has a definitive answer to that question, outside of the Yongbyon nuclear plant, the now-disabled nuclear test site close to the Chinese border, and the missile test and fabrication plants. That's just not good enough.

The Prospects for a Settlement

A peace process is required if war is to be avoided, which means the two major protagonists must talk to each other. That started in March 2018, with secretary of state–designate Mike Pompeo travelling twice to Pyongyang, first secretly and then overtly. This culminated in the Singapore summit, which gave birth to the sparse joint statement signed by Trump and Kim. This low base is intended as the foundation for a settlement, to be thrashed out subsequently. The size of the task is indicated by the JPCOA deal with Iran, which dedicated 110 pages to nuclear issues alone, in addition to hundreds of pages of annexes. Negotiating such a deal will take months, followed in close order by the final and most difficult phase – implementation. This will likely stretch a decade or more, and could fall apart at any time.

What shape would a settlement take that would assuage US concerns about nuclear proliferation and Pyongyang's concerns about regime change, economic strangulation, and the need to generate development assistance while also mitigating the complete distrust between the two parties? Trust grows from actions rather than words. The deal would need to be front-end loaded with early wins but with a long tail. Even this must be carefully co-ordinated. Some of Pyongyang's unilateral acts, such as the destruction of the nuclear test site, have generated as much suspicion as goodwill, with their limited transparency to technical experts.

Of all the 'deals' done with Pyongyang, the Agreed Framework was the only one that worked. Some claim that its ultimate failure shows that no deal is possible. I argue that it shows that any deal that works must resemble it. The Agreed Framework halted Pyongyang's nuclear programme for a short decade. What went wrong? It was a lack of ownership. Steven Bosworth, KEDO's first director, commented, 'The Agreed Framework was a political orphan within two weeks of its signature'. A new deal will need clear parentage, ownership, and a set of godparents invested in the birth. Its durability will only be as strong as its guarantors.

In 1973, the Sunningdale Agreement was signed in an attempt to end the armed struggle in Northern Ireland. It collapsed less than a year later. But the Good Friday Agreement, made a quarter of a century after that, closely shadowed Sunningdale. Seamus Mallon, deputy leader of Northern Ireland's Social Democratic and Labour Party, forecast at the time that what would emerge from any successful talks would be 'Sunningdale for slow learners'. With respect to Pyongyang, it is likely that any future deal will be an 'Agreed Framework for slow learners'.

The North is not offering overnight denuclearisation. The last, best chance of that came and went in 2011. Today its bargaining position is much stronger. Then Washington was looking to buy out the prospect and potential of nuclear weapons. Now Pyongyang has a complete nuclear deterrent to sell, or so it claims.

Whether that is entirely true is not proven. Testing a convention-ally armed missile over the deep South Pacific would mean war. For the US, the best case is that the North remains in the grey zone in terms of capability: certainly able to crash a missile near Washington, but almost incapable of hitting the US capital with a nuclear weapon due to inadequate payload capacity, a lack of re-entry technology, and a primitive guidance system. Why wouldn't the price be that much higher?

Kim's unilateral suspension of the nuclear programme in his New Year's address opened the floodgates to a cascade of diplomacy, from the Winter Olympics to a North-South Summit, a date with Trump, and forays to Beijing and Dalian to meet President Xi. For a country whose leaders have not travelled outside the close orbit of China, Russia, and Mongolia for 34 years, this was globetrotting.

Pyongyang has two minimum demands of the US and one of the wider world. From Washington it seeks promises to desist – don't threaten; don't undermine; don't sanction, block, or interfere. These will be delivered through a cast-iron security guarantee – preferably verifiable and irreversible – granting legitimacy and respect; not impeding the easing or removal of UN and international sanctions; and lifting the veto on Pyongyang's membership in the World Bank and international financial institutions. South Korea and the rest of the world will do the heavy financial lifting providing humanitarian, development assistance, and foreign investment.

En route to hard negotiations following a soft summit, Pyongyang is working harder, with the pre-summit moratorium on weapons testing, the destruction of the nuclear test site, the promise to dismember missile testing facilities, and renewed co-operation on the search for the remains of Korean War UNC soldiers missing in action. In exchange, Trump has agreed to suspend the joint military exercises.[3] The next step, rationally, would be to take the Yongbyon nuclear reactor offline, thus limiting the amount of weapons-grade plutonium Pyongyang has at its disposal. Subsequently, North Korea should then re-join the NPT and allow IAEA inspections.

Here is the first problem: Pyongyang is chary of re-joining the NPT. It's was all too intrusive last time around. They worry about two things: requests to visit prison camps and the sheer volume of visits that the IAEA would deem technically necessary for the IAEA to give Pyongyang a clean bill of health. For them, denuclearisation is purely a bilateral issue between Pyongyang and Washington – without interference even from Seoul. Inspections, when we finally get to that point, will be US-led and with a footprint and frequency that results from a political accommodation rather than technical necessity. Quite how the rest of the world will respond to such neglect of the normal channels is unclear.

Yet, while early gestures are crucial in setting tone, irreversible actions are the crucial test. Will the dismantling of Yongbyon mean the delivery of energy projects, interim energy supplies – electricity from South Korea – or a peace settlement? The global civil nuclear industry would be happy to fund and partner in the process; after the 2011 Fukushima Daiichi disaster in Japan, one more nuclear accident and the civil nuclear industry is dead. One obvious option to bridge the energy gap would be to return to the promised LWRs of the Agreed Framework, matching with Pyongyang's nuclear machismo and compressing the timeframe for delivery of a major project to ease the North's energy deficiency, since the groundwork at the Kumho site near Sinpo is already virtually complete. It might be possible to mitigate Washington's instinctive aversion by substituting for one of the two reactors with a renewable energy programme, including a serious element of utility-scale big energy. The obvious candidate is a major tidal-power scheme. The west coast of the Korean Peninsula has the high tidal range necessary for a scheme that, suitably designed, could provide twice the capacity of one LWR. With their experience constructing the 8-kilometre West Sea Barrage between 1981 and 1986, North Korea could do the bulk of the work in house, with only the largest turbines supplied from abroad.

While the overall shape of a settlement depends on Washington and Pyongyang, the delivery process and denouement require a wider set of players as guarantors, donors, or both. The reason for that is twofold: bolstering the political load and paying the bill. The North needs a massive shot of resources to kick-start its economy but is all too well aware that Washington will barely be a provider at all, let alone the sole provider. If the precedent of the Agreed Framework is anything to go by, Washington may only chip in small change. Yet any acceptable settlement will require substantial assistance in solving the problem of energy insufficiency, which is far worse than it was in 1994. This requires considerable financial resources. The initial cost estimate for the two LWRs to fulfil the Agreed Framework promise was $4.5 billion (€3.9 billion). This had risen significantly by the time the project was effectively abandoned in 2002, creating a funding gap that was never filled.

The White House acknowledges the need for donors. As they put it, the US will have saved the world from the dangers of a nuclear-armed North Korea and the world needs to pay its share of the costs. That bill will be at least two or three times higher than in 1994. Donald Trump will never accept the US contributing real money to such a project. Neither will Congress. Seoul expects to cover up to 70 per cent of the overall costs, but will require partners. Beijing could chip in with a branch of its Belt and Road Initiative (which could even connect the South), and Moscow can serve its own interests. Moon Jae-in's 'New Northern Policy', aimed at economic cooperation with countries to the north, and Putin's 'New Eastern Policy', to develop Russia's far east, fit like pieces of a jigsaw puzzle, with new railways, roads, and pipelines spanning the North.

Second is the need for guarantors and policing. Almost from the minute the Agreed Framework was signed, some in Washington attempted to expand its terms. This predilection remains. Trump's rejection of the JCPOA deal with Iran means that no unilateral guarantee from Washington or letter from President Trump will serve. For Pyongyang, the final political deal will need buttressing and reinforcement by as big and influential a multilateral group as possible, to relieve the risk of future unilateral action by the US. The Security Council would be ideal.

The same is true for reaching a peace settlement to replace the 1953 armistice. This must come first. Kim's confidence-building measures have focused on hardware. Washington cannot respond in kind, but it can move politically. The armistice was signed by the UN Command, on the one side, and the KPA and CPV on the other. Syngman Rhee refused; he wanted Washington to fight on till final victory. The armistice is a political nightmare and a lawyer's dream: the only thing the UN Command shares with the UN is a set of initials. For those running the show, it is an entirely independent franchise.

In January 2018, as we saw, the US called a conference in Vancouver to assemble a 'coalition of the willing', ready to return to the battlefield. Now the talk is of a settlement. It is in the North's interest to make the settlement as sturdy as possible and the process multilateral – to widen the circle, and not just to Seoul. The North seemed to realise that when it rejected a trilateral declaration at the Singapore summit. This widening could start by bringing in China alongside South Korea. A US–ROK–DPRK–China declaration at the UN that 'the war is over' would be one device. Alternately, the circle could be widened further by revisiting and tweaking the format of the 1954 Geneva talks, where the Soviet Union, France, and the United Kingdom were added to the attempt to resolve stand-offs in Vietnam and the Korean Peninsula. The EU could substitute for the latter two. The attraction here is that Moscow is in and Tokyo out. Even Beijing seems to have finally woken up to the pernicious role of Abe's Tokyo and now rarely suggests the Six-Party Talks format.

Despite worries, such a settlement would neither legitimise the North's nuclear weapons nor invalidate UN sanctions. The danger is for Pyongyang to allow Washington to try to turn settlement into a formal peace treaty. Such a treaty would require ratification by the US

Congress, which is not to be trusted on such an issue. The settlement would be held hostage, on the one side, to Democratic Party legislators who want to frustrate Trump and his domestic agenda and, on the other side, to Republicans and some Democrats who have legislatively tied improving relations with the North to denuclearisation and human rights concerns. However, when the required agreement is produced, it will be more robust and resilient and give Pyongyang more confidence if it is sanctioned by the Security Council rather than marooned in the US Senate.

Pompeo's July visit to Pyongyang illustrated quite how thwart the process will be. He got his opposite number – who was, as expected, Kim Yong Chol – but that was about it. The two sides were totally at odds and had cross-purposes. Pyongyang was expecting news on the delivery of what was agreed in the Singapore Declaration, namely, a statement that the war is over. This was supposed to be the first stage of a three-stage process, which would be followed by a peace settlement and the subsequent withdrawal of US troops. It was also supposed to be the first step towards putting in place the promised security guarantees for the North.

Instead Pompeo was the demander, with a shopping list that included the requirement of a full disclosure and inventory of the North's nuclear holdings, inspections, and CVID, or 'complete, verifiable, irreversible' denuclearisation – whose very initials are an anathema to Pyongyang – and inspections. It was this cavalier approach that people such as Vice Chairman Ri Su Yong saw as 'gangsterism'. 'How can Washington imagine we can contemplate allowing inspections when we are still at war! We still trust Trump's promises but his adjutants are reverting back to their old ways'. Warnings that if Pompeo is pushed out of the game they get Bolton seemingly fell on deaf ears. Subsequent visits to Brussels and the UN found him very despondent.

Trump subsequently tweeted that there was no time limit on denuclearisation, but failed to answer what happens on sanctions. The UN's stack of sanctions resolutions promises relief as progress is made towards denuclearisation, not enduring in perpetuity to the end. Pyongyang is adding that to its list of complaints – it has frozen tests and dismantled and destroyed facilities and what have the Americans ever done for it? An easily reversible moratorium on joint military exercises and the forward march of peace halted. Recurring summits may be required to maintain momentum. The Kim-Trump show may become a series.

A decade ago – after Iraq – my political preference for the North was 'changing the regime' over 'regime change'. Ten years later, with the Libyan experience in the interim and seeing Pyongyang's changing face, I have no reason to question that judgement. I hope, for the sake of the people on the Peninsula, that at the end of another decade all of us end up on the right side of that future.

Notes

1. Introduction

1. Scott A. Snyder, 'The Motivations Behind North Korea's Pursuit of Simultaneous Economic and Nuclear Development', *Asia Unbound*, Council on Foreign Relations, 20 November 2013, www.cfr.org/blog/ motivations-behind-north-koreas-pursuit-simultaneous-economic- and-nuclear-development.
2. Andrei Lankov, 'The Limits of North Korea's Meager Economic Growth', *NK News*, 6 February 2017, www.nknews.org/2017/02/the- limits-of-north-koreas-meagre-economic-growth.
3. *Ronin* is the Japanese term for a samurai lacking a master.
4. Treaty on the Non-Proliferation of Nuclear Weapons, United Nations, 2–27 May 2005, www.un.org/en/conf/npt/2005/npttreaty.html.
5. Interview, August 2016, Honolulu.
6. United Nations Human Rights Council, 'Report of the Commission of Inquiry on Human Rights in the Democratic People's Republic of Korea', 7 February 2014, www.ohchr.org/EN/HRBodies/HRC/ CoIDPRK/Pages/ReportoftheCommissionofInquiryDPRK.aspx.
7. Personal communication from senior EEAS official.
8. UK Ministry of Defence, answer to Written Parliamentary Question 123796, by Stephen Kinnock, MP, 29 January 2018.

2. Drawing the Iron Curtain

1. George Orwell, *The Complete Works of George Orwell*, vol. 13 (London: Secker & Warburg, 1998), 317.
2. Ha Young Kim, *Kukche chuui sigak eso pon hanbando* [The Korean Peninsula from an Internationalist Perspective] (Seoul: Chaekbulae, 2002), 234–35.
3. Suzy Kim, *Everyday Life in the North Korean Revolution, 1945–1950* (New York: Cornell University Press, 2013).
4. Andrew C. Nahm, *Korea: Tradition and Transformation* (Seoul: Hollym, 1988).

5. Quoted in Adrian Buzo, *The Making of Modern Korea* (London: Routledge, 2002), 63.

6. Documents in the South Korean government archives from 1949 and 1950, including letters and memoranda by Rhee and Chang Myun (then South Korean ambassador in Washington), military reports, and even a strategic map for attack on North Korea illustrate the military adventurism of Rhee's administration. Democratic People's Republic of Korea, *Facts Tell: Secret Documents Seized by North Korea from the South Korean Government Archives*, (Honolulu: University Press of the Pacific, 2001).

7. Formosa is where Chiang Kai-Shek retreated from mainland communist China. It refers to today's Taiwan but was then called by its Portuguese name (*ilha formosa*), meaning 'beautiful island'.

8. Joseph S. Bermudez, *North Korean Special Forces*, 2nd ed. (Annapolis, MD: Naval Institute Press, 1988), 36–37.

9. United Nations, 'Security Council Resolutions – 1950', www.un.org/docs/scres/try/scres50.htm.

10. Truman claimed that the decision to go to war in Korea was the hardest decision of his presidency. If so, he made it quickly. See John Dickerson, 'The Hardest Job in the World', *Atlantic* (May 2018): 46–63.

11. Jed Mercurio, *Ascent* (London: Vintage Random House, 2007). The novel follows the career of Yevgeni Yerevin from MiG 'ace' in Korea to the moon. See also Leon Krylov and Yuriy Tepsurkaev, *Soviet MiG-15 Aces of the Korean War* (Oxford: Osprey, 2008).

12. Chen Jian, quoted in in Chuck Downs, *Over the Line: North Korea's Negotiating Strategy* (Washington, DC: AEI Press, 1999), 24.

13. Kim Il Sung, 'Temporary Strategic Retreat and the Tasks of Party Organisations', *Selected Works of Kim Il Sung*, vol. 6 (Pyongyang: Foreign Languages Publishing House, 27 September 1950).

14. Red Cross Society of China, *Out of their Own Mouths* (Red Cross: Peking, 1952) has some not entirely incredible descriptions of UNC atrocities from US POWs.

15. Red Cross, *Out of their Own Mouths*, 223–24.

16. This Pulitzer-winning book by three investigative journalists details the July 1950 incident at No Gun Ri. Charles J. Hanley, Sang-Hun Choe and Martha Mendoza, *The Bridge at No Gun Ri: A Hidden Nightmare from the Korean War* (New York: Henry Holt, 2002).

17. Robert Leckie, quoted in Downs, *Over the Line*, 29.

18. C. Turner Joy, *How Communists Negotiate* (New York: Macmillan, 1955), 18.

19. Ha Jin, *War Trash* (New York: Pantheon, 2004).

20. As a partial counter to *War Trash*, see Hal Vetter, *Mutiny on Koje Island* (Rutland, VT: Tuttle, 1965).

21. Condron returned to Britain in the 1960s, as the Sino-Soviet schism divided the Communist world, and remained active in the pro-Soviet Communist Party of Great Britain; see Alan Winnington, *Breakfast with Mao* (London: Lawrence and Wishart, 1986). For stories from the US perspective, see Virginia Pasley, *21 Stayed* (New York: Farrar, Straus and Cudahy, 1955) or, from the Chinese side, Andrew Condron, Richard Corden and Larance Sullivan (eds.), *Thinking Soldiers* (Peking: New World Press, 1955).

22. Eugene Kinkead, *Why They Collaborated* (London: Longmans, 1960). This is the British edition of a book published in the United States in 1959. The British, in contrast, were more hard-headed. See UK Ministry of Defence, *The Treatment of British Prisoners of War in Korea* (London: HMSO, 1955).

23. Kongdan Oh and Ralph C. Hassig, *North Korea Through the Looking Glass* (Washington, DC: Brookings Institution, 2002), 7.

24. John Halliday and Bruce Cumings, *Korea: The Unknown War* (London: Viking, 1988).

25. Downs, *Over the Line*, 34.

26. Churchill's remark was quoted in *Monthly Review* (April 1997).

3. Kim's Korea

1. Victoria Kim, 'Korean Diaspora in Uzbekistan', *Journal of the Royal Asiatic Society China* 77 (August 2017), 48–55, particularly note 18.

2. Kim Il Sung, 'Our People's Army Is an Army of the Working Class, an Army the Revolution; Class and Political Education Should Be Continuously Strengthened', speech delivered to People's Army cadres on 8 February 1963, in Kim Il Sung, *Selected Works*, vol. 3, 519.

3. Kim Il-pyong, *Communist Politics in North Korea* (New York: Praeger, 1975), 65–76.

4. The conspiracy is detailed in chapter 4 of Andrei Lankov, *Crisis in North Korea: The Failure of De-Stalinization 1956* (Honolulu: University of Hawaii Press, 2005).

5. Sonia Ryang, *Reading North Korea* (Cambridge, MA: Harvard University Press, 2012).

6. Kim Il Sung, 'On Some Problems of Our Party's *Juche* Idea and the Government of the Republic's Internal and External Policies, Answers to a Japanese Journalist for *Mainichi Shimbun* on September 17, 1972',

in Kim Il Sung, *On Juche in Our Revolution*, vol. 2 (Pyongyang: Foreign Languages Publishing House, 1975), 425–36.

7. Vladimir Lenin, 'Our Foreign and Domestic Position and Party Tasks', speech delivered to the Moscow Gubernia Conference of the RCP(B), 21 November 1920, translated by Julius Katzer, www.marxists.org/archive/lenin/works/1920/nov/21.htm.

8. Kim Il Sung's speech at the Fourth Supreme People's Assembly, 16 December 1967. See Kim Il Sung, *Works*, vol. 21 (Pyongyang: Foreign Languages Publishing House, 1985), 414.

9. The last Marx and Lenin kept watch over Kim Il Sung Square from the face of the Ministry of Foreign Trade until five years ago. It was explained that the portraits had gone for repair. Few expect them to reappear.

10. Ryang, *Reading North Korea*, 25.

11. Unlike in East Germany after the war, there is no evidence that the Soviets sought reparations.

12. Tessa Morris-Suzuki, *Exodus to North Korea: Shadows from Japan's Cold War* (Lanham, MD: Rowman & Littlefield, 2007).

13. A disappointing performance forced the Plan to be extended for a further three years.

14. Kim Il Sung, 'Every Effort for the Country's Reunification and Independence and for Socialist Construction in the Northern Half of the Republic', *Works*, vol. 1, 510.

15. N. Vreeland and R.S. Shinn, *Area Handbook for North Korea* (Washington, DC: Library of Congress, 1976), 225.

16. Andrea M. Savada, *North Korea: A Country Study*, 4th ed. (Washington, DC: Library of Congress, 1994), 126; also see Vreeland and Shinn, *Area Handbook*, 224.

17. Savada, *North Korea*, 114–15.

18. Kim Il Sung, 'Let Us Embody the Revolutionary Spirit of Independence, Self-Sustenance and Self-Defence More Thoroughly in All State Activities', speech at the first session of the Fourth Supreme People's Assembly, 16 December 1967, *Works*, vol. 4, 557.

19. Kim Il Sung, 'On the Immediate Tasks of the Government of the Democratic People's Republic of Korea', *Works*, vol. 3, 399.

20. It was the thin silver lining in the cloud of advances in labour-process innovation. See Harry Braverman, *Labour and Monopoly Capital: The Degradation of Work in the Twentieth Century* (New York: Monthly Review Press, 1974).

21. Kim Il Sung, in fact, boasted that the number of technical personnel increased from 497,000 in 1970 to 1 million in 1976. Kim Il Sung, 'New Year Address 1976', *Rodong Shinmun*, 1 January 1976.

22. The GDP growth rate in North Korea was 5.4 per cent in 1975, 3.8 per cent in 1980, -3.7 per cent in 1990, -7.6 per cent in 1992, -4.6 per cent in 1995, -3.7 per cent in 1996, -6.8 per cent in 1997, -1.1 per cent in 1998. Estimated by the Bank of Korea. See Ministry of Unification of the Republic of Korea, *Pukhanihae 2000* [Understanding North Korea 2000] (Seoul: Ministry of Unification, 2001), 153.

23. Savada, *North Korea*, 91.

24. See table 5.3, 'Changes in Occupational Structure among North Korean People', in T.H. Ok and H.Y. Lee, *Prospects for Change in North Korea* (Berkeley: University of California Press, 1994), 267.

25. Savada, *North Korea*, 59; Vreeland and Shinn, *Area Handbook*, 54.

26. Ok and Lee, *Prospects for Change*, 228, 267.

27. It wasn't that different in the South at the time, with massive discrimination and repression against those tainted with any family history of 'leftism'. For a specific example, see the introduction to Yi Mun-yol, *My Meeting with My Brother* (New York: Columbia University Press, 2017), or, more generally, Namhee Lee, *The Making of Minjung: Democracy and the Politics of Representation in South Korea* (Ithaca, NY: Cornell University Press, 2007).

28. Robert A. Scalapino and Chong-sik Lee, *North Korea: The Building of the Monolithic State* (Berwyn, PA: KHU Press, 2017), 325.

29. Kim Il Sung, 'Let Us Defend the Socialist Camp', *Rodong Shinmun*, 28 October 1963.

30. Adrian Buzo, *The Guerilla Dynasty: Politics and Leadership in North Korea* (Boulder, CO: Westview Press, 1999), 57–79.

31. *Rodong Shinmun*, 'Thwart the Manoeuvres to Split the International Communist Movement', 19 April 1964.

32. Kim Il Sung, 'The Present Situation and the Tasks of Our Party', report to the 5 October 1966 conference of the Korean Workers' Party, *Works*, vol. 4, 378.

33. Bon-hak Koo, *Political Economy of Self-Reliance: Juche and Economic Development in North Korea*, 1961–1990 (Seoul: Research Center for Peace and Unification of Korea, 1992), 123.

34. Kim Jong Il expressed his concern about the US–China rapprochement and the real intention of the US in Nixon's visit to China. See Kim Jong Il, 'Let Us Inspire the Young People with the Spirit of Continuous Revolution', speech to the senior officials of the Youth-Work Department of the Central Committee of the Workers' Party of Korea and of the Central Committee of the LSWY on 1 October 1971, in *Works*, vol. 2, 282.

35. A chronology of North Korea's stamps across the years show alternations between pro-Soviet and pro-Chinese issues that may give a better reflection of relations than official announcements. See *Korean Stamp Catalogue (1946–1998)* (Pyongyang: Korean Stamp Corporation, 1998).

36. Website of the Non-Aligned Movement, www.dirco.gov.za/foreign/ Multilateral/inter/nam.htm.

37. Benjamin R. Young, 'North Korea and the American Radical Left', Woodrow Wilson Center, North Korea International Documentation Project, 6 February 2013, www.wilsoncenter.org/publication/north-korea-and-the-american-radical-left.

38. Arunrasmy Norodom and Julio A. Jeldres, *A Life Dedicated to Cambodia* (Phnom Penh: HRH The Princess Royal Norodom Arunrasmy, 2012).

39. Sonia Ryang, *North Koreans in Japan: Language, Ideology and Identity* (Boulder, CO: Westview Press, 1977).

40. Kim Il Sung, 'For the Independent Unification of Korea', Report at the Celebrations of the 15th Anniversary of the August 15 Liberation, 1960.

41. Kim Il Sung, 'Independent Unification'.

42. Democratic Front for Reunification of the Fatherland, 'The Committee for Peaceful Reunification of the Fatherland Knew the Truth about the Abduction and Detention of Kim Dae Jung, a Democratic Prisoner of South Korea', Pyongyang, 16 September 1973.

43. Daniel P. Bolger, *Scenes from an Unfinished War: Low-Intensity Conflict – Korea, 1966–69* (Fort Leavenworth, KS: US Army Command and General Staff College, Combat Studies Institute, 1991).

44. Savada, *North Korea*, 261–62.

45. The list of people who were purged in the charge of opposition to the hereditary succession plan is shown in the 'chronology of purges by Kim Il Sung' in I.S. Lee, *North Korea: The Land That Never Changes* (Seoul: Naewoe Press, 1995), 19.

46. For a detailed study of the leadership in North Korea, see Soyoung Kwon, 'Changes in the Composition and Structures of the North Korean Elite', *International Journal of Korean Unification Studies* 12, no. 2 (2003).

4. Famine, Markets, Refugees, and Human Rights

1. Nicholas Eberstadt, Marc Rubin, and Albina Tretyakova, 'The Collapse of Soviet and Russian Trade with North Korea, 1989–1993', *Korean Journal of National Unification* 4 (1995): 87–104.

2. Stephan Haggard and Marcus Noland, *Famine in North Korea: Markets, Aid and Reform* (New York: Columbia University Press, 2007).

3. Andrew Natsios, *The Politics of Famine in North Korea* (Washington, DC: US Institute of Peace, 1999).

4. World Food Programme, 'Democratic People's Republic of North Korea', 2018, www1.wfp.org/countries/democratic-peoples-republic-korea.

5. Food and Agriculture Organisation of the United Nations and World Food Programme, 'Special Report, FAO/WFP Crop and Food Supply Assessment Mission to the Democratic People's Republic of Korea', 22 December 1995.

6. Haggard and Noland, *Famine in North Korea.* 130.

7. European Parliament, Resolution on the Famine in North Korea, 23 October 1997 (OJ C 339, 10.11.1997), 153.

8. European Parliament, Resolution on the Food Crisis in North Korea, 12 March 1998 (OJ C 104, 6.4.1998), 236.

9. See the report of the Parliament ad hoc delegation that visited the Democratic People's Republic of Korea in December 1998, PE 229.331.

10. Material in this section was first published as Glyn Ford, 'Through the Looking Glass: Alice in Asia', *Soundings* 18 (Summer/Autumn 2001), 75–76.

11. European Parliament, Resolution on the Food Crisis in North Korea, 3 December 1998; see also Resolution on Relations between the European Union and the Democratic People's Republic of Korea, 23 March 1999.

12. UNICEF, 'Analysis of the Situation of Children and Women in the Democratic People's Republic of Korea', October 2003, http: //www.unicef.org/dprk/situationanalysis.pdf.

13. Kate Pound Dawson, 'DPRK Seeks Shift in Aid to Grow Economy, Prevent Hunger', *Voice of America News*, 30 September 2004.

14. Glyn Ford, 'Feeding the Famine: The European Union's Response to North Korea', *38 North*, 12 July 2011.

15. Quoted in Bradley K. Martin, *Under the Loving Care of the Fatherly Leader: North Korea and the Kim Dynasty* (New York: Macmillan, 2006), 517.

16. For detailed description of change inside North Korea, see Food and Agriculture Organisation of the United Nations and World Food Programme, 'Special Report, FAO/WFP Crop and Food Supply Assessment Mission to the Democratic People's Republic of Korea', 11 November 2004, www.wfp.org/content/dpr-korea-faowfp-crop-and-food-supply-assessment-mission-november-2004.

17. Kim Jong Il, 'Historical Lesson in Building Socialism and the General Line of Our Party', speech delivered 3 January 1992, published in *Rodong Shinmun*, 4 February 1992, and broadcast on the same day by KCNA, transcribed by *FBIS*, East Asia, 92–024, 5 February 1992, 11–24.

18. Kim Jong Il, 'Historical Lesson', 23.

19. Kongdan Oh and Ralph Hassig, *North Korea Through the Looking Glass* (Washington, DC: Brookings Institution, 2000), 30.

20. Speech given by Kim Jong Il on the 50th Anniversary of Kim Il Sung University, quoted in Martin, *Under the Loving Care*, 831n21.

21. *Rodong Shinmun*, 'Let Us See and Solve All Problems from a New Perspective and a New Height', 9 January 2001. The so-called 'innovation in thinking and work attitude' in building an economically prosperous country, however, first appeared in a *Rodong Shinmun* editorial on 4 January 2001.

22. USA for UNHCR, 'What Is a Refugee?' n.d., www.unrefugees.org/ refugee-facts/what-is-a-refugee.

23. Baek Jieun, *North Korea's Hidden Revolution: How the Information Underground Is Transforming a Closed Society* (New Haven, CT: Yale University Press, 2017).

24. Daniel Gordon (dir.), *The Game of Their Lives* (London: BBC, 2002).

25. I met and paid Kang Chol Hwan for an interview around 2002.

26. Blaine Harden, *Escape from Camp 14* (London: Pan, 2015).

27. Song Jiyoung, 'Why Do North Korean Defector Testimonies So Often Fall Apart?' *Guardian,* 13 October 2015, www.theguardian.com/ world/2015/oct/13/why-do-north-korean-defector-testimonies-so-often-fall-apart.

28. Blaine Harden, *Rescapé du Camp 14* (Paris: Belfond, 2012).

29. Mary Ann Jolley, 'The Strange Story of Yeonmi Park', *Diplomat,* 10 December 2014, https://thediplomat.com/2014/12/the-strange-tale-of-yeonmi-park/.

30. Antony Barnett, 'Revealed: The Gas Chamber Horror of North Korea's Gulag', *Guardian,* 31 January 2004, www.theguardian.com/world/2004/ feb/01/northkorea.

31. KCNA, 'Western "Standards of Human Rights" Cannot Work', 5 August 1993.

32. This is based on the Vienna Declaration of the European Union of 10 December 1998.

33. For reference, see: Bertin Lintner, 'Shop Till You Drop', *Far Eastern Economic Review,* 13 May 2004; Andrew Ward, 'Hermit Kingdom Peeps Cautiously Out of Its Shell', *Financial Times,* 12 February 2004;

Jonathan Watts, 'How North Korea Is Embracing Capitalism by Any Other Name', *Guardian*, 3 December 2003; Anthony Faiola, 'A Crack in the Door in North Korea', *Washington Post*, 24 November 2003; James Brooke, 'Quietly, North Korea Opens Markets', *New York Times*, 21 November 2003; Anthony Faiola, 'North Korea Shifts Toward Capitalism', *Washington Post*, 14 September 2003.

34. US Congress, 'North Korea: Status Report on Nuclear Program, Humanitarian Issues, and Economic Reforms' 23 February 2004.

5. Kim Jong Un

1. Andrei Lankov, 'Is Byungjin Policy Failing? Kim Jong Un's Unannounced Reform and Its Chances of Success', *Korean Journal of Defence Analysis* 29, no. 1 (2017), 26.
2. Daniel Tudor and James Pearson, *North Korea Confidential: Private Markets, Fashion Trends, Prison Camps, Dissenters and Defectors* (Rutland, VT: Tuttle, 2015), 58.
3. Lankov, 'Is Byungjin Policy Failing?' 31.
4. Tudor and Pearson, *North Korea Confidential*, 177.
5. In reality it's a decent tarmacked road and no more, but nevertheless of a superior standard to the remaining roads in Rason.
6. The 2007 North–South Summit did discuss the possibility of further SEZs linked to the South, but nothing came of the proposals, as President Roh Moo-hyun's successor, Lee Myung-bak, adopted a hard-line strategy towards the North.
7. Andray Abrahamian, Geoffrey K. See, and Wang Xingyu, *The ABCs of North Korea's SEZs* (Washington, DC: US-Korea Institute at SAIS, 2014).
8. Lankov 'Is Byungjin Policy Failing? 28.

6. Daily Life in North Korea

1. Private communication with a Politburo member, September 2014.
2. Baek Jieun, *North Korea's Hidden Revolution: How the Information Underground Is Transforming a Closed Society* (New Haven, CT: Yale University Press, 2017).
3. Kim Chaek was a partisan who fought alongside Kim Il Sung and was killed in 1951 during the Korean War. One of the very few outside the Kim family to be so honoured, he has, in addition to the university, a stadium, a steel works, and a city in his name.
4. Ryang, *North Koreans in Japan*.

5. In September 2017 the BBC launched a Korean-language channel for the first time. Quite what persuaded them of a gap in this already over-crowded market is unclear. George Orwell wasted most of the war years producing talks for the BBC's India Service and failed to discover any listeners after the war.

6. Kim Il Sung, 'On Creating Revolutionary Literature and Art', speech to workers in the field of literature and art, 7 November 1964, *Works*, vol. 4, 163.

7. Byungmook Lim, Jongbae Park, and Changyon Han, 'Attempts to Utilize and Integrate Traditional Medicine in North Korea', *Journal of Alternative and Complementary Medicine* 15, no. 3 (March 2009).

8. World Health Organization, *World Malaria Report 2017* (Geneva: World Health Organization, 2018), www.who.int/malaria/publications/world-malaria-report-2017/en/.

9. Associated Press, 'No College for North Korean Smokers,' *Taipei Times*, 13 June 2006, www.taipeitimes.com/News/lang/archives/2006/06/13/2003313383.

10. The eighteen-month mango cult, starting in 1968, is just one bizarre exemplar. See Alfreda Murck (ed.), *Mao's Golden Mangoes and the Cultural Revolution* (Zurich: Museum Rietberg Zürich, Scheidegger & Spiess, 2013).

11. Pyongyang too has its 'communist crimes'. James Church (pseud.) has published six books so far in his Inspector O series. The first, *Corpse in the Koryo* (2007), is a warning for the Western delegations that normally stop in the Koryo Hotel when they visit Pyongyang.

12. For detailed history, organisation, and function of the Ministry of People's Security and its bureaus, see Jon Hyun-Jun, *A Study of the Social Control System in North Korea: Focusing on the Ministry of People's Security* (Seoul: Korea Institute for National Unification, 2003).

13. These include Camp 11 (women-only, in Jeung-san in South Pyongan Province); Camp 33 (for juvenile delinquents, in Sook-chon in South Pyongan Province); Camp 55 (Hyongje mountain area in Pyongyang); Camp 66 (Dong-rim in North Pyongan Province); Camp 77 (Dan-chon in North Hamgyong Province); and Camp 88 (Wonsan in Kangwon Province).

14. See David Hawk, *The Hidden Gulag,* 2nd ed. (Washington, DC: Committee for Human Rights in North Korea, 2012). They include Camp 14 (Kaechon, South Pyongan Province); Camp 15 (Yodok family camp, South Hamgyong Province); Camp 16 (Hwasong, North Hamgyong Province); Camp 18 (Puk-chang Kun, South Pyongan

Province); Camp 22 (Huiryong in North Hamgyong Province); and
Camp 25 (Chongjin family camp, North Hamgyong Province).

15. Ali Lameda, *A Personal Account of a Prisoner of Conscience in the Democratic People's Republic of Korea* (London: Amnesty International, 1979).

7. The Nuclear Factor

1. Jeffrey Lewis, 'Patriot Missiles Are Made in America and Fail Everywhere', *Foreign Policy* (28 March 2018).

2. This has been the standard Party line for a decade and more.

3. Christine Kim and Ben Blanchard, 'North Korea Missile Technology Not Perfected Yet: South Korea', Reuters, 13 August 2017, www.usnews. com/news/world/articles/2017-08-13/north-korea-still-needs-time-to-perfect-re-entry-technology-south-korea-vice-defense-minister.

4. US State Department Senior Official, personal communication, July 2017.

5. Excerpt from Central Intelligence Agency, 'Estimate of North Korea Missile Force Trends', in *Department of Defense, Proliferation and Response* (Washington, DC: US Government Printing Office, 2002).

6. North Koreans are now Hollywood's favourite villains. They have replaced a long line of others. The choice is driven by politics and, more recently, economics. For obvious reasons, in the 1940s the villains were Germans – and Japanese – who gave way to the Russians and their fellow travellers with the Cold War. The Japanese returned for a walk-on part in the eighties as Tokyo's economy threatened to hollow out American industry, while the Russians gave way to the Chinese with the collapse of the Soviet empire. Films after 9/11 played to Muslim terrorists, but the North has led the recruitment of evildoers to the screen. The 2012 remake of the 1984 Soviet-invasion thriller *Red Dawn* was originally intended to have Chinese Red Army parachutists descending on Washington State, but the threat to box-office takings there saw the North Koreans brought on as last-minute substitutes.

In the 1950s three films featured North Korea, and in the subsequent 30 years there have been another three – one every decade (in 1962 it was *The Manchurian Candidate*). North Koreans took off as screen villains from the beginning of this century, with 15 films in the first decade and a second 15 in the subsequent five years. Save for a handful of South Korean films – *Joint Security Area* (2000) and *The Berlin File* (2013) – North Koreans have been depicted with few saving graces. They torture Pierce Brosnan's James Bond in *Die Another Day* (2002) and Angelina Jolie in *Salt* (2010). They are cartoon tyrants in *Team America: World Police* (2004) and the infamous *The Interview* (2014), while in *Olympus Has Fallen* (2013), Morgan Freeman sees them take down the White House, brutally murdering dozens of staff.

TV is little better, as series throw North Koreans into the mix. Kim Jong Il got a cameo on *South Park* (2003) and the remade *Hawaii 5-0* (2010), now passing into its ninth season, sees North Korea and North Koreans as a regular feature. Series two of *Blindspot* (2016) has Pyongyang plotting a sneak nuclear attack on the US mainland, and the fifth season of *30 Rock* (2010) has Alec Baldwin rescuing his kidnapped wife from North Korea. It's spreading into novels, too: David Baldacci's *The Target* (New York: Macmillan, 2014) features a crazed North Korean assassin from the prison camps. Adam Johnson's *The Orphan Master's Son* (New York: Random House, 2012) is a very different story, but twice I've had people try to discuss elements of the book with me as if it were real. I've had to say, 'It's a novel!'

7. Michelle Nichols, 'North Korea Says Linking Cyber Attacks to Pyongyang Is "Ridiculous"', Reuters, 19 May 2017, www.reuters.com/ article/us-cyber-attack-northkorea/north-korea-says-linking-cyber-attacks-to-pyongyang-is-ridiculous-idUSKCN18F1X3.

8. Theresa Locker, 'You Can Now Install the Original North Korean Operating System RedStar 3.0', *Motherboard*, 7 January 2015, https:// motherboard.vice.com/en_us/article/pgaxa9/you-can-now-install-the-north-korean-operating-system-redstar-30; Dan Goodin, '>10,000 Windows Computers May Be Infected by Advanced NSA Backdoor', *Ars Technica*, 21 April 2017, https://arstechnica.com/information-technology/2017/04/10000-windows-computers-may-be-infected-by-advanced-nsa-backdoor.

9. Mark Bowden, 'The Worst Problem on Earth: Here's How to Deal with North Korea. It's Not Going to be Pretty', *Atlantic* (July/August 2017), 66–77.

10. This point was made by William Perry, the former Defence Secretary, at the State Department; and by Philip W. Yun, who served as a State Department official from 1994 to 2001. Quoted from my meeting with Perry and Yun at the Asia Pacific Research Center, Stanford University, on 3 February 2005.

11. Scott Sagan, 'The Korean Missile Crisis', *Foreign Affairs* (November/ December 2017).

12. Carter tried to repeat his trick in October 2017. Both Trump and Pyongyang said no.

13. Robert A. Wampler (ed.), 'North Korea's Collapse? The End is Near – Maybe', *National Security Archive Electronic Briefing Book* 205, 26 October 2006.

14. *Rodong Shinmun*, 4 April 2001; 11 May 2001; 20 June 2001.

15. Julian Borger, 'Two Minutes to Midnight: How US Diplomatic Failure Sped Up North Korea's Nuclear Race', *Guardian*, 30 March 2018.

16. CNN, 'Rumsfeld: North Korea May Have Nuclear Weapons Already', 17 October 2002, www.cnn.com/2002/US/10/17/us.nkorea/.

17. In the KCNA report, the North Korean Foreign Ministry stated that the DPRK was 'entitled to possess not only nuclear weapons but any type of weapon more powerful than that so as to defend its sovereignty and right to existence from the ever-growing nuclear threat by the US', KCNA, 25 October 2002; for details of the controversial 'confession', see 'North Korean Nuclear 'Admission' in Doubt', BBC News, 18 November 2002, http://news.bbc.co.uk/2/hi/asia-pacific/2487437.stm.

18. I spoke to Kang Suk Ju in October 2013 and James Kelly in August 2017 about this meeting. Both held the line, although Kelly added that, come what may, Congress would never have approved the imminent transfer of sensitive nuclear technology to Pyongyang.

19. The term the US constantly uses is *pre-emptive*, to forestall an attack, which has some legal basis in international law. In reality, any such attack would at best be *preventive*, to stop the process of them beginning to acquire nuclear weapons. This has no legal basis. I use the appropriate term.

20. William Langewiesche, 'The Point of No Return', *Atlantic* (January/February 2006), 111.

21. A cargo ship with aluminium destined for the North Korean firm Nam Chon Gang. See Georg Mascolo, 'Nuclear Smuggling: A Smoking Gun', trans. by Margot Bettauer Dembo, *Der Spiegel*, 7 July 2003, www.spiegel.de/international/spiegel/nuclear-smuggling-a-smoking-gun-a-256226.html.

22. The sixth – and possibly fifth – test may have used a mixed charge of plutonium and HEU, plus tritium, to both boost the yield and eke out limited supplies of weapons-grade plutonium. The claim was that they had a new standard weapon for mass production to fit on the Hwasong. See Jeffrey Lewis, 'North Korea's Nuke Program is Way More Sophisticated Than You Think', *Foreign Policy* (9 September 2016).

23. Nuclear Threat Initiative, 'North Korea', updated July 2017, www.nti.org/learn/countries/north-korea/delivery-systems/.

24. Andrea M. Savada (ed.), *North Korea: A Country Study* (Washington, DC: Library of Congress, 1994), 259–60.

25. Norodom Sihanouk, *Shadow Over Angkor: Memoirs of His Majesty King Norodom Sihanouk of Cambodia*, vol. 1 (Phnom Penh: Monument Books, 2005), 152.

26. John Sweeney, *North Korea Undercover* (London: Bantam, 2014); and my review: Glyn Ford, 'Close Shave for Sweeney Tosh', *Tribune*, 9 May 2014.

27. Nuclear Threat Initiative, 'Libya Nuclear Chronology', last updated February 2011, www.nti.org/media/pdfs/libya_nuclear.pdf.

28. Julian Borger, 'Two Minutes to Midnight: Did the US Miss Its Chance to Stop North Korea's Nuclear Programme?' *Guardian*, 30 March 2018, www.theguardian.com/news/2018/mar/30/north-korea-us-nuclear-diplomacy-agreed-framework-1999-pyongyang-mission.

29. John Bolton, *Surrender Is Not an Option: Defending America at the United Nations* (New York: Simon & Schuster, 2008), 103.

30. The US is building a three-tier anti-ballistic-missile defence system. The lower tier is the TMD, designed to defend against short-range missiles. This system was jointly developed and deployed by the US and Japan. The second level is THAAD, which is devised to destroy intermediate to large missiles. The third tier is NMD, which consists of long-range anti-ballistic missiles based in the US.

31. Constitution of Japan, November 3, 1946; the Japanese government's official English translation is available at https://japan.kantei.go.jp/constitution_and_government_of_japan/constitution_e.html.

32. Lewis, 'Patriot Missiles'.

33. Chris Mooney, *The Republican War on Science* (New York: Basic Books, 2005).

34. Quoted in Hans M. Kristensen and Robert S. Norris, 'Chinese Nuclear Forces, 2011', *Bulletin of the Atomic Scientists* 67, no. 6 (2011): 81–87.

35. Léonie Allard, Mathieu Duchâtel, and François Godement, *Preempting Defeat: In Search of North Korea's Nuclear Doctrine* (Berlin: European Council on Foreign Relations, 22 November 2017).

36. Under South Korea's Presidential Election Act (1987), the president is directly elected for one non-renewable five-year term.

37. Responding to criticisms raised by North Koreans of the term 'Sunshine Policy', the name was later changed to a 'Reconciliation and Cooperation Policy' towards North Korea.

38. *China Daily*, 'Kim Jong-il Wishes to Visit Seoul – Report', 4 July 2004, www.chinadaily.com.cn/english/doc/2004-07/04/content_345372.htm.

39. For the contents and achievements of Kim Dae Jung administration's 'Sunshine Policy' towards North Korea, see Ministry of Unification,

Promoting Peace and Cooperation (Seoul: Ministry of Unification, Republic of Korea, 2003). Also visit the website: www.unikorea.go.kr.

40. Condoleeza Rice, *No Higher Honor: A Memoir of My Years in Washington* (New York: Crown, 2011), 2; Robert Gates, *Duty: Memoirs of a Secretary at War* (New York: Alfred A. Knopf, 2014), 416.

41. Choe Sang-hun, 'Despair Overwhelmed Former South Korean Leader Embroiled in Scandal', *New York Times*, 23 May 2009, www.nytimes.com/2009/05/24/world/asia/24roh.html.

42. I was at Masrikryong on 1 February 2018 and saw the South's skiers before they left.

43. Private sources in Beijing and Pyongyang.

8.   Foreign Affairs

1. Shortly after the release of US citizen Otto Warmbier, the Ministry of Foreign Affairs informed the Swedish Embassy that it was no longer considered the 'protecting power' for US citizens.

2. Technically, the DPRK ambassador to the EU is not accredited to Brussels, which would require unanimity in the council. Only the First Secretary and the rest are accredited as they only require a qualified majority.

3. David Cyranoski, 'DNA Is Burning Issue as Japan and Korea Clash over Kidnaps', *Nature* 433 (3 February 2005).

4. Quoted in Gavan McCormack, 'Disputed Bones: Japan, North Korea and the *Nature* Controversy', *Asia-Pacific Journal* 3, no. 4 (27 April 2005), https://apjjf.org/-Gavan-McCormack/1949/article.html.

5. *Nature* 'Politics Versus Reality', editorial, *Nature* 434 (17 March 2005), www.nature.com/articles/434257a.

6. Twelve members of the Japanese Communist League – Red Army Faction hijacked Japan Airlines Flight 351 in an attempt to defect to Cuba. Armed with samurai swords and pipe bombs, they seized the plane in the name of the iconic working-class boxer Joe Yabuki from the manga *Ashita no Joe*. The plane didn't have the range to cross the Pacific and they ended up in Pyongyang. One of the hijackers was Moriaki Wakabayashi, bass player with the cult rock band Les Rallizes Dénudés and a hard-core fan of Liverpool FC. Another member of the band overslept and missed the hijacking. No one was killed or injured.

7. Jane Perlez and Yufan Huang, 'China Says Its Trade with North Korea Has Increased', *New York Times*, 13 April 2017, www.nytimes.com/2017/04/13/world/asia/china-north-korea-trade-coal-nuclear.html.

8. Reality failed to match rhetoric. A Chinese diplomat serving in their Pyongyang embassy at the time reported that relations were frigid in the extreme.
9. State Department official, personal communication, December 2017.
10. Ben Kesling and Alistair Gale, 'Trump's North Korean Obstacle: Sanctions Are Unevenly Enforced' *Wall Street Journal*, 25 April 2017.
11. KCNA
12. European Union, *EU – Democratic People's Republic of Korea (DPRK) Country Strategy Paper 2001–2004*, n.d., http://eeas.europa.eu/archives/docs/korea_north/docs/01_04_en.pdf.

9. Conclusion

1. Apart from procedural matters, the UNSC has passed eleven sanctions resolutions between 2006 and 2018: two in 2006, two in 2009, one in 2013, one in 2016, four in 2017, and one in 2018.
2. Rex Tillerson, speech at the Atlantic Council's Korea Foundation Forum, 12 December 2017, Washington, DC.
3. *Guardian*, 'US and South Korea to Announce Suspension of "Large-Scale" Military Drill', 17 June 2018, www.theguardian.com/world/2018/jun/17/us-south-korea-north-korea-large-scale-military-drills-trump.

Bibliography and Further Reading

Abrahamian, Andray. *North Korea and Myanmar: Divergent Paths* (Jefferson, NC: McFarland & Co., 2018).

Adams, Clarence. *An American Dream: The Life of an African American Soldier and POW Who Spent Twelve Years in Communist China,* edited by Delia Adams and Lewis H. Carlson (Amherst: University of Massachusetts Press, 2007).

Akaha, Tsuneo (Ed.). *The Future of North Korea* (London: Routledge, 2002).

Albright, David, and Kevin O'Neill (Eds.). *Solving the North Korean Nuclear Puzzle* (Washington, DC: Institute for Science and International Security, 2000).

Albright, David. *Peddling Peril: How the Secret Nuclear Trade Arms America's Enemies* (New York: Free Press, 2010).

An, Tai Sung. *North Korea in Transition: From Dictatorship to Dynasty* (Westport, CT: Greenwood Press, 1983).

Armstrong, Charles K. *The North Korean Revolution, 1945–1950* (Ithaca, NY: Cornell University Press, 2003).

Armstrong, Charles K. *Tyranny of the Weak: North Korea and the World, 1950–1992* (Ithaca, NY: Cornell University Press, 2013).

Baek Jieun. *North Korea's Hidden Revolution: How the Information Underground is Transforming a Closed Society* (New Haven, CT: Yale University Press, 2016).

Beal, Tim. *North Korea: The Struggle Against American Power* (London: Pluto Press, 2005).

Beal, Tim. *Crisis in Korea: America, China and the Risk of War* (London: Pluto Press, 2011).

Bechtol, Bruce E. Jr. *Red Rogue: The Persistent Challenge of North Korea* (Washington, DC: Potomac Books, 2007).

Bechtol, Bruce E. Jr. *The Last Days of Kim Jong-Il: The North Korea Threat in a Changing Era* (Washington, DC: Potomac Books, 2013).

Becker, Jasper. *Rogue Regime: Kim Jong Il and the Looming Threat of North Korea* (New York: Oxford University Press, 2005).

Bender, Xiomara. *North Korea: The Power of Dreams* (Berlin: Kehrer, 2016).

Bermudez, Joseph S. Jr. *North Korean Special Forces,* 2nd ed. (Annapolis, MD: Naval Institute Press, 1998).

Bermudez, Joseph S. Jr. *The Armed Forces of North Korea* (London: I.B. Tauris, 2001).

Bijl, William van der, and R.J.C.M. de Groen. *The World According to Kim Jong Il* (Utrecht: Centre for Korean Studies, Leiden University, 2004).

Bleiker, Roland, *Divided Korea: Towards a Culture of Reconciliation,* (Minneapolis: University of Minneapolis Press, 2005).

Bolger, Daniel P. *Scenes from an Unfinished War: Low-Intensity Conflict in Korea, 1966–1969* (Leavenworth, KS: Combat Studies Institute, 1989).

Bonner, Nick. *Made in North Korea: Graphics from Everyday Life in the DPRK* (London: Phaidon, 2017).

Bonner, Nick, and Anna Barraclough. *Common Ground* (Beijing: Koryo, 2010).

Boynton, Robert S. *The Invitation-Only Zone* (New York: Farrar, Straus and Giroux, 2016).

Breuer, William B. *Shadow Warriors: The Covert War in Korea* (New York: John Wiley, 1996).

Breen, Michael. *Kim Jong-Il: North Korea's Dear Leader,* 2nd ed. (New York: John Wiley, 2012).

Burn, Ellen, and Jacques Hersh. *Socialist Korea: A Case Study in the Strategy of Economic Development* (New York: Monthly Review Press, 1976).

Bussey, Charles M. *Firefight at Yechon: Courage and Racism in the Korean War* (Lincoln: University of Nebraska Press, 1991).

Buzo, Adrian. *The Guerrilla Dynasty: Politics and Leadership in North Korea,* (London: I.B. Tauris, 1999).

Buzo, Adrian. *The Making of Modern Korea* (London: Routledge, 2002).

Carlin, Robert L., and Joel S. Wit. *North Korean Reform: Politics, Economics and Security* (London: IISS, 2006).

Caprio, Mark E. *Japanese Assimilation Policies in Colonial Korea 1910–1945* (Seattle: University of Washington Press, 2009).

Carpenter, Ted Galen, and Doug Bandow. *The Korean Conundrum: America's Troubled Relations with North and South Korea* (New York: Palgrave, 2004).

Caruthers, Susan L. *Cold War Captives: Imprisonment, Escape and Brainwashing* (Berkeley: University of California Press, 2009).

Casey, Steven. *Selling the Korean War: Propaganda, Politics and Public Opinion 1950–1953* (New York: Oxford University Press, 2008).

Cha, John H., and K.J. Sohn. *Exit Emperor Kim Jong-il* (Bloomington, IN: Abbott Press, 2012).

Cha, Victor. *The Impossible State: North Korea, Past and Future* (New York: HarperCollins, 2012).

Cha, Victor, and David C. Kang. *Nuclear North Korea: A Debate on Engagement Strategies* (New York: Columbia University Press, 2003).

Chang, Gordon G. *Nuclear Showdow: North Korea Takes On the World* (New York: Random, 2006).

Chen, Jian. *China's Road to the Korean War: The Making of the Sino-American Confrontation* (New York: Columbia University Press, 1994).

Chen, Jian. *Mao's China and the Cold War* (Chapel Hill: University of North Carolina Press, 2001).

Coles, T.J. *Fire and Fury: How the US Isolates North Korea, Encircles China and Risks Nuclear War in Asia* (West Hoathly, UK: Clairview, 2017).

Coleman, Craig S. *American Images of Korea* (Seoul: Hollym, 1990).

Condron, Andrew M., Richard G. Corden, and Larance Sullivan. *Thinking Soldiers: By Men Who Fought in Korea*, (Peking: New World Press, 1955).

Cope, Julian. *Japrocksampler: How the Post-War Japanese Blew Their Minds on Rock 'n' Roll* (London: Bloomsbury, 2007).

Corera, Gordon. *Shopping for Bombs: Nuclear Proliferation, Global Insecurity and the Rise and Fall of the A.Q. Khan Network* (London: Hurst, 2006).

Corfield, Justin. *Historical Dictionary of Pyongyang* (London: Anthem Press, 2014).

Cornell, Erik. *North Korea Under Communism* (London: Routledge Curzon, 2002).

Crane, Charlie. *Welcome to Pyongyang* (London: Chris Boot, 2007).

Csoma, Mozes. *From North Korea to Budapest: North Korean Students in the Hungarian Revolution in 1956* (Seoul: Jimoondang, 2016).

Cucullu, Gordon. *Separated at Birth: How North Korea Became the Evil Twin* (Guilford, UK: Lyons Press, 2004).

Cummings, Bruce. *The Origins of the Korean War*, 2 volumes (Princeton, NJ: Princeton University Press, 1981 [vol 1], 1990 [vol 2]).

Cummings, Bruce. *North Korea: Another Country* (New York: New Press, 2004).

Cummings, Bruce, Ervand Abrahamian, and Moshe Ma'oz. *Inventing the Axis of Evil: The Truth about North Korea, Iran, and Syria* (New York: New Press, 2004).

Cunningham, Cyril. *No Mercy, No Leniency: Communist Mistreatment of British and Allied Prisoners of War in Korea* (Barnsley, UK: Leo Cooper, 2000).

Cwiertka, Katarzyna J. *Cuisine, Colonialism and Cold War: Food in Twentieth-Century Korea* (London: Reaktion Books, 2012).

Daniels, Anthony. *The Wilder Shores of Marx: Journeys in a Vanishing World* (London: Hutchinson, 1991).

Danisman, Hasan Basri. *Korea 1952: Situation Negative! An Account of Service with the Turkish Brigade* (Istanbul: Denizler Kitabevi, 2002).

Danziger, Nick. *Above the Line: People and Places in the DPRK (North Korea)* (London: British Council, 2014).

Delisle, Guy. *Pyongyang: A Journey in North Korea* (Montreal: Drawn & Quarterly, 2005).

Demick, Barbara. *Nothing to Envy: Real Lives in North Korea* (London: Granta, 2010).

Democratic People's Republic of Korea. *Facts Tell: Secret Documents Seized by North Korea from the South Korean Government Archives* (Honolulu: University Press of the Pacific, 2001).

Dowdey, Patrick (Ed.). *Living Through the Forgotten War: Portrait of Korea* (New York: Wesleyan University & Korea Society, 2003).

Fahy, Sandra. *Marching Through Suffering: Loss and Survival in North Korea* (New York: Columbia University Press, 2013).

Fehrenbach, T.R. *This Kind of War* (Washington, DC: Brassey's, [1963] 1994).

Fischer, Paul. *A Kim Jong-il Production* (London: Viking, 2015).

Ford, Glyn. 'Through the Looking Glass: Alice in Asia', *Soundings* 18 (Summer/Autumn 2001): pp. 64–81.

Ford, Glyn. 'North Korea in Transition', *Soundings* 43 (Winter 2009): pp. 125–34.

Ford, Glyn. 'Continuity through Change: North Korea's Second Succession', *Soundings* 52 (Winter 2012): pp. 113–25.

Ford, Glyn. 'The Pyongyang Paradox', *Soundings* 67 (Winter 2017–18): pp. 135–46.

Ford, Glyn, with Soyoung Kwon. *North Korea on the Brink: Struggle for Survival* (London: Pluto, 2008).

Frazier, Robeson Taj. *The East is Black: Cold War China in the Black Radical Imagination* (Durham, NC: Duke University Press, 2015).

French, Paul. *North Korea: The Paranoid Peninsula, A Modern History* (London: Zed Books, 2005).

French, Paul. *North Korea: State of Paranoia* (London: Zed Books, 2014).

Funabashi, Yoichi. *The Peninsula Question: A Chronicle of the Second Korean Nuclear Crisis* (Washington, DC: Brookings, 2007).

Gavroussenko, Tatiana. *Soldiers on the Cultural Front: Developments in the Early History of North Korean Literature and Literary Policy* (Honolulu: University of Hawaii Press, 2010).

Goncharov, Sergei, N., John W. Lewis, and Xue Litai. *Uncertain Partners: Stalin, Mao, and the Korean War* (Stanford, CA: Stanford University Press, 1993).

Ha Tae Keung. *The Great Successor: Kim Jong Un* (Seoul: Hungry Dictator Press, 2012).

Haggard, Stephan, and Marcus Noland. *Famine in North Korea: Markets, Aid, and Reform* (New York: Columbia University Press, 2007).

Haggard, Stephan, and Marcus Noland. *Hard Target: Sanctions, Inducements, and the Case of North Korea* (Stanford, CA: Stanford University Press, 2017).

Hanley, Charles, J., Cho Sang-hun, and Martha Mendoza. *The Bridge at No Gun Ri: A Hidden Nightmare from the Korean War* (New York: Henry Holt, 2001).

Harden, Blaine. *Escape from Camp 14* (London: Pan, 2015).

Harden, Blaine. *The Great Leader and the Fighter Pilot: The True Story of the Tyrant Who Created North Korea and the Young Lieutenant Who Stole His Way to Freedom* (Basingstoke, UK: Mantle, 2015).

Harris, Mark Edward. *Inside North Korea* (San Francisco: Chronicle Books, 2007).

Harrison, Selig S. *Korean Endgame: A Strategy for Reunification and US Disengagement* (Princeton, NJ: Princeton University Press, 2002).

Harrold, Michael. *Comrades and Strangers: Behind the Closed Doors of North Korea* (New York: John Wiley, 2004).

Hartley, Tim. *Kicking Off in North Korea: Football and Friendship in Foreign Lands* (Talybont: Y Lolfa, 2016).

Hartman, Eddo. *Setting the Stage: North Korea* (Furnes: Hannibal, 2017).

Hastings, Max. *The Korean War* (London: Papermac, 1993).

Hassig, Ralph, and Kongdan Oh. *The Hidden People of North Korea: Everyday Life in the Hermit Kingdom* (Lanham, MD: Rowman & Littlefield, 2015).

Heather, David, and Koen de Ceuster. *North Korean Posters* (London: Prestel, 2008).

Helgesen, Geir, and Hatla Thells. *Dialogue with North Korea? Preconditions for Talking Human Rights with a Hermit Kingdom* (Copenhagen: Nias Press, 2013).

Hoare, James E. *Historical Dictionary of the Democratic People's Republic of Korea* (Lanham, MD: Scarecrow Press, 2012).

Hooper, Beverley. *Foreigners Under Mao: Western Lives in China, 1949–1976* (Hong Kong: Hong Kong University Press, 2016).

Hwang, Su-kyoung. *Korea's Grievous War* (Philadelphia: University of Pennsylvania Press, 2016).

Institute of South-North Korea Studies. *The Human Rights Situation in North Korea: The Reality of Self-Styled Paradise* (Seoul: Institute of South-North Korea Studies, 1992).

International Institute for Strategic Studies. *North Korea's Weapons Programmes: A Net Assessment* (London: IISS, 2004).

International Scientific Commission for the Investigation of the Facts Concerning Bacterial Warfare in Korea and China. *Report* (Prague: Hsinhua News Agency, 1952).

Iverson, Shepherd. *Stop North Korea! A Radical New Approach to the North Korean Standoff* (Tokyo: Tuttle Publishing, 2017).

Jäger, Sheila Kiyoshi. *Brothers at War: The Unending Conflict in Korea* (London: Profile Books, 2013).

Jang, Jin-sung. *Dear Leader* (London: Rider, 2014).

Jenkins, Charles Robert, with Jim Frederick. *The Reluctant Communist: My Desertion, Court-Martial, and Forty-Year Imprisonment in North Korea* (Berkeley: University of California Press, 2008).

Jon, Chol Nam. *A Duel of Reason between Korea and US: Nuke, Missile and Artificial Satellite*, (Pyongyang: Foreign Languages Publishing House, 2000).

Jo, Am, and An Chol Gang (Eds.). *Korea in the 20th Century* (Pyongyang: Foreign Languages Publishing House, 2002).

Jung, Chang Hyun. *Kim Jong Il in North Korea* (Seoul: Joongang Books, 2009).

Kang, Chol Hwan and Pierre Rigoulot. *The Aquariums of Pyongyang* (London: Atlantic, 2006).

Kang, Hyok. *This is Paradise! My North Korean Childhood* (London: Abacus, 2005).

Kang, Minsoo (Trans.). *The Story of Hong Gildong* (London: Penguin, 2016).

Kim, Suzy. *Everyday Life in the North Korean Revolution, 1945–1950* (Ithaca, NY: Cornell University Press, 2013).

Kim, Sung Chull. *North Korea Under Kim Jong Il: From Consolidation to Systemic Dissonance* (Albany, NY: State University of New York Press, 2006).

Kim, Suk Hi, Terence Roehrig, and Bernhard Seliger. *The Survival of North Korea: Essays on Strategy, Economics, and International Relations* (Jefferson, NC: McFarland & Co., 2011).

Kim, Samuel S. *North Korean Foreign Relations in the Post-Cold War Era* (Hong Kong: Oxford University Press, 1998).

Kim, Kyoung-soo. *North Korea's Weapons of Mass Destruction: Problems and Prospects* (Seoul: Hollym, 2004).

Kim, Joungwon. *Divided Korea: The Politics of Development 1945–1972* (Seoul: Hollym, 1997).

Kim, Victoria. 'The Korean Diaspora in Uzbekistan', *Journal of the Royal Asiatic Society China* 77 (2017): pp. 48–55.

Kinkead, Eugene. *Why They Collaborated* (London: Longmans, 1959).

Kirk, Donald. *Korea Betrayed: Kim Dae Jung and Sunshine* (New York: Palgrave Macmillan, 2009).

Kirkbride, Wayne A. *Panmunjom: Facts about the Korean DMZ* (Seoul: Hollym, 2011).

Korean Film Export and Import Corporation. *Korean Film Art* (Pyongyang: Korfilm, 2016).

Korean Institute for National Unification. *Change on the Korean Peninsula: The Relevance of Europe* (Seoul: KINU, 2001).

Koryo. *Art of the DPRK: Promoting North Korean Film* (Beijing: Koryo, 2010).

Krylov, Leonid, and Yuriy Tepsurkaev. *Soviet MiG-15 Aces of the Korean War* (Oxford: Osprey, 2008).

Kurtzman, Harvey. *Corpse on the Imjin* (Seattle: Fantagraphics, 2012).

Lankford, Dennis. *I Defy!* (London: Allan Wingate, 1954).

Lankov, Andrei. *From Stalin to Kim Il Sung: The Formation of North Korea 1945–1960* (New Brunswick, NJ: Rutgers University Press, 2002).

Lankov, Andrei. *Crisis in North Korea: The Failure of De-Stalinisation, 1956* (Honolulu: University of Hawaii Press, 2005).

Lankov, Andrei. *Essays on Daily Life in North Korea* (Jefferson, NC: McFarland & Co, 2007).

Lankov, Andrei. *The Real North Korea: Life and Politics in the Failed Stalinist Utopia* (Oxford: Oxford University Press, 2013).

Lee, Chae-jin. *China and Korea: Dynamic Relations* (Stanford, CA: Hoover Institute, 1996).

Lee, Namhee. *The Making of Minjung: Democracy and the Politics of Representation in South Korea* (Ithaca, NY: Cornell University Press, 2007).

Lee, Seung Hyok. *Japanese Society and the Politics of the North Korean Threat* (Toronto: University of Toronto Press, 2016).

Lee, Soon Ok. *Eyes of the Tailless Animals* (Bartlesville: Living Sacrifice Books, 1999).

Lee, Wan Bom. *Korean History 1945–1948* (Seoul: Academy of Korean Studies Press, 2007).

Li, Xiaobing. *China's Battle for Korea: The 1951 Spring Offensive* (Bloomington, IN: Indiana University Press, 2014).

Li, Xiaobing, Allan R. Millett, and Bin Yu. *Mao's Generals Remember Korea* (Lawrence, KS: University Press of Kansas, 2001).

Li, Yuk-sa (Ed.). *The Speeches and Writings of Kim Il Sung, with a Foreword by Eldridge Cleaver* (New York: Grossman, 1972).

Ling, Laura, and Lisa Ling. *Somewhere Inside: One Sister's Captivity in North Korea and the Other's Fight to Bring Her Home* (New York: William Morrow, 2010).

Liu, Yuan. *Journey Through North Korea* (Beijing: China Book Publishing House, 2010).

Logie, Andrew. *The Answers: North Korea* (Singapore: Marshall Cavendish, 2012).

Lone, Stewart, and Gavan McCormack. *Korea Since 1850* (Melbourne: Longman Cheshire, 1993).

MacDonald, Callum. *Britain and the Korean War* (Oxford: Basil Blackwell, 1990).

Magnum. *Korea as Seen by Magnum Photographers* (New York: Norton, 2009).

Mahoney, Kevin. *Formidable Enemies: The North Korean and Chinese Soldier in the Korean War* (Novato, CA: Presidio, 2001).

Malkasian, Carter. *The Korean War 1950–1953* (Oxford: Osprey, 2001).

Martin, Bradley K. *Under the Loving Care of the Fatherly Leader: North Korea and the Kim Dynasty* (New York: Thomas Dunne Books, 2004).

Mazarr, Michael J. *North Korea and the Bomb: A Case Study in Nonproliferation* (New York: St Martin's Press, 1996).

McEachern, Patrick. *Inside the Red Box: North Korea's Post-Totalitarian Politics* (New York: Columbia University Press, 2010).

Mauser, Philipp (Ed.). *Pyongyang: Architectural and Cultural Guide*, 2 volumes (Berlin: DOM Publishing, 2012).

Michishita, Narushige. *North Korea's Military-Diplomatic Campaigns, 1966–2008* (London: Routledge, 2010).

Ministry of Defence (UK). *Treatment of British Prisoners of War in Korea* (London: HMSO, 1955).

Moltz, James Clay, and Alexandre Y. Mansourov. *The North Korean Nuclear Program: Security, Strategy, and New Perspectives from Russia* (New York: Routledge, 2000).

Morris-Suzuki, Tessa. *Exodus to North Korea: Shadows from Japan's Cold War* (Lanham, MD: Rowman & Littlefield, 2007).

Moskin, J. Robert. *Turncoat, An American's 12 Years in Communist China*, (Englewood Cliffs, NJ: Prentice Hall, 1968).

Myers, B.R. *Han Sŏrya and North Korean Literature: The Failure of Socialist Realism in the DPRK* (Ithaca, NY: Cornell University, 1994).

Myers, B.R. *The Cleanest Race: How North Koreans See Themselves – and Why It Matters* (New York: Melville House, 2010).

Myers, B.R. *North Korea's Juche Myth* (Busan: Sthele Press, 2015).

Natsios, Andrew S. *The Great North Korean Famine: Famine, Politics, and Foreign Policy* (Washington, DC: United States Institute of Peace, 2001).

National Human Rights Commission of Korea. *International Seminar on North Korean Human Rights* (Seoul: NHRCK, 2005).

Noland, Marcus. *Avoiding the Apocalypse: The Future of the Two Koreas* (Washington, DC: Institute for International Economics, 2000).

Noland, Marcus. *Korea After Kim Jong-il* (Washington, DC: Institute for International Economics, 2004).

Norodom, Arunrasmy, and Julio A. Jeldres. *A Life Dedicated to Cambodia* (Phnom Penh: HRH The Princess Royal Norodom Arunrasmy, 2012).

Norodom, Sihanouk. *Shadow Over Angkor: Memoirs of His Majesty King Norodom Sihanouk*, vol. 1 (Phnom Penh: Monument, 2005).

North Korea Modernisation Research Group. *North Korea: Development, Human Rights, and Democracy* (Seoul: Kyungnam University Press, 2010).

Oberdorfer, Don. *The Two Koreas: A Contemporary History* (London: Little, Brown and Co, 1998).

O'Hanlon, Michael, and Mike Mochizuki. *Crisis on the Korean Peninsula: How to Deal with a Nuclear North Korea* (New York: McGraw-Hill, 2003).

Oh, Kongdan and Ralph C. Hassig. *North Korea Through the Looking Glass* (Washington, DC: Brookings Institution Press, 2000).

Park, Myungkyu, Bernhard Seliger, and Park Sung-jo (Eds). *Europe–North Korea: Between Humanitarianism and Business?* (Berlin: Lit Verlag, 2010).

Pasley, Virginia. *21 Stayed: The Story of the American GIs Who Chose Communist China – Who They Were and Why They Stayed* (New York: Farrar, Straus and Cudahy, 1955).

PETRA. *The Hermit Country: Today's Art from the Democratic People's Republic of Korea* (Padova, Italy: PETRA, 2007).

Petrisor, Adelin. *A Weekend in Pyongyang, North Korea* (Seoul: Hollym, 2016).

Portal, Jane. *Art Under Control in North Korea* (London: Reaktion Books, 2005).

Pratt, Keith. *Korean Painting* (Oxford: Oxford University Press, 1995).

Pritchard, Charles L. *Failed Diplomacy: The Tragic Story of How North Korea Got the Bomb* (Washington, DC: Brookings Institution Press, 2007).

Radiopress. *North Korea Directory* (Tokyo: Radiopress), annual publication, 1998–2018.

Red Cross Society of China. *Out of Their Own Mouths* (Peking: Red Cross Society of China, 1952).

Richardson, Sharon (Ed.). *Perspectives on U.S. Policy Toward North Korea: Stalemate or Checkmate?* (Lanham, MD: Lexington Books, 2006).

Righetti, Nicolas. *The Last Paradise: North Korea* (New York: Umbrage Editions, 2003).

Riley, John W., and Wilbur Schramm. *The Reds Take a City* (New Brunswick, NJ: Rutgers University Press, 1951).

Rimjin-gang. *News from Inside North Korea* (Osaka: AsiaPress, 2010).

Rocha, João. *Kim Jong Il Looking at Things* (Paris: Jean Boîte, 2018).

Rodong Shinmun. Thwart the Manoeuvres to Split the International Communist Movement (Pyongyang: Foreign Languages Publishing House, 1964).

ROK-EU Forum on Peaceful Unification. *Korean Unification and the Role of the European Union* (Seoul: National Unification Advisory Council, 2015).

Roughneen, Dualta. *North Korea On the Inside, Looking In* (Oakamoor, UK: Bennion Kearny, 2014).

Ryang, Sonia. *North Koreans in Japan: Language, Ideology, and Identity* (Boulder, CO: Westview Press, 1997).

Ryang, Sonia. *Reading North Korea: An Ethnological Inquiry* (Cambridge, MA: Harvard University Press, 2012).

Saccone, Richard. *Negotiating with North Korea* (Seoul: Hollym, 2003).

Scalapino, Robert A., and Lee Chong-sik. *Communism in Korea: Part II: The Society* (Berkeley: University of California Press, 1972).

Scalapino, Robert A., and Lee Chong-sik. *North Korea: Building the Monolith – Selected Chapters from* Communism in Korea (Berwyn, PA: KHU Press, [1972] 2017).

Schönherr, Johannes. *North Korean Cinema: A History* (Jefferson, NC: McFarland & Co, 2012).

Schrift, Melissa. *Biography of a Chairman Mao Badge: The Creation and Mass Consumption of a Personality Cult* (New Brunswick, NJ: Rutgers University Press, 2001).

Selectman, Muriel. *What's Left? What's Right? – A Political Journey via North Korea and the Chinese Cultural Revolution* (Kibworth, UK: Matador, 2014).

Shen, Zhihua. *Mao, Stalin, and the Korean War: Trilateral Communist Relations in the 1950s* (London: Routledge, 2003).

Shim, David. *Visual Politics and North Korea: Seeing Is Believing* (London: Routledge, 2014).

Shu Guang Zhang. *Mao's Military Romanticism: China and the Korean War, 1950–1953* (Lawrence: University Press of Kansas, 1995).

Simmons, Wendy E. *My Holiday in North Korea: The Funniest/Worst Place on Earth* (New York: Rosetta Books, 2015).

Sigal, Leon V. *Disarming Strangers: Nuclear Diplomacy with North Korea* (Princeton, NJ: Princeton University Press, 1998).

Snyder, Scott. *Negotiating on the Edge: North Korean Negotiating Behaviour* (Washington, DC: United States Institute of Peace Press, 1999).

Smith, Hazel. *North Korea: Markets and Military Rule* (Cambridge: Cambridge University Press, 2015).

Smith, Hazel, Chris Rhodes, Diana Pritchard, and Kevin Magill (Eds.). *North Korea in the New World Order* (Basingstoke, UK: Macmillan, 1996).

Springer, Chris. *Pyongyang The Hidden History of the North Korean Capital* (Budapest: Entente, 2003).

Springer, Chris. *North Korea Caught in Time: Images of War and Reconstruction* (Reading, UK: Garnet, 2010).

Suh, Dae-sook. *Kim Il Sung: The North Korean Leader* (New York: Columbia University Press, 1988).

Suh, Jae-jung (Ed.). *Origins of North Korea's Juche: Colonialism, War, and Development* (Lanham, MD: Lexington Books, 2013).

Sutiagin, Yuri, and Igor Seidov. *MiG Menace Over Korea: The Story of Soviet Fighter Ace Nikolai Sutiagin* (Barnsley, UK: Pen & Sword, 2009).

Sweeney, John. *North Korea Undercover: Inside the World's Most Secret State* (London: Bantam, 2013).

Szalontai, Balazs. *Kim Il Sung in the Khrushchev Era: Soviet-DPRK Relations and the Roots of North Korea Despotism, 1953–1964* (Washington, DC: Woodrow Wilson Center Press, 2005).

Tančič, Matjaž. *3DPRK* (Beijing: Koryo, 2012).

Takashi, Nada. *Korea in Kim Jong Il's Era* (Pyongyang: Foreign Languages Publishing House, 2000).

Thompson, Reginald. *Cry Korea: The Korean War: A Reporter's Notebook* (London: Reportage Press, [1951] 2009).

Triplett II, William C. *Rogue State: How a Nuclear North Korea Threatens America* (Washington, DC: Regnery Publishing, 2004).

Tudor, Daniel. *Korea: The Impossible Country* (Tokyo: Tuttle Publishing, 2012).

Tudor, Daniel. *Ask a North Korean: Defectors Talk About Their Lives inside the World's Most Secretive Nation* (Tokyo: Tuttle Publishing, 2017).

Tudor, Daniel, and James Pearson. *North Korea Confidential: Private Markets, Fashion Trends, Prison Camps, Dissenters and Defectors* (Tokyo: Tuttle Publishing, 2015).

US Committee for Human Rights in North Korea. *Failure to Protect: A Call for the UN Security Council to Act in North Korea* (Washington, DC: DLA Piper and US Committee for Human Rights in North Korea, 2006).

Vetter, Hal. *Mutiny on Koje Island* (Rutland, VT: Charles E. Tuttle, 1965).

Winnington, Alan. *Breakfast with Mao: Memoirs of a Foreign Correspondent* (London: Lawrence and Wishart, 1986).

Wit, Joel S., Daniel B. Poneman, and Robert L. Gallucci. *Going Critical: The First North Korean Nuclear Crisis* (Washington, DC: Brookings Institution Press, 2004).

World Korean Forum (Brussels). *The New Era of Korea and the European Union* (Seoul: Korean Global Foundation, 2010).

World Korean Forum (Sydney). *East-Asia Community in a Multi-Polar Era: The Cooperation & Role of Korea-Australia* (Seoul: Korean Global Foundation, 2011).

World Korean Forum (Manila). *Achieving the Asia Vision: Peace and Prosperity through Korean Reunification* (Seoul: Korean Global Foundation, 2012).

World Korean Forum (Vancouver). *Cooperation and Challenges of the Asia-Pacific Era* (Seoul: Korean Global Foundation, 2013).

World Korean Forum (London/Paris). *The Way Towards Korean Reunification* (Seoul: Korean Global Foundation, 2015).

World Korean Forum (Almaty). *Unstable Korea and East Asia Present and Future: Peace Collaboration Coexistence Order in Ethnic Multicultural World Era* (Seoul: Korean Global Foundation, 2017).

Yoo, Byong-yong. *Korea in International Politics: 1945–1954: Britain, the Korean War, and the Geneva Conference* (Seoul: Jinmoondang, 2003).

Films

The Spy Gone North (2018). Directed by Yoon Jong-bin, Seoul.

The Berlin File (2013). Directed by Ryoo Seung-wan, Seoul.

Comrade Kim Goes Flying (2012). Directed by Kim Gwang Hun, Nicholas Bonner, and Anja Daelemans, UK.

Crossing the Line (2006). Directed by Koryo, Beijing.

The Game of Their Lives (2002). Directed by Koryo, Beijing.

Heaven's Soldiers (2005). Directed by Min Joon Ki, Seoul.

Joint Security Area (2000). Directed by Park Chan Wook, Seoul.

The Manchurian Candidate (1962). Directed by John Frankenheimer, USA.

Northern Limit Line (2015). Directed by Kim Hak-soon, Seoul.

One Minute to Zero (1952). Directed by Tay Garnett, USA.

Silmido (2003). Directed by Kang Woo Suk, Seoul.

A State of Mind (2004). Directed by Koryo, Beijing.

Team America: World Police (2004). Directed by Trey Parker, USA.

Plus, of course, Pyongyang's own substantial output!

Index